RAISING FINANCE
FOR YOUR BUSINESS

If you want to know how. . .

100 Ways to Make Your Business a Success
A resource book for small businesses

Starting Your Own Business
*The bestselling guide to planning and building
a successful enterprise*

Mastering Book-Keeping
*A complete guide to the principles and
practice of business accounting*

Voices of Experience
The professional's guide to making great presentations

howtobooks

Send for a free copy of the latest catalogue to:

How To Books
Spring Hill House, Spring Hill Road
Begbroke, Oxford OX5 1RX
email: info@howtobooks.co.uk
http://www.howtobooks.co.uk

RAISING FINANCE FOR YOUR BUSINESS

A nuts and bolts guide for SME owners and managers

MARK BLAYNEY

howtobooks

To Pat and my parents for all their support

Published by How To Books Ltd,
Spring Hill House, Spring Hill Road
Begbroke, Oxford OX5 1RX
Tel: (01865) 375794. Fax: (01865) 379162
email: info@howtobooks.co.uk
http://www.howtobooks.co.uk

British Library Cataloguing in Publication Data
A catalogue record for this book is available from the British Library

ISBN 13 978 1 84528 127 4
ISBN 10 1-84528-127-6

Cover design by Baseline Arts, Oxford
Produced for How To Books by Deer Park Productions, Tavistock, Devon
Typeset by PDQ Typesetting, Newcastle-under-Lyme, Staffs.
Printed and bound by Cromwell Press Ltd, Wiltshire

NOTE: The material contained in this book is set out in good faith for general guidance and no liability
can be accepted for loss or expense incurred as a result of relying in particular circumstances on
statements made in the book. The laws and regulations are complex and liable to change, and readers
should check the current position with the relevant authorities before making personal arrangements.

Contents

List of Illustrations

Introduction

Turnover is vanity
Profit is vanity
Cash is king

Do any of these feel like you?

- Is your business struggling to find enough funds to get you off the ground?
  - If so, your business idea will remain just that, an idea.

- Is your business in the financial position to take advantage of all the opportunities that are open to it?
  - If not, your business is being held back by its financing arrangements.

- Is your business being restricted by the facilities your bank will offer?
  - If so, you're not in control of your business, your bank manager is.

- Can your business afford to pay all its bills as and when they fall due?
  - If not, your business is insolvent (don't panic, but do get advice).

In any business, finance, the cash that is critical to your business is absolutely vital, from allowing you to start-up through to enabling you to grow, survive and thrive.

And if you have any of the above problems, you have a financing problem that you need to deal with.

Cash is the lifeblood of your business and knowing how to raise it, manage it, and use it efficiently and effectively is as vital to your business as knowing how to make and sell your products, because if you can't manage your cash and finances then either you may not get the chance to run a business in the first place, or you might one day even lose it all.

However, financing a business, by which I mean both raising and managing the cash that is both:

◆ generated inside the business; and
◆ introduced into the business from outside

is an area that many business owners shy away from for reasons that are quite understandable.

It's an area that is obviously 'financial' and driven by 'numbers'; but 'numbers' are things many people feel uncomfortable dealing with. As a businessperson you probably did not go into business in order to juggle figures or interpret accounts, but rather to be able to make and sell your products and develop your firm.

Finance and accounts are often seen as complex issues where you require professional guidance on the issues involved and the options open to you. It's also an area where as a smaller business you are very often dealing with very large businesses such as banks and other financial institutions, where it can feel at times that they hold all the cards.

The good news is that this book is on your side. It has been written for the owner managers of small and medium-sized businesses.

The purpose of this book is to help you as a business owner:

- understand how much and what sorts of finance your business needs (and why);

- identify what options are open to you when it comes to raising this finance; and

- choose the most appropriate form of finance for both you and your business, on the most appropriate terms.

To do so, this book is dedicated to making this area of management accessible and understandable to every business owner.

Financing a business inevitably involves looking at financial matters, which includes having some understanding of accounting and accounts, what they are, how they are put together and what they can tell you. But rest assured you do *not* have to be an accountant in order to understand accounts.

This book will show you how to pick out the key details and how to use the information in your business's accounts to help you understand and manage your business and its finances.

Finance, like any other area of business, has its own jargon, shorthand, abbreviations and TLAs (three letter acronyms) that those in the profession use, but which often act as a barrier to exclude those not in the know. This book will explain the meaning of terms like 'gearing' and 'liquidity' in plain English as they arise in the text and these definitions are repeated in the glossary at the end of the book. It will also show how concepts such as security work in practice. This will help you to manage your relationships with financial professionals and advisers by showing them that you know your 'assets' from your 'LBO'

(leveraged buy out) and can talk to them in the language that
they understand.

Unfortunately you will find that some words such as 'capital' can
have a number of related but slightly different meanings
depending on the context. Where these differences are important I
have tried to make this clear.

It is also true to say that this is not designed to be a corporate
finance textbook or academic exercise in accounting theory, so the
definitions used will be down to earth and aimed at providing
non-accountants with useful day-to-day tools.

In order to make this approach as straightforward as possible,
this book is divided into three sections.

A: UNDERSTANDING YOUR BUSINESS'S FINANCES

The starting point in the first section is understanding your
business's financial needs; how to manage these by managing the
funding generated internally within the business and its
requirement for external finance; and the issues to watch out for
in respect of raising any such finance.

If you are familiar with accounts and financial issues you may
wish to skip this section and concentrate on the more detailed
information in the subsequent sections.

B: THE SOURCES OF EXTERNAL BUSINESS FINANCE

The middle section provides detailed information on what many
people will think about when they think about finance, the
different sources of external funding that may be available for
your business, and how to go about raising these.

As finance is an area where things can change rapidly, this section will not attempt to give chapter and verse on the specifics of what is currently available, as this type of information will soon become out of date. Instead it will give you an understanding of the main types of finance that are available, the principles that underlie how they operate and information on how to access the relevant sources.

C: SPECIFIC FINANCING SITUATIONS

The last section provides a series of detailed briefings on the issues surrounding the financing of some specific types of business situations such as a start-up, an acquisition, property development or a turnaround.

While these chapters are written to be stand alone briefings they will tend to assume some familiarity with the concepts covered in the previous sections.

So, if you've ever wanted to say bye-bye to your bank manager, this is the book for you.

Acknowledgements

I am grateful to my colleagues at Creative Business Finance Limited (www.creativefinance.co.uk) and in particular Stuart Hare and Graeme Funnell for their help and support in writing this book, much of which would not have been possible without their years of experience and detailed knowledge of how to raise business finance, and particularly their expertise in the areas of property development finance, commercial property bridging loans and commercial mortgages.

I am also grateful for the company's permission to reproduce a variety of application forms and finance check sheets that I have put together for use by the company's clients. As you will see I include a number of these in the second section so as to provide you with tools for raising finance.

A

UNDERSTANDING YOUR BUSINESS'S FINANCES

$$\left(1\right)$$

Why Does Your Business Need Cash?

The question in the chapter title probably appears simplistic. The answer is obviously to pay for things: suppliers for **stock**, staff for their wages, utilities for services, the bank for the **mortgage** on the premises or the landlord, the taxman, the photocopier rental people, the **leases** on the equipment. And so on, right down to yourself as a business owner since you need a salary, **dividends** or drawings for the time and effort you put in to running the business, otherwise what is the point?

Yet it's a good question to start with, since it helps to start to illustrate the different uses for cash in your business and how it impacts on the types of finance you need.

INVESTMENT AND WORKING CAPITAL

It is when you start to think about what you need cash for in your business that you can see it divides into two different areas.

The first is what you could see as the long-term investment in the business. This can take many forms. It could be investment in physical **assets** such as machinery, or in buying the business's factory or offices, or in less tangible things such as research and development in order to produce intellectual property, or in long-term marketing to develop a brand, or even in training in order to develop staff skills and resources.

These can all be seen as long-term investments in the business's future, which require a long-term commitment of funds to achieve results and where a payback is going to come over many years.

These are in contrast to the shorter-term requirement to finance the day-to-day trading of the business, the buying in of stock and the meeting of the day-to-day running costs of the business, including the cost of staff wages in order to be able to sell goods or services on to customers.

The working capital cycle

This shorter term activity and requirement to make payments actually forms part of a larger cycle of activities in the business which accountants refer to as the **working capital cycle**. This concept is illustrated in the diagram in Figure 1 of a cash pump which shows how a business's working capital cycle is like a person's heart, pumping the business's lifeblood of cash around its system in a virtuous circle.

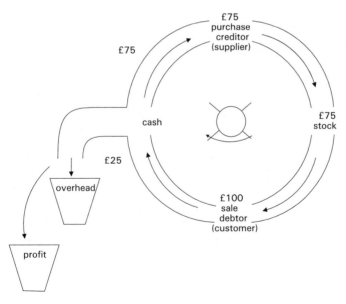

Fig. 1. The working capital cycle.

Imagine for a moment a business which only undertakes a single transaction at a time, buying in goods and selling them on, and which operates on credit. You can see that starting at the top of the circle the business will buy goods from a supplier (a purchase) at a cost of £75 and in doing so it creates somebody who is owed money, known in accounting terminology as a **creditor** (it may help you in thinking this through to use the American term of '**payable**' as this is more descriptive).

The goods that the business has bought then form the business's stock (at a value of £75, being the price the business has bought them at) until it sells them.

When the business then sells these goods to a customer at £100 it creates somebody who then owes the business money (a **debtor** in English accounting terminology, a '**receivable**' in American).

In due course you would expect the debtor to pay the business in order to clear their **debt** of £100 and this means that the business is then holding cash. As the business has sold the goods for a higher price than it has bought them for from the supplier, the cash received in from the sale is then sufficient to both pay off the supplier (the creditor or payable) and generate a surplus or **contribution** of £25 which can go firstly towards the costs of running the business known as its **overheads**, and then once these have all been paid represents profit.

Of course very few businesses only deal in a single transaction at a time. So if you imagine many transactions happening over a period, all at different stages in the cycle, it may be easier to think of this cycle as actually being a pump, spinning round and sucking in cash from your customers as they pay their debts.

Management of the working capital cycle
Looking at Figure 1 you can see that some of this flow stays in the pipe to go back round to the start of the cycle to pay the suppliers.

You can also see that the surpluses generated by this process are then pouring out of this system, each drop making a contribution towards filling a bucket that represents the total cost of your overheads. And once this first bucket is filled so that your overheads are covered, the overflow from this into the second bucket represents your profits which can be used to invest in the business or to pay off borrowings.

In this simplified example, the business is able to obtain credit terms from its supplier that are long enough to allow it to both sell the goods in question and receive the cash in time to pay the supplier. As a result the business in this example has no need of funding to support its working capital cycle. Of course in practice few businesses are in such a fortunate position and the degree to which a business requires financing in order to trade is determined by its actual **terms of trade** with its suppliers and customers.

This is, however, an important concept. Management of the working capital cycle, and the degree to which there is a **funding gap** that needs to be covered by other sources of finance, is critical in determining how much cash your business needs and this will be looked at in more detail in Chapters 3 and 4.

Long-term investment and short-term working capital

Of course in practice the distinction between long-term investment and short-term **working capital** can be more difficult to make. For example is your advertising a long-term investment in building your brand? Or is it a shorter-term requirement in order to ensure your working capital cycle is rolling around day-to-day?

Similarly the cost of your machinery and your premises, while clearly long-term investments, are also a necessary cost in the short-term in order to manufacture your goods and to be able to operate.

Nevertheless, it is a useful distinction to try to keep in mind, since one of the first principles of financing a business is that the nature of the finance used needs to match the characteristics of what the finance is required for.

So, for example, if you have a long-term asset such as a machine that is going to cost £100,000, where the business is going to obtain the benefits of that machine in terms of a cash profit it can generate over many years at say £50,000 a year, for say a useful life of ten years, then the business has a choice about its approach to funding this asset.

◆ It could look to pay £100,000 immediately in cash. This has the advantage that the business does not have an outstanding payable of £100,000 and so it has eliminated any risk that it might not be able to pay for the machine at a future date. But it also means that the business will be out of pocket for two years until the machine has made sufficient profits to reimburse this expenditure (or in fact it is likely to be more since it may take time for the sales to actually turn into the cash).

◆ It could look to pay the machine off in, say, just over two years, allowing for some interest costs by using all the profit that it generates to cover its costs until it's completely paid for. However, this means that the business will not be seeing a return in the form of increased profits for at least the first two years. Agreeing these terms also means that the business is taking a risk, since what happens if for some unknown reason the machine does not generate a cash profit of £50,000 a year in the first few years? The business will then be committed to making up the difference from some other source of funds.

◆ Perhaps the more appropriate way of funding the asset is by way of long-term funding over, say, five to eight of the ten years of the machine's useful life so that the payments for that funding can be made broadly over the useful life of the asset. This in turn means that the profits that can be made from the machine can be relied on to generate cash with which to make the payments in respect of investment in it.

Funding for investment tends to be long term and relatively stable in that payment dates are set on a monthly or quarterly basis, while interest rates may vary up and down with the underlying bank base rate. It is, however, relatively easy for the business to project forward the payments it is going to need to make over the foreseeable future to fund this asset that it's going to use during this period.

This can be contrasted with the financing that might be needed to support the company's working capital cycle. As the level of the company's business changes from day-to-day and week-to-week the funding it may need is also likely to vary, since if turnover is growing the company may need to acquire more stock from suppliers and may have more money tied up in debtors who have not yet paid. Working capital funding therefore needs to be flexible and capable of changing over relatively short periods of time to meet the trading needs of the business.

For businesses in the UK this has typically in the past meant using a bank **overdraft** facility where the company's current account is expected to **swing** into overdraft as funding is required, returning into credit again as the profitable transactions turn into surplus cash. In this way the overdraft provides a very short-term facility which can be increased as the business's demand for funding requires. Indeed overdrafts are actually much more short-term funding than many businesses realise; bank overdrafts are actually repayable on demand by the bank.

This general approach to financing is referred to as **matching**, since it looks to match the type of finance to the useful life of the asset or length of the requirement so that the following are possible.

- Long-term assets or funding requirements are financed with funding that is structured on a longer-term basis providing longer-term security and stability for the business. It does not make much sense, for example, to finance the purchase of a building that may have a useful life of, say, 50 years out of an overdraft that is theoretically repayable tomorrow.

- Short-term assets or funding requirements should be met with short-term flexible funding that can be 'retired' when not required so that you are not paying for what you do not use. It would not make much sense, for example, to fund a temporary requirement for working capital that may only last a month or so by taking out a mortgage on the business's premises that ties you into repaying a loan over ten, 15 or even 25 years, long after the need for the cash has gone.

WHO NEEDS THE MONEY? YOUR BUSINESS'S LEGAL STATUS

Before considering finance in much more detail, it is probably worth thinking first about who or what your business is that is going to need finance, since the form that you choose can have a significant impact on how the business's finance works.

This is not the place for a lengthy discussion on the various forms of corporate structure available to the business owner, but it is necessary to understand just who is the business.

In business on your own

You – You can obviously set up in business on your own and begin trading in your own right, buying in goods and selling them on (having notified the Inland Revenue that you are starting up). If you do so you are said to be acting as a **sole trader** in that you, the **proprietor**, are trading in your own name (and even if you use a business name, 'Southern Widgets', you will actually need to open bank accounts and enter into transactions as 'Joe Smith, trading as Southern Widgets'). This is because from a legal point of view, you and the business are one and the same.

On the upside you own all the business's assets personally, including whatever cash it may hold, and when the business makes a profit, this forms part of your personal income on which you will need to account to the Inland Revenue. On the downside, you are also personally responsible for all the business's **liabilities**, including any money it has borrowed and if the business does not pay its bills or make its repayments, the supplier or lender involved will sue you personally to recover their money as you are the business.

The advantages of this approach to you when looking at financing a business is that since you are the business, all of your resources can be used to raise money for the business and lenders do not have to worry, for example, about distinguishing between assets owned by you and those owned by the business.

The disadvantage of this approach to you as an individual is that since you are the business, you have no protection if things go wrong, as you have unlimited personal liability for the company's debts, including any borrowings. You obviously also cannot attract investment into the business from outsiders as there is no vehicle separate from you as an individual for an investor to invest in.

In business with others

Sometimes of course you may not go into business on your own, but may do so with one or more colleagues in which case you may form a **partnership**.

A partnership does have a certain status as an entity distinct from the individual partners that make it up (it has, for example, to file a partnership tax return), but for the purposes of financing, being a partner is very similar to being a sole trader in that you have unlimited personal liability for the partnership's debts including repayment of any borrowings. The difference here is '**joint and several liability**' where each partner is liable to an unlimited degree for the whole of the partnership's debts while your ownership of the assets is restricted to your share of the partnership's **capital** (see Chapter 2).

As with an individual, when it comes to raising finance, a partnership is not an appropriate structure through which to try to raise most forms of investment, as there is no separate entity outside the individual partners in which an investor can obtain a stake in return for their investment.

The fact that a partnership is actually a collection of individuals, rather than a legal entity in its own right, can make raising finance from lenders more difficult than for an individual. A lender has to deal with all the partners and assets will have to be held in the names of all the partners. The position is then complicated as new partners may be admitted to the partnership, or existing partners may retire or leave, and these entries and exits will have to be dealt with by way of the partnership deed which is its constitution. If the partnership has not agreed such a deed then the partnership will be governed by the provisions of the Partnership Act 1890 which will, for example, mean that in the event of the death or departure of one of the partners, the partnership formally comes to an end, which obviously if you were acting as a lender to a partnership could cause you a certain amount of concern.

Since neither sole traders nor partnerships have to file public or audited accounts showing how the business is doing in the way that companies do, this can also make lenders more cautious in dealing with them.

Limited Liability Partnership

A recent variation of the partnership which has come in over the last few years is the **limited liability partnership (LLP)**. This is something of a cross between a partnership (since it is constituted and taxed as a partnership), and a limited liability company (since it has to file annual accounts at Companies House).

The advantage of this form of partnership for the participants is that your liability for the business's debts can be limited to a specified amount, thus separating for the first time your personal assets and liabilities from those of the business.

The disadvantage when it comes to raising finance is that the lenders can no longer take automatic comfort from your personal abilities to repay any borrowings from resources outside the business, and can therefore be expected to take a more critical and cautious view of lending to the business.

In business as someone else

The final form a business can take is a **limited liability company** identified by the words:

♦ limited (or Ltd) after its name, the basic form of company also known as a '**private company**'; or

♦ public limited company (or PLC), which is essentially a special type of limited liability company which has chosen to comply with a number of rules concerning the size of its **share capital** and how it is governed, which then entitle it to offer its shares for sale on a stock market (to be **listed**) assuming that it fulfils the stock market's criteria for entry (see Chapter 12).

A company is owned by shareholders who may either have subscribed for the initial shares offered when it was formed, or may have bought shares subsequently.

In contrast with a sole trader or a partnership, a limited liability company is regarded by the law as a legal person, separate from the shareholders who own it. It may therefore enter into contracts in its own right, can hold assets and incur liabilities, sue and be sued, all in its own name. The limitation of liability means that the liability of the owners of the business (its shareholders) for the company's debts is limited to the amount of any unpaid parts of the share capital that they own. This difference is illustrated in Figure 2.

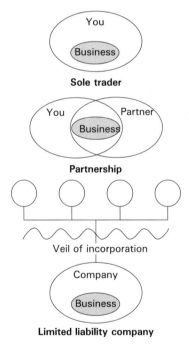

Fig. 2. Liability for debts.

There are some companies that are limited by guarantee, but these are rare, and are not normally used for commercial trading. Instead they are used to form trade associations or other bodies that may need to have a corporate personality.

To decide which is the best form of business organisation for you, you should talk to your accountant as, for example, the effect of tax can be very different. However, my view in general would be that the ability to separate your personal position from the business and its risks means that you should always strongly consider trading through a limited liability company.

Pros and cons for raising finance
From the point of view of raising finance this distinction between the owners and the company has both advantages and disadvantages.

- Since the company shares can be sold, or more shares issued, this provides a mechanism whereby other people can invest money into the business in a way that is impossible for a sole trader and difficult for a partnership.

- Because the company has a legal life of its own, independent of those of the shareholders, it can survive them and pass on from generation to generation, so the party with which a lender or investor is dealing is potentially immortal.

- As the price for allowing shareholders to limit their liability in this way, a company has to file public accounts on a regular basis so that third parties dealing with it, such as suppliers or lenders, can assess its financial performance and position.

The separation of personal and business assets can also be advantageous since through the publicly filed accounts, lenders and investors can obtain a clear picture of what assets and liabilities the company has. But on the other hand, this also restricts the assets available with which to repay lenders if difficulties arise, as the owner's assets are now separated from those of the business. This may also lead lenders and investors to feel that the owner has less commitment to the business.

This separation is known as the **veil of incorporation** as it screens the business owner from the liabilities of the business. If the company as a separate legal person gets into difficulties, and is not able to pay its bills or can't repay its borrowings, then this is the company's problem, and in general the business owner will not be personally liable. There are some exceptions to this.

◆ The first is that the protection which the limitation of liability gives is obviously one that is potentially open to abuse. So **insolvency** legislation provides mechanisms whereby if a company fails insolvently, the directors may potentially be held liable for the liabilities run up by a company they have been controlling.

◆ The second is where the directors or shareholders have personally guaranteed a liability of the company. This situation arises where a lender (who will be well aware of this issue), or sometimes another supplier such as a landlord or equipment hire company, insists on the directors or shareholders providing a **personal guarantee** (**PG**) in order to provide the loan or equipment. They do so in order to be able to try to claim against the guarantors in the event that they suffer a shortfall in payment by the company.

The issues surrounding personal guarantees are discussed in more detail in Chapter 7.

Making the shareholders liable for the liabilities of a company in this way is known as piercing the veil of incorporation (or corporate veil).

TWO SPECIAL CASES

Having drawn the distinction between the normal uses of finance in a business, there are two special cases which it is worth discussing at this stage.

Funding losses

In Figure 1 the working capital cycle is spinning out cash from the completion of each of its trading transactions, to contribute towards first covering the business's overheads and then towards its eventual profits.

However, if the working capital cycle is not generating enough flow with which to fill the first bucket in the cash pump diagram representing the business's total overhead costs, then at the end of the trading period the gap between the level of funds generated and the top of the bucket will represent a loss suffered by the business.

However, if the overheads have to be paid then cash has to come into the business from somewhere with which to make up the gap and fill the bucket. The business will be demanding funds with which to cover these losses.

Even worse, in some cases the working capital cycle can be running so badly that actually there is not enough cash to go back round to the start of the cycle.

And if you've ever had an airlock build up in pipes in your house you'll know that it starts by restricting the flow around the system and eventually causes it to dry up altogether. The same process will affect the cashflows in your business and once the cash, which is the lifeblood of your business, ceases to flow, your business will die from a business heart attack.

As will be covered in Chapters 3 and 4, managing your working capital cycle is vital for the financial health of your business.

Defined benefit or final salary pension schemes

A specific issue has arisen at the time of writing, due to changes in the law in relation to the types of pension schemes that provide a pension based on levels of earnings and periods of service, so known as defined benefit or final salary pension schemes.

This change has come about following situations where pension schemes have been unable to cover the liabilities due to a business's employees following the failure of the employer, together with the significant deficits that some schemes are believed to have, due in part to poor performance of their investments over the past few years.

If your business operates a defined benefit or final salary pension scheme the likelihood is that your business will need to raise cash to invest in the scheme and to pay increased running costs.

Within the next three years, the trustees of every scheme will be required to have reviewed the scheme's funding requirement, which is to say the money that you as an employer need to put into it. This is likely to go up because the basis on which it has to be calculated is changing from what was known as the **minimum funding requirement (MFR)** introduced after the Maxwell scandal, to the **pension protection fund (PPF)** measure which is significantly higher.

To give you an idea of the scale of this problem, in one case being quoted by professionals involved in the area, the deficit to be made up under the MFR basis was £3 million. The deficit under the PPF measure, however, was approximately £600 million (and in this case the deficit for buy out basis, probably the most expensive measure of pension scheme liability, was estimated at £1.6 billion). As you can see, the impact of changing the measure of the scheme's liabilities can suddenly produce a significant increase in the deficit that will need to be covered.

The legislation goes on to say that the pension scheme will be allowed only ten years in which to achieve funding of the PPF level required.

The likelihood is, therefore, that as an employer who will be required to ensure the scheme is properly funded, you are likely to receive a cash call over the next ten years from any such scheme.

At the same time, the new pension protection fund has been set up to act as a safety net for schemes where the employer fails while the scheme still has a deficit. This fund is to be financed by way of a levy on all defined benefit pension schemes which do not meet the PPF funding level. This levy will be calculated on the basis of the size of your scheme and its deficit multiplied by a risk factor which will be based on your business's credit rating as at March 2006. The worse your credit rating, the higher the risk factor and the higher the bill the scheme may expect to receive when the first invoices arrive in August 2007.

So if your scheme has a deficit on the PPF measure you will be faced with the prospect of:

◆ paying in funds to bring it up to this level, over at most the next ten years; while

◆ paying a levy to the PPF.

The good news, however, is that this problem only applies to defined benefit pension schemes. It does not apply to defined contribution (also known as money purchase) schemes. So one strategy may be to attempt to cease to provide a final salary pension scheme. You can in theory buy out the scheme members' benefits (a Section 75 buy out), but in practice the cost of this will usually be more than the funding required to meet the PPF criteria. You may, however, be able to incentivise members to voluntarily transfer their benefits out of a final salary scheme and into a money purchase scheme at a lower cost than bringing an existing scheme into line with the funding required. This will of course still take cash.

If your business has a defined benefit or final salary pension scheme, as a matter of urgency I would suggest you should:

- take advice on the impact of these changes in legislation on your business's position; and

- consider how you're going to fund the cost of whatever action you may need to take.

For advice you will need to speak to an appropriately qualified Independent Financial Adviser. If you would like a referral to an adviser please contact me at mark@theoss.freeserve.co.uk.

2

Understanding Your Business's Accounts

Understanding and managing the finances of your business must involve understanding and managing your business's accounts.

This is an area where many people feel uncomfortable and which many business owners shy away from, seeing accounting as a technical and complex area.

The purpose of the remainder of this section is to provide an overview of what the accounts can tell you as an owner manager and to provide some tools (ratio analysis) that you can use to extract useful information with which to manage your business and its finance requirements.

If you are familiar with reading accounts you may therefore wish to skip this and the following chapter. If not, you may wish to work through each subsection of these two chapters to ensure that you are comfortable with each element, what it is showing you and why. You may also find it useful to revisit these two chapters at a later date.

WHAT ARE ACCOUNTS AND WHY ARE THEY IMPORTANT?

A set of accounts is simply a record of:

- the business's trading performance over a period, a **profit and loss** account;

- a snapshot of its financial position at the end of a period of trading showing its assets and liabilities, a **balance sheet**.

Accounts have two principal uses.

- They are a means of providing you as the business owner with understanding and control of how the business is performing. As such they can be produced annually, quarterly, monthly or even weekly if that is how detailed the control of the business needs to be. Accounts in this sense (prepared primarily for internal consumption and known as **management accounts**) are part of what is known as a business's management information systems (or MIS), where they may be tied into other reports such as key data (eg, orders in the pipeline, production efficiencies, wastage rates), compared with budgets, to see whether the business is on track, and used as the basis for **cashflow forecasting** to establish the finance required.

- They are also a means of communicating how the business is doing to third parties who may need to know, such as the tax man, the bank, or suppliers who you would like to give you credit. As shown in Chapter 1, part of the price of limitation of liability is a requirement to publicly file annual accounts so that people who are dealing with a limited liability company can assess its financial position.

HOW ARE ACCOUNTS PREPARED?

Accounts are prepared from the books and records kept by the business and will generally be prepared in accordance with what is known as UK **Generally Accepted Accounting Practice (GAAP)**.

UK GAAP is the overall term for what you might think of as the rules of the game in that, in order to make accounts as easy to interpret as possible, it dictates:

◆ the basic assumptions which it will be expected that any set of accounts should follow;

◆ a standardised approach to laying out the information so that one set of accounts looks more or less like another. The accounts shown below show a simple profit and loss and balance sheet for Widget Co Ltd that might form its management accounts.

Widget Co Ltd Profit and loss account		12 months to 31 Dec 05 (£000)	12 months to 31 Dec 04 (£000)
Sales		1,000	750
Cost of sales		−500	−325
Gross profit		500	425
		50%	57%
Overheads			
Wages and salaries	−190		−125
Rent	−50		−50
Heat, light and power	−50		−40
Telephones	−35		−30
Postage, printing, stationery	−20		−15
Audit	−10		−7
Bad debt provision	−25		−5
Total		−380	−272
Operating profit		120	153
Depreciation		−25	−25
Bank interest		−20	−15
Net profit before tax		75	113
Tax		−25	−35
Net profit after tax		50	78

You'll find that published sets of accounts, the formal sets that are prepared for filing at Companies House, may look different from this because, for example, the overheads will normally be consolidated into a single figure, thus showing much less detail than in the management accounts.

Widget Co Ltd Balance Sheet	As at 31 Dec 05 (£000)	As at 31 Dec 04 (£000)
Fixed assets		
Cost	250	250
Less depreciation	− 100	− 75
Net book value	150	175
Current assets		
Stock	90	60
Debtors	200	150
Cash at bank/petty cash	2	2
	292	212
Current liabilities		
Overdraft	− 61	− 37
Trade creditors	− 150	− 101
PAYE/NI	− 3	− 3
VAT	− 22	− 15
Mortgage (current element)	− 50	− 50
Corporation tax	− 25	− 30
	− 311	− 236
Net current liabilities	− 19	− 24
Long-term liabilities		
Mortgage	− 50	− 100
Net assets	81	51
Shareholder funds		
Share capital	− 2	− 2
P&L a/c BF	− 49	− 11
P&L for period	− 30	− 38
	− 81	− 51

If you're not familiar with accounting practice there are a small number of these key underlying assumptions that you need to be aware of to make sense of any set of accounts. There may be occasions where a set of accounts deviates from one of these key assumptions, but if so this should always be clearly indicated in the accounts so that the readers are aware of this.

In a published set of accounts the policies and specific assumptions made, such as **depreciation** policy, will be set out in the first of the notes to the accounts.

The four key **accounting concepts** are as follows.

1 Prudence

Accounts should be prepared prudently. This means first, that they should not anticipate profit before it has been earned, so sales should not be recognised in turnover until the goods or services have been supplied and normally the invoice raised.

Secondly, losses should be recognised as soon as possible, by providing for the costs or writing down any asset whose value has been impaired as soon as appropriate. So you should recognise the expense of suffering a bad debt or needing to write off obsolete stock as soon as you become aware of the problem.

2 The accruals concept (or the matching basis)

Accounts should also be prepared on the basis that costs should be matched to the relevant sales or periods. So, for example, if the company has bought three widgets during the year and has sold two of them, then the cost of the two that have been sold will appear in the profit and loss account as the costs of the goods sold, so matching the cost to the relevant sales during that period. The cost of the third will be carried forward as part of the stock in the balance sheet to be matched against the relevant sale when this occurs at some point in the future.

In the same way, overhead costs should be matched to the relevant periods. For example, if the company is billed quarterly for its electricity, but the year end to which the accounts are drawn up comes two months through a quarter, then the company should accrue a cost in its profit and loss and a matching liability in creditors (shown as an accrual) for two-thirds of a normal quarter's electricity bill.

This principle operates in reverse as well in that if, for example, the company has paid an insurance premium in January covering the 12 months of the calendar year, but it draws up its accounts to the end of June, then it has actually paid six months of the following year's costs during the current year. This is dealt with by deducting half of the insurance premium paid from the cost in the profit and loss account, and showing this balance as an asset called a prepayment, as part of the business's **current assets**, under the overall heading of debtors.

Where an item such as a machine is to be used over a number of periods the approach is therefore to record the item in the balance sheet as an asset, and to then spread the cost over the years when it will be used by way of a depreciation charge.

3 Historical cost convention

The assumption is that costs incurred by a business and perhaps more importantly the value of the assets on its balance sheet, are generally recognised at the original cost when they were bought. So for instance the stock used in the example at the beginning of Chapter 1 had a value of £75 because this was the cost of the goods when they were bought from the supplier.

Obviously an asset may in time have a very different value from its original purchase price (a used car may be worth significantly less, a building may be worth significantly more). For most accounting purposes, however, the cost of the asset will continue to be shown at its original purchase price. Any reduction in value is shown separately as an expense by way of a depreciation charge or a provision (as discussed above). Where assets such as a property may have increased in value it may sometimes be possible to shows this increase in value in the accounts, the increase being clearly identified as a revaluation **reserve**.

One of the criticisms of sets of accounts, and in particular of the balance sheet, is that because of the historical cost convention, this statement of assets and liabilities can actually have very little relation to the value of the business's assets. This is particularly true if you are looking at say financial businesses holding a range of investments. Within the accounting profession, and the process of developing international accounting standards, there therefore appears to be a move away from this convention and towards the process of showing assets at closer to their actual market value (known as **mark to market**).

Within the owner managed sector, other than in respect of revaluing properties, this issue does not normally arise to any great degree.

4 Going concern
Most accounts are prepared on the assumption that the business will continue to trade into the future and is therefore a **going concern**.

This is important because where a company ceases to trade the following happen.

◆ It incurs (crystallises) a number of costs which it would not normally face, such as redundancy payments to employees or termination charges in contracts.

◆ The value of its assets have to be marked down to their actual realisable value in the open market, so for example, **work in progress** which cannot be completed may have to be treated as completely worthless.

There are also two practices which should be used in preparing most accounts, as follows.

Consistency
So as to make accounts easy to read and comparable from year to year, a business's accounts should as far as possible be prepared on a consistent basis. This means both how they are laid out and key assumptions (such as for example the rate of depreciation) should not be changed.

For example, depreciating a piece of machinery costing £100,000 over three years gives a cost of depreciation in the P&L of £33,333 per year. Changing the period to five years reduces this cost to £20,000 per year, giving an instant apparent profit improvement of £13,333 per year, whereas in reality nothing different has actually happened.

Minimum of netting off
It is good practice when preparing accounts not to net off assets and liabilities, but to show both. So for example, you might have

a piece of machinery which is an asset valued at £100,000 on which you owe money on a lease of £40,000.

You could show the value of this machinery as:

- a net asset of £60,000
- but you should really show both:
  - the asset of £100,000; and separately
  - the liability of £40,000.

WHAT IS IN EACH PART OF THE ACCOUNTS?

To explain how these assumptions and practices operate, this chapter will look at a simple profit and loss account (P&L) for Widget Co Ltd, while the next chapter will look at Widget Co Ltd's balance sheet.

In doing so this chapter will touch briefly on profitability. While this is not the focus of this book, profitability is important for financing a business as it acts as the basis on which to attract investment and to support the ability of a business to repay loans.

A profit and loss account is a statement showing the sales and expenses for a period of trading between two balance sheet dates.

In the case of Widget Co Ltd, its P&L covers a period of the year's trading showing the results for the year to the end of December 2005. For comparison purposes it also shows the results for the previous period which in this case is also a full year. This obviously makes comparison of this year's performance against last year's easier.

Widget Co Ltd's profit and loss account is made up of the following.

- **Sales (**or **turnover)** which represents the business's total sales that relate to the period. Where a businesses is registered for **Value Added Tax (VAT)**, both the sales and all of the costs shown in the profit and loss account are always stated exclusive of the VAT.

- **Costs of sales (CoS** or sometimes **COGS, Cost of Goods Sold)** are the costs to the company in buying in materials or producing things, of the goods or services that have been sold which make up the turnover.

  This is an area where the matching concept comes into play since during any particular period the goods sold may not be the goods actually purchased during that period. So for example the cost of goods sold in this case represents:

Opening stock at the beginning of the period (brought forward)	60
Purchases in the period *	530
Total	590
Less closing stock at the end of the period (carried forward)	−90
Cost of the goods sold in the period	500

  * You will not see the purchases figure on the face of the accounts, but since in this case you know both the opening and closing stock values and the cost of sales this missing figure of purchases can be calculated.

- **Gross profit (GP or gross margin)** is the profit that the company has made by selling the goods or services, before having to pay its overheads. Thinking back to the cash pump diagram in Chapter 1, this represents the £25 generated by having sold the £75 purchase for £100, and the business illustrated in the diagram in Chapter 1 would be said to have a **gross profit percentage** of 25% (being £25/£100).

In the case of Widget Co Ltd, its gross profit is £500,000 on a turnover of £1,000,000 which gives it a gross profit percentage of 50%. As a measure of how much profit is generated from trading to contribute towards paying the business's overheads, this gross profit percentage figure is the first important ratio for analysing a set of accounts.

◆ The **overheads** are the general costs that the company incurs by being in business. Many of these, from its audit fees through to its wages and salaries, are obvious items that it is having to pay for.

Some overheads are, however, not items that you buy, but are provisions for costs that you may incur. An example of this is a bad debt provision. You obviously don't go out and buy a bad debt, but the cost of suffering one is an expense that the business has to cover if it occurs.

Widget Co Ltd has decided to split its overheads into two sections, and can therefore calculate an **operating profit** designed to see how much the trading activities of the business are generating, before thinking about depreciation which is a non-cash item, and the costs of financing.

The basis on which Widget Co Ltd has calculated this operating profit is also known as **EBITDA (earnings before interest, tax, depreciation and amortisation)**. EBITDA is important, as it is often used by financial institutions as a way of measuring the underlying profitability of a business on a quasi cash basis when thinking about how much debt it may be able to service.

◆ **Net profit** is the profit that the company has left after covering the overheads out of the gross profit. This can be stated before and after tax.

Elsewhere within a published set of accounts there should be a note showing how the profit and loss account ties up with the item on the balance sheet which is labelled as the profit and loss.

This is because the net profit made each year after tax can either be:

◆ distributed to the owners as a sole trader's or partner's drawings or shareholder's dividends; or

◆ retained in the business, appearing as part of the owner's capital or shareholder's funds as a profit and loss reserve.

The working below shows how Widget Co Ltd's shareholders have divided the net profit made during the year of £50,000 into a £20,000 distribution of a dividend to the shareholders and have left £30,000 in the business.

Widget Co Ltd Movement on reserves	12 months to 31 Dec 05 (£000)	12 months to 31 Dec 04 (£000)
Net profit after tax	50	78
Distributed by way of dividend	−20	−40
Retained for year	30	38

WHAT INFORMATION CAN YOU FIND IN THE PROFIT AND LOSS ACCOUNT?

The key information provided by the profit and loss account is obviously profitability, or at its simplest: does the business make money?

This is important for financing because in the long term it is profits that turn into business cash through the operation of the working capital cycle.

It is therefore profits that generate the ability to:

◆ repay loans;
◆ provide a return for investors for having put their money into the business.

So, the greater the profitability of the business the easier it is likely to be to:

◆ generate finance internally from the business;
◆ raise money externally when required.

So it is important to be able to 'read' a profit and loss account and understand what it is saying about profitability. To help with this the rest of this chapter will cover:

◆ horizontal and vertical analysis;
◆ types of cost;
◆ gross profit, contribution and **break-even**;
◆ interest cover;
◆ cost drivers;
◆ profit improvement;
◆ breaking the business down.

Horizontal and vertical analysis

As a starting point in understanding any set of P&L accounts, horizontal and vertical analysis can be used to spot the trends in turnover and costs over time.

Widget Co Ltd Profit and loss account Horizontal analysis	12 months to 31 Dec 05 (£000)	12 months to 31 Dec 04 (£000)	Change
Sales	1,000	750	33.3%
Cost of sales	−500	−325	53.8%
Gross profit	500	425	17.6%
	50%	57%	
Overheads			
Wages and salaries	−190	−125	52.0%
Rent	−50	−50	0.0%
Heat, light and power	−50	−40	25.0%
Telephones	−35	−30	16.7%
Postage, printing, stationery	−20	−15	33.3%
Audit	−10	−7	42.9%
Bad debt provision	−25	−5	400.0%
Total	−380	−272	39.7%
Operating profit	120	153	
Depreciation	−25	−25	0.0%
Bank interest	−20	−15	33.3%
Net profit before tax	75	113	
Tax	−25	−35	−28.6%
Net profit after tax	50	78	

Horizontal analysis (as above) compares the levels of income and expenditure across years to see the relative degrees of change that have taken place in each item, which can be expressed as a percentage.

To compare more than two years, treat the first one as your base point (so all items equate to 100%) and express the numbers in other years as percentages compared with this, so that the level of change can be seen.

This type of approach is useful for showing how revenues and costs are changing over time (but you must be careful to adjust for inflation effects over longer periods).

Widget Co Ltd Profit and loss account Vertical analysis	12 months to 31 Dec 05 (£000)		12 months to 31 Dec 04 (£000)	
Sales	1,000	100.0%	750	100.0%
Cost of sales	−500	50.0%	−325	43.3%
Gross profit	500	50.0%	425	56.7%
Overheads				
Wages and salaries	−190	19.0%	−125	16.7%
Rent	−50	5.0%	−50	6.7%
Heat, light and power	−50	5.0%	−40	5.3%
Telephones	−35	3.5%	−30	4.0%
Postage, printing, stationery	−20	2.0%	−15	2.0%
Audit	−10	1.0%	−7	0.9%
Bad debt provision	−25	2.5%	−5	0.7%
Total	−380	38.0%	−272	36.3%
Operating profit	120	12.0%	153	20.4%
Depreciation	−25	2.5%	−25	3.3%
Bank interest	−20	2.0%	−15	2.0%
Net profit before tax	75	7.5%	113	15.1%
Tax	−25	2.5%	−35	4.7%
Net profit after tax	50	5.0%	78	10.4%

Vertical analysis (as above) shows how the figures for each element of the P&L is changing as a percentage of that year's sales. This is useful for understanding how much of the business's sales each category of expenditure is consuming in each year.

In the case of Widget Co Ltd, from horizontal analysis you would want to know why the bad debt provision has grown by 400% over the year.

However from the vertical analysis you can see that the bad debt cost is still only 2.5% of sales; the more immediate issue is the increase of cost of sales to 50.0% of sales from 43.3%.

This process can help you to understand how your business is performing and start to indicate some areas to investigate. In Widget Co Ltd's case you can see that:

◆ sales have increased by a third (33.3%);

◆ but costs of sales have gone up by 53.8% to 50% of the sales price (from 43.3%), so the gross margin being achieved has been squeezed from 56.7% to 50%.

So have extra sales been achieved simply by reducing prices, or by aggressive discounting?

Whatever the reason, this is bad news as instead of a gross profit of £570,000, which might have been expected from the increased turnover based on last year's gross profit, the business is only generating £500,000, a £70,000 shortfall.

There has also been a significant rise in bad debts. Why is this? Is it that in chasing for more sales the business is being less careful about who it is selling to and how much risk there is that they will not pay?

The operating overheads have otherwise risen reasonably in line with sales (at 38% against 36.3%) and if it weren't for that increase in bad debt they would have been bang on target.

The result is that despite an increase in turnover, the company's profit has gone down (from £153,000 to £120,000 at operating profit level), largely as a result of a fall in contribution.

The company needs to take a look at what is happening to its sales and margins.

This approach can be particularly helpful if you have information from other companies in the same sector against which to compare your performance (**benchmarking**) to see what this might tell you about your relative levels of efficiency.

Types of costs

To really understand your business's profitability, you must first understand its cost structure.

If you imagine for example a shop, you can see that in the same way as its funding requirements can be split into working capital and investment, its trading costs fall into two broad categories.

◆ The costs of buying goods in for sale, where the level of purchases will broadly move (vary) up and down in line with the level of sales.

◆ The day-to-day costs of being in business that have to be met each day irrespective of the level of sales on that day, such as the rent and rates, heating and lighting bills and so on.

These types of cost should be familiar by now from looking at both the working capital cycle and the profit and loss account as the cost of sales and overheads respectively.

This is, however, a slight oversimplification as for most businesses there are essentially three types of costs for any business.

	Variable level of cost varies closely with changes in the level of sales	**Fixed** do not vary in the short term as sales fluctuate

Direct costs
relate directly to the
cost of producing or
acquiring goods for sale
	• raw materials/
	  purchases
	• piecework wages
	• overtime pay
	• factory energy costs
		• normal factory
		  wages
		• machinery costs and
		  depreciation
		• factory rent

Indirect costs general costs of being in business, not directly related to particular costs of trading		• auditors' fees • admin staff's wages • directors' fees • interest on loans*

* Not the loan principal (sometimes called the capital) element, which is simply repayment of the amount borrowed in the first place and so is not an expense that appears in the profit and loss account.

Fixed costs are of course not fixed in the long term (you can move factory, or hire and fire factory staff), and will eventually reflect levels of production and activity.

As already shown however, the profit and loss account divides costs only into two broad areas:

♦ **costs of sales** (CoS) which will include all **variable direct costs**;
♦ **overheads** which will include all **fixed indirect costs**.

This can lead to a problem in interpreting accounts, as businesses differ as to how they deal with analysing **direct fixed costs** between costs of sales and overheads.

At present Widget Co Ltd's accounts CoS figure simply shows the costs of materials. But the company makes, installs and repairs widgets, all of which require labour and in fact £100,000 of its wages overhead actually relates to its production workers.

So it could restate its P&L to show this cost as part of its cost of sale as follows:

	As per current treatment	Restated
Sales	1,000	1,000
Cost of sales		
Cost of goods sold	− 500	− 500
Production labour		− 100
Total cost of sales	− 500	− 600
Gross profit	500	400
Gross profit %	50%	40%
Overheads	− 380	− 280
Operating profit	120	120

This obviously also illustrates why consistency in how accounts are prepared is important. Changing how the item is shown could give a very misleading picture when compared with last year's results if you were not aware of what had been done.

It is also something to be careful of when attempting to benchmark your performance against a competitor's accounts.

This approach can be extended to include all relevant direct overheads such as factory rent, power costs and even depreciation of the production machinery, depending on how sophisticated an analysis your business requires.

The reason this is important is that if you do not include all your direct costs in calculating your cost of sales, you risk underestimating your costs when it comes to setting prices or tendering for contracts. The result for businesses of continuously selling at less than their true cost of manufacture (ie at a loss) is inevitably failure. It is generally best practice therefore to include direct costs as fully as possible in establishing your costs of sales.

The exception to this is if your production volumes swing significantly between periods. In this case you will need to be careful in using cost of sales to establish a meaningful contribution figure for sales, and you may find it best to treat all fixed costs as overheads for the purpose of calculating break-even levels (see below).

Gross profit and break-even

One of the principal reasons that an understanding of the cost structure is important in calculating your gross profit and gross profit percentage is that these are then used to calculate break-even.

In the diagram of the working capital cycle in Chapter 1 (Figure 1), the business bought its supplies at £75 and sold these on at £100, thereby generating a £25 contribution towards its overheads for every transaction completed. While this tells us that that business has a gross profit percentage of 25% (£25/£100) we do not know the level of overheads that it needs to cover.

We do, however, know Widget Co Ltd's overheads and its cost of sales. So if Widget Co Ltd sells each of its widgets for £100, then from the above its average cost of sales per widget are:

Raw materials	(£50)
Labour and manufacturing costs	(£10)
Its gross profit per widget is	40%
So its contribution per widget is	£40

On the same basis, Widget Co Ltd has operating overheads of £280,000 per year, plus a further £45,000 in depreciation and interest, giving a total of £325,000.

As its gross profit per widget (or contribution towards covering overheads) is £40 per widget, it has to sell 8,125 widgets a year (£325,000/£40) before the total contribution is sufficient to cover all the overheads, or break-even.

Its break-even turnover is therefore £812,500 per year (£100 selling price per widget x 8,125). If it sells less than this it will make a loss, if it sells more it will make a profit.

The above break-even has used accounting figures based on costs taken from the profit and loss accounts. It is often useful to redo this exercise to calculate a cash break-even by stripping out the key costs that do not represent cash (eg depreciation) and replacing this with real cash items (eg total loan payments).

Widget Co Ltd's overheads include charges of £25,000 for depreciation and £20,000 for bank interest. Looking at the balance sheet, the amount due to the bank in respect of the mortgage has reduced (from £150,000 at the end of last year to £100,000 at the end of this) so this must mean that the company has repaid £50,000 of capital during the year.

So the company's overheads restated on a cash basis are:

Overheads	£325,000
Less depreciation	£(25,000)
Add capital payment	£50,000
Total	£350,000

As a result its break-even turnover on a cash basis is 8,750 (£350,000/£40) widgets a year or £8,750,000.

Interest cover

Another key ratio for lenders is the ratio of:

$$\frac{\text{profit before interest}}{\text{interest}}$$

This shows the sensitivity of available profit in covering interest payments (eg to the bank), in Widget Co Ltd's case:

$$\frac{£95,000}{£20,000} = 4.75$$

So a lender to this business knows that the business's profits have to fall to almost a fifth of its present levels before the interest cannot be paid.

Cost drivers

The relative level of a business's costs compared with its competitors will be due to a number of factors, of which some of the most common are listed below. If your analysis is suggesting that the business's costs are out of line with those of its competitors these are the areas you might look at for opportunities to cut expenditure. Be alert, however, for the common pitfalls of poorly applied cost reductions, where disruption and other problems brought about outweigh the planned saving:

◆ economies of scale (sometimes bigger is better);

◆ capacity utilisation (the business is paying for that plant and those people, whether they are earning for it or not);

◆ learning curves (the more it does of something, the better at it the business should become);

◆ location (relative local costs and transportation costs);

◆ purchasing (how good at buying is the business?);

◆ operating efficiency;

◆ investment (eg in automation or training);

◆ waste management.

Profit improvement
As you start to think about break-even calculations, something becomes very clear. To improve profits, you can do any or all of three things:

◆ increase turnover;
◆ increase margin (gross profit percentage);
◆ reduce overheads.

If you can do all three, the effects multiply. So if Widget Co Ltd could achieve a 10% improvement in each of these areas, the overall effect would be an incredible 93.3% increase in profit.

	Original	10% improvement	Result	
Sales	1,000	100	1,100	
Gross profit %	40%	4%	44%	
Gross profit	400		484	
Overheads	−280	28	−252	
Operating profit	120		232	93.3% increase

Breaking the business down

To see what is happening to a business it is often helpful to break performance down by individual area (known as a **profit centre**), at least at gross profit and contribution level, even if it is impractical to separately allocate overheads.

Looking more closely at Widget Co Ltd, a more detailed set of management accounts might therefore show:

	£000
Sales	
Widget sales	750
Installation	240
Widget repairs	10
	1,000
Cost of sales	
Materials	−500
Production wages	−60
Installation wages	−25
Repair shop wages	−15
	−600
Gross profit	400
Gross profit %	40%

However, by breaking this down into different areas of activity (profit centres), a clearer picture emerges of where the company really makes (or loses) its money:

	Widget sales	Installation	Repairs
Sales	750	240	10
Cost of sales	−560	−25	−15
Gross profit	190	215	−5
Gross profit %	25%	90%	−50%

This analysis stops at gross profit level. However, you could go further, identifying and allocating overheads to each area and apportioning any overheads which cannot be directly linked to a particular part of the business on an appropriate basis so as to find an operating or a net profit for each area.

By capturing enough information in your accounting system you can apply this approach to establishing the profitability of different areas of your business, as well as to individual customers or groups of customers, or individual orders, contracts or products.

3

Assets and Liabilities

The second key financial statement is the **balance sheet**. There are two reasons why it is called a balance sheet. The first is that this is a snapshot at the end of a period of trading of the business's:

◆ **assets**, things that are owned by the business which have a value; and

◆ **liabilities**, the business's obligations to pay money to others.

It is therefore a statement of the balances on these accounts at the end of a period.

As it is a statement of the business's assets and liabilities, the balance sheet is sometimes seen as a statement of the business's worth. This is, however, a dangerous assumption as in accounting terms it is simply a list of balances.

For example, the balance sheet values of assets (at historical cost, as discussed in the last chapter) are unlikely to provide you with an accurate reflection of their current market value. It also takes no account of business assets such as goodwill or brand awareness, which have a value, but generally do not appear on the balance sheet.

Widget Co Ltd's balance sheet as shown in Chapter 2 consists of the following.

- **Fixed assets** such as property, plant and machinery, motor vehicles, or even some intangible assets which the company owns and will use over a number of years. These are shown at the cost of acquisition, less the depreciation accumulated over the years to show a **net book value**, which is essentially the remaining cost of the asset to be written off to the profit and loss as the asset is used.

- Any **investments** in subsidiary companies would be shown separately.

- **Current assets**, which are those assets such as debtors (or to use the American term **receivables**), stock and cash in hand and at the bank which should be used in trading the business over the next 12 months.

- **Current liabilities** are all the creditors (or payables in American parlance) which are due and payable within the next 12 months. This will include normal trade creditors, balances due to the Crown in respect of VAT or **PAYE/NI** (tax deducted from employees' wages under Pay As You Earn and employees' and employers' contributions to National Insurance), the proportion of the capital of long-term loans, **hire purchase** and leases that are due to be paid during this period, and the total of any bank overdraft (as these are always repayable on demand).

- **Net current assets** (or in this case, liabilities) is the total of the current assets less the current liabilities, and broadly represents the working capital of the business.

- **Long-term liabilities** are all creditor balances due after periods longer than a year.

- **Net assets** is the sum of the fixed and current assets and investments, less the current and long-term liabilities.

The second reason why it is called a balance sheet is that it should balance. That is to say that the value of the net assets (which should normally be a positive number) will then in the case of a limited liability company match the value of the **shareholders' funds** which consist of:

◆ the **share capital**, which are the funds introduced to the company by the shareholders;

◆ the **P&L account** or **retained profits**, which is essentially the sum of money left in the business from profits over this and previous years;

◆ any **other reserves** such as will have been created, for example, by a revaluation of the company's property.

For a partnership the net assets will be matched by the total of the partners' capital and current accounts.

If the balance sheet does not balance in this way it shows that there is a fundamental problem in the business's bookkeeping system.

WHAT DOES THE BALANCE SHEET TELL YOU?

If the profit and loss account tells you about the business's profitability, then the balance sheet tells you about its financial position and in particular the following.

Financial stability

How risky are the finances? This means looking at its:

- **liquidity**, which can show how much risk the business has of running out of cash in the short term; and

- **gearing**, which shows how reliant on, and exposed to, borrowed money the business is.

Financial efficiency

How well is the business managing the cash it needs?

This means looking at its:

- stock turn and debtor and creditor days, which brings us back to the working capital cycle;
- return on capital employed; and
- return on investment.

UNDERSTANDING FINANCIAL STABILITY

Liquidity

Sometimes a business's balance sheet will show a very positive position, but it still has financial problems in meeting its bills. This can be because it has its cash tied up in **illiquid** assets. For example, a business had a balance sheet that showed net assets of well over £10m. However, looking more closely at the make up of the assets, £12m of this asset base was farming land which could not be used as such to meet day-to-day payments required by the business and so the business had a liquidity problem.

Liquidity is an indication of the business's likely ability to pay its current liabilities. Quite simply it measures: does it have enough cash to hand?

The basic measure is the **liquidity** or the **current ratio** which divides:

◆ the current assets, the cash and the assets that should turn into cash over the next 12 months such as the debtors and the stock; by

◆ the current liabilities, the sums that need to be paid over the next 12 months:

$$\frac{\text{current assets (debtors, stocks and cash)}}{\text{current liabilities (trade creditors, VAT, PAYE, overdraft etc)}}$$

Simplistically, one would expect that a ratio of more than one would indicate financial stability, and significantly less than one would indicate problems. Whilst this is generally a safe working hypothesis, you must compare the ratio calculated against that of other businesses in the same industry as in some sectors an apparent low liquidity is normal. As for all ratios discussed in this book, what you need to know for any figures calculated is:

◆ whether for your industry the ratio is relatively good or bad, so why not obtain a copy of your competitors' accounts from Companies House and benchmark your ratios against theirs; and

◆ what the trend is over time (in this case, increasing or decreasing liquidity).

In the case of Widget Co Ltd the answer is 0.94 which would suggest that the company has reasonable liquidity:

$$\frac{90 + 200 + 2}{311} = 0.94$$

In order to generate cash at a known value, however, stock must first be sold. Stock is therefore less liquid than debtors and cash, and is therefore less reliable for meeting existing liabilities than these assets.

For example, an importer of summer goods had a poor season, and was left at the end of September with stock at a value equal to almost half the normal annual turnover and little or no prospects of sales until the following spring. While the current ratio still showed a reasonable position, the trading position worsened over October and November, as the debtors paid and the cash was used to meet overheads and pay some creditors. Despite having stock (a current asset) the business obviously had a liquidity problem.

The **acid test** (N ratio) measure of liquidity therefore excludes stock to see how readily the business can pay its current liabilities from the cash and near cash assets on hand:

$$\frac{\text{debtors and cash}}{\text{current liabilities}}$$

Again the trend over time (improving or worsening) and relative performance to the norm for your industry is as important, if not more so, than the actual number.

In the case of Widget Co Ltd the answer is 0.65 which might start to give some cause for concern:

$$\frac{200 + 2}{311} = 0.65$$

By contrast a shop which is buying on credit and selling for cash will typically have no debtors, but will still have a large value of creditors. You would therefore expect most shops to show a very low acid test measure; however, you would also expect most shops to be able to turn stock into cash fairly quickly, so in this sector a low ratio is not necessarily a cause for concern.

Gearing

Gearing (also known by the American term **leverage**) measures how financially exposed the company is by looking at to what extent the business's long-term finance is based on borrowed money rather than the shareholders' funds or **equity**. There are a number of different ways to calculate a gearing figure. The simplest is:

$$\frac{\text{Long-term loans}}{\text{Shareholders' funds}}$$

Again, the importance of the figures lies less in the absolute number, and more in how it compares with other businesses in the sector and the long-term trends.

Now you may well want and need to gear up your business by borrowing funds to invest in plant or to fund increasing working capital requirements caused by growth. This may, for example, allow you to expand your business faster than you could otherwise manage by putting in more of your own money or retaining profits generated. If you can borrow money to fund trading that makes you an additional profit of well in excess of the interest charge involved then it may well make sense to do so.

Indeed some businesses fail because their level of trading expands faster than their supply of funding to meet the funding gap, a problem known as **overtrading**.

However, this is at a risk as interest charges on long-term loans will need to be paid whatever the profits generated by the business. So, the higher the gearing (ie the greater the proportion of the business's long-term funding that is borrowed money), the higher the financial risk of the business.

Widget Co Ltd's gearing is:

$$\frac{\text{Long-term loans (the mortgage)} \quad £100,000}{\text{Total capital employed (shareholders' funds)} \quad £81,000} = 1.23$$

However, last year the gearing ratio was 2.94 (£150,000/£51,000), so the company has degeared by paying off £50,000 of its long-term debt and building up its shareholders' funds by retaining profits in the business, rather than paying these out by way of a dividend to shareholders. This action has reduced the financial risk of the business.

So have Widget Co Ltd's directors decided that things are becoming a bit more difficult, and decided to cut their interest costs and reduce the business's financial risks by using cash generated by the business to pay down its long-term debt?

Widget Co Ltd must pay £20,000 a year interest on its debt or default on its loan. By contrast, its competitor Thingumy Ltd, whose finances are more highly geared and is borrowing at the same interest rate of 20%, has to find £35,000 a year:

	Widget Co Ltd (£000)	Thingumy Ltd (£000)
Long-term loans	100	175
Shareholders' funds	81	6
Total 'capital employed'	181	181
Interest at 20%	20	35

So if times are getting hard, Thingumy Ltd will be more financially stretched by having to meet its interest payments (and don't forget, also its repayments of the principal elements) than Widget Co Ltd.

So why is Thingumy Limited taking this risk? The shareholders of Thingumy limited have only had to invest £6,000 in shareholders' funds and are using £175,000 of someone else's money which they have borrowed to fund their business. Widget Co Ltd's shareholders have much more of their own money tied up in the business (£81,000) as they are less reliant on borrowed cash.

You therefore need to balance the advantage gained by being able to borrow against the risk that this may pose to your business if things slow down.

UNDERSTANDING FINANCIAL EFFICIENCY

Cash is a critical resource for your business. As I hope will be becoming clear, a given level of trading for your business will require a certain amount of cash, so if your business is growing you will need to either:

- raise more cash to support this level of trading; or
- improve the efficiency with which you manage cash so that each pound can support more trading.

Calculating how efficiently a business's working capital is being managed is a matter of calculating the stock, debtor and creditor days as below. Again the trends over time and how these compare with your competition can provide important information.

There are a number of ways that these ratios can be calculated (eg you can take the year end figure for the balance concerned, or you can take an average of the opening and closing balance to get an average balance for the year).

In some ways, so long as you are consistent, it doesn't really matter. What is important is seeing the overall picture, and being consistent in approach when doing so over time, to monitor changes and trends or to benchmark against competitors.

The key ratios (and the way I prefer to calculate these) are as follows.

Stock days

$$\frac{\text{Stock at year end}}{\text{Purchases}} \quad \frac{90}{530} \times 365 = 62$$

On average Widget Co Ltd is holding stocks equivalent to two months' worth of purchases and this stock represents cash tied up in the business. So perhaps the company should investigate why it is carrying this amount of stock.

By looking more closely it may be possible to further calculate the following.

◆ Raw material days (say in the company's case 21). Is the business purchasing raw materials in over-large volumes to get good prices? If so, is this an efficient use of the cash available? How long does it take to get a delivery of raw materials? If these can be bought for next day delivery why hold three weeks' worth of supplies?

◆ Work in progress (**WIP**) days (say these are ten). Is this realistic? Does it really take ten days on average to make a widget? If it should only really take three days does this mean there is an inefficiency on the shopfloor which is tying up cash?

◆ Finished goods days (say these are 31). Now the business may need to hold a large range or quantity of finished goods in order to ensure it is able to give customers the service they want by always having the widget they want in stock. But is there cash tied up in lines that are rarely asked for? And if it takes ten days on average to make an item of stock, why does the business need to have 31 days' worth of finished items on hand?

Debtor days

Once you have made a sale to your customers you then have to collect payment and until the customer pays, this is more cash tied up in the business:

$$\frac{\text{Debtors at year end}}{\text{Sales (+ VAT if applicable so as to be comparable with debtors)}} = \frac{200}{1{,}175} \times 365 = 62$$

So it is taking Widget Co Ltd about two months on average to obtain payment from its customers. There may be ways that the company can speed up the process by improved credit control, introducing tighter payment terms (eg 14 days not 30), offering settlement discounts (eg X% if paid within 14 days of invoice). It may also be worthwhile calculating this figure for some of its individual key customers to see if it can spot any particularly bad payers who are pushing the average up and targeting these for particular action.

However, it can be an important part of your service to customers to offer credit terms. If you don't, customers may go elsewhere to buy from suppliers who do.

The company might also explore raising money against its debtor book by either **invoice discounting** or **factoring**, where it obtains an advance of normally 60% to 80% of the invoice value when the sale is made, with the balance of the invoice value being received (less the lenders' charges) once the customer pays. The pros and cons of these types of finance are set out in Chapter 9.

Creditor days

The other side of the coin of course is that you also have to pay your suppliers:

$$\frac{150}{(530 + 50 + 50 + 35 + 20 + 10) \times 1.175} \times 365 = 67$$

Trade creditors at year end
Purchases and purchased overheads
(eg rent, power etc) + VAT if applicable
so as to be comparable with trade creditors

So Widget Co Ltd is taking 67 days on average to pay its suppliers. In effect this is a free loan of cash from the suppliers to the company. So could Widget Co Ltd eke out its own cash by taking advantage of this loan for longer by taking longer to pay?

Possibly, but what risks is it then running of suppliers putting the company on stop, or taking legal action to recover their cash which may make obtaining credit in future more difficult?

Managing your working capital is therefore a matter of:

◆ measuring and tracking where you stand; and

◆ taking action to manage how much cash is tied up in working capital; but

◆ balancing the costs and consequences of the actions:
  – cutting down on stock frees up cash, but may cause customer service levels and operating efficiencies to suffer;
  – reducing the level of credit to customers saves cash, but may lose you sales;
  – taking longer to pay suppliers conserves cash, but can cost you in missed settlement discounts and disruptions as you go on stop.

It is important though to appreciate that different industries and businesses will have very different profiles. For example, Widget Co Ltd is obviously a manufacturer of widgets, selling these to other businesses on credit so it will have both stock and debtors.

A services business selling say consultancy to other firms will probably have debtors, but other than unbilled time on any project is unlikely to have any 'stock'.

By contrast, a shop will carry a lot of stock, after all, that's what they are there for, to have stock of the item the customer wants when they come in to buy it. However, shops will normally be selling for cash and so have few or no debtors. But even here there may be things that a shop can do to limit its investment in stock.

◆ Can it buy items on sale or return? So if a line does not move, it can go back to the supplier and the shop is not stuck with cash tied up in items which are not selling.

◆ Can it let out pitches in its premises to concessions which will sell their own goods and pay the shop a mix of rent for the pitch and a commission on value sold?

◆ Can it sell on commission for the suppliers, so that the stock in the shop doesn't actually belong to it and the business only has to pay the supplier for an item out of the proceeds when it is actually sold?

Taking Widget Co Ltd's figures from above you can quickly see in Figure 3 where the business's requirement for trading finance comes from:

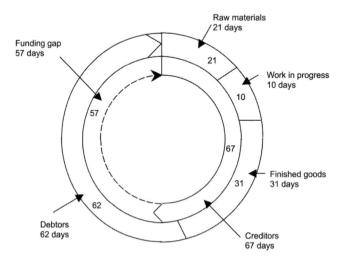

Fig. 3. Breakdown of trading finance.

From the moment the company buys something until it pays for it is on average some 67 days. But on average from the moment it buys the raw material the company takes 21 days before it goes into production, which takes 10 days, and the finished item then sits on the books for a further 31 days before being sold. So 62 days have ticked by before the goods purchased have actually made it through to a sale, meanwhile the company only has another five days left before the company is to pay the supplier.

Yet it is going to be a further 62 days from the point of sale before the company has the cash in from the customer, leaving a funding gap of on average 57 days which needs to be filled by borrowing.

This may be easier to see by looking at Whatsit Ltd, which only deals with one item at a time. Its current transactions are summarised below:

01/01   Purchases a whatsit at £100,000 on one month's credit
31/01   Pays supplier for whatsit
28/02   Sells whatsit at 200% mark up on one month's credit after normal two months in stock
31/03   Customer pays £300,000

Plotting these transactions over time we can show how borrowing requirement to fund this working capital cycle is £100 over two months:

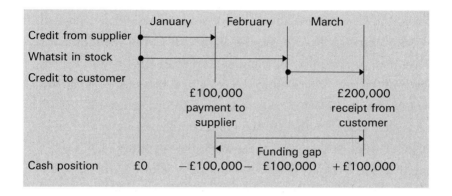

On average therefore it will be another month after the supplier wants paying for the goods before Whatsit Ltd sells them and a further month before the cash comes in from its customer. So Whatsit Ltd has to fund two months' worth of working capital from somewhere.

A bank would see this as an appropriate use of an overdraft facility which will swing back into credit as the transaction unwinds into realised profit and cash. However, in practice:

◆ Whatsit Ltd will need to agree the facility in advance with the bank;

◆ and it will need to offer some other **security** such as personal guarantees as the bank will be unlikely to lend against 100% of stock value without security agreed.

Recognising the nature of the business's funding requirement is therefore a critical first step to planning how you will manage its cash requirements by working capital management.

Reducing the requirement to tie up cash in working capital will mean that whatever cash is available will be available to fund a higher level of trading. In the case of Whatsit Ltd, its management could reduce its borrowing requirements to nothing if they can do the following.

- Reduce the investment in stock and debtors if it:
  - only bought in the whatsit when it had a firm order and could ship it straight out (a back-to-back deal), then the debtor would pay at exactly the same time as the creditor was due; or
  - only stocked what it could sell in a month for cash; or
  - took all its whatsits on a sale or return basis where they could be returned if they did not sell;
  - took all its whatsits on a consignment stock basis where, while it physically held the whatsits on site, the business only bought them from the supplier when a customer took one.

- Replace bank lending with supplier credit:
  - by taking three months' credit which would match the date of receipt and payment.

- Or a mixture:
  - eg take two months' credit from suppliers and only stock items which turn over in a month.

If you are anticipating expanding your business, you will need to ensure that you put in place the finance required to cover the funding gap as this expands with it. Businesses that expand faster than their financing is able to keep up with eventually run out of cash and fail through 'overtrading'.

RETURN ON CAPITAL EMPLOYED

The different activities of different parts of the business will generate different levels of profit and require different levels of investment. They will therefore produce different rates of return on the assets (capital) employed in that area of the business.

Widget Co Ltd has a manufacturing arm making widgets for sale to third parties, an installation business and a repair division. If the analysis of profitability is extended to include overheads, by making an assumption as to how overheads are allocated or apportioned between the divisions, it is possible to find a net profit for each division.

It may also be possible to allocate the assets used to each division (eg the vans may be allocated to installation, the bulk of the factory and the raw material stock to production and so on) to estimate the assets each division employs.

	Widget sales (£000)	Installation (£000)	Repair (£000)	Total (£000)
Return				
Sales	750	240	10	1,000
Gross profit	190	215	−5	400
Overheads	−150	−110	−20	−280
Operating profit	40	105	−25	120
Depreciation and interest	−25	−15	−5	−45
Net profit before tax	15	90	−30	75
Assets employed				
Fixed assets	100	40	10	150
Stock	60	20	10	90
Debtors	135	60	5	200
Cash		2		2
Total	295	122	25	442
Return on assets employed	5%	74%	−120%	17%

This exercise allows you to calculate the return you are getting by investing money in each part of the business.

$$\frac{\text{Net profit before tax}}{\text{Total assets employed}}$$

So in the case of Widget Co Ltd, if there is cash to invest it would appear to make sense to try to expand the installation side of the business as this generates a much higher return than production.

Occasionally this type of analysis will suggest that you may be best off disposing of some aspect of the business, such as the repair arm which is tying up cash only to make a loss. This in theory should allow you to redeploy resources to areas where you'll get a high return. However, before planning to shut any operation you do need to be careful as you must ensure that you are not simply removing some contribution towards the overall overheads, which will then need to be borne by the remaining parts of the business.

Again, if your accounting system can be set up to capture the relevant data this can be a useful exercise to do on a key customer by key customer basis, or for individual large contracts.

RETURN ON INVESTMENT

A related concept is the one of return on investment, which is the profits generated by the business (usually shown before tax) divided by the shareholders' funds invested in the business.

This also helps to explain why the owners of Thingumy Ltd have decided to gear up or leverage their company, as it shows how borrowings act as a multiplier of the investor's return:

	Widget Co Ltd	Thingumy Ltd
EBITDA	120	120
Depreciation	− 25	− 25
Interest	− 20	− 35
Profit before tax	75	60
Shareholders' funds	81	6
Return on investment	93%	1,000%

By using borrowed money rather than their own, the owners of
Thingumy Ltd have made the company more financially risky as
it has lower profits through a higher interest cost and a greater
exposure to default on its borrowings in times of difficulty.

However, in doing so they have increased their return from a
business generating exactly the same level of underlying trading
profits as Widget Co Ltd; which is giving them 1,000% return on
the cash they have invested compared with the 93% return
enjoyed by Widget Co Ltd's owners.

HAVING FAITH IN NUMBERS

If you are not familiar with reading accounts there are some
general rules that you should bear in mind throughout these
chapters.

◆ The trends in the numbers (say over time, such as growth, or in
   comparison with other similar businesses known as
   benchmarking) tend to be more important than any individual
   absolute figure.

◆ Do not be fooled into thinking that the numbers are ever
   absolutely true as any set of accounts will always be a matter
   of judgement. For example, a company should provide for its

bad debts, which means recognising the cost of the bad debts in its P&L and reducing the value of debtors on the balance sheet. But how much it should prudently provide is a matter for the directors' judgement.

◆ The numbers are produced as a result of how the business is being run; they are symptoms and evidence of what is happening, not the cause. As a result the numbers by themselves don't tell you what you need to know; they are guides to help you work out the questions to ask and consider what plans to put in place.

◆ So the numbers should be used to plan your actions for the future by setting quantified and measurable financial targets for the business (eg reducing its average debtor payment time to 45 days by the end of the year) as part of your plan for your business, and you can then use the numbers to monitor your progress.

◆ The actions you will have to take to make these financial results appear will, though, be real actions in the real world. They may include setting tight credit terms for the customers, issuing statements, picking up the telephone to chase in the money when it is due and putting customers on stop if they don't pay.

How Much Cash Does Your Business Need?

As you will have seen your business needs money to cover its requirements for:

- working capital to allow it to trade from day-to-day and to meet its overheads, which will include funding for payments to the business's directors and owners for their work in the business; and

- investment to allow it to develop and survive into the longer term, which will include funding for payments to give investors in the business a return and repay borrowings.

You will always need more than you think as these two real life examples show:

- The management bought out a specialist manufacturer that was turning over approximately £13 million. Within a year turnover had increased significantly, with prospects of hitting £20 million as a result of the failure of one of its main competitors. As a result within a year the business was seriously overtrading and came very close to collapse, only being saved by a **sale and leaseback** of its property (see Chapter 8) which released approximately £1 million of cash.

- At the same time (and only 20 miles down the road) the managers of an electronics business had bought their plant out of a receivership. Unfortunately in their case, rather than turnover recovering from the receivership level of £30 million to the expected £40 million, things got worse, falling to closer to £20 million. Given the business's high overheads this translated into severe losses and as a result the business failed again within 18 months.

The business's cash requirement will result from the complex interaction of its profitability, which generates cash, with its requirement for cash to meet its working capital and investment needs.

So how do you understand how this is working in your business, and then how do you establish what levels of funding you are likely to need going forwards?

The answer is that:

◆ to understand what is happening to the finances of your business as you trade you need to draw up a **statement of source and application** of funds; and

◆ to establish how much finance you are likely to need you need to draw up a **cashflow forecast**.

STATEMENT OF SOURCE AND APPLICATION OF FUNDS

Profitability is all very well, but it is actually cash that pays the bills. Sometimes it can be difficult to see whether the business is actually generating cash or not and if so, what is happening to it.

A statement and source of application of funds (**SSAF** or Source & Apps and now more properly known as a cashflow statement) can be used to demonstrate where the money has come from (the sources) and gone to (the applications).

In my view this is one of the best ways to obtain an overview of your business's performance. In my experience it also mirrors the way bank managers tend to read accounts. They are, however, notoriously difficult to get to balance and you may find it easiest to ask your accountant to prepare it for you.

The beauty of the SSAF is that it provides a link that shows what has happened to the profit generated by or introduced into the business.

So for Widget Co Ltd, the company has apparently produced a net profit after tax of £50,000, yet the company's overdraft has gone up by £24,000. So where has the cash gone?

A simple statement of source and application of funds can help explain (see page 71).

The net profit after tax for the year is after having suffered a £25,000 charge for depreciation, which is obviously not a real cash item. So adding this back, you find the net funds generated from operations ie the cash you would expect to see generated by these profits as a source of funding for the business of £75,000.

However, you know that £20,000 of this has been applied to paying out a dividend so this is no longer available for the business.

Then you can see that over the year the level of debtors and stock has gone up by a total of £80,000. As shown in the last chapter this translates into £80,000 more cash absorbed by the business tied up in stock and debtors than in last year. These funds have therefore been applied to building up assets.

Widget Co Ltd
Statement of source and
application of funds
12 month period to 31 December 2005

				Source	Applications
				Where the cash	
				comes from	has gone
Funds generated from operations					
Profit after tax				50	
Add back depreciation				25	
Net funds generated from operations				75	
Dividends paid					20
Balance sheet movements	**BF**	**CF**	**Move-ment**		
Stock	60	90	30		30
Debtors	150	200	50		50
Trade creditors	−101	−150	−49	49	
PAYE/NI	−3	−3	0		
VAT	−15	−22	−7	7	
Corporation tax	−30	−25	5		5
Mortgage	−150	−100	50		50
				131	155
					−24
Balanced by movements in bank and cash					
Overdraft	−37	−61	−24		
Cash at bank/petty cash	2	2	0		
					24

On the creditors' side of the balance sheet, trade creditors and the sum due for VAT have also gone up by a total of £56,000, but credit given by a trade creditor or by the Crown is in effect a loan to the business so it is a source of funds. If these organisations did not give you this extra credit then you would have had to spend (ie apply) more cash during the year to keep the balances down to the level that were brought forward from last year.

Meanwhile the balance due to the Crown for corporation tax has gone down by £5,000 while £50,000 of the mortgage debt has been paid off. So the company has applied funds generated by the business to reducing these liabilities.

The result of all these movements is that the company has required an extra £24,000 with which to make ends meet, which has come from increasing the company's overdraft, which is exactly what has happened.

CASHFLOW FORECASTING

To predict what your financing requirements are likely to be you need to prepare a cashflow forecast. This will be a vital document, for:

◆ actively managing the cash in your business to extract maximum trading 'value' from it;

◆ obtaining and maintaining support from lenders for whatever facilities you may need.

Cashflow forecasting is essentially straightforward as you are dealing with real cash movements into and out of the business, not more abstract accounting transactions, such as accruals, prepayments or depreciation.

Forecasts can be prepared on, say, a monthly basis for the coming year, or for more detailed control on a weekly basis (say for 13 weeks), or in some crisis situations they have to be done on a daily basis. Obviously:

◆ the further into the future you are projecting, the more uncertain the outcome is likely to be;

◆ the longer the periods used to forecast, the greater the danger that the results may hide a mid-period spike, where for example the figure at the end of the month in your monthly forecast may look acceptable as it is within your overdraft limit, but this is hiding the fact that the PAYE payment due mid-month will push you well over the limit.

For any cashflow forecast, all you are looking to calculate is:

- the cash you are going to get *in* that period;
- less the cash you are going to pay *out* that period;
- to give a **net** movement ('flow') of cash into or out of the business.

Adding the net inflow (or deducting the net outflow) of cash to the balance held at the start of the period gives the balance at the end as shown below:

	Period 1 £000	Period 2 £000
Cash in	100	100
Less cash out	−50	−125
Net cash in (out) flow	50	−25
Balance brought forward	25	75
Balance carried forward	75	50

Widget Co Ltd has produced a cashflow forecast as shown in Figure 4. This type of forecast lends itself to being set up on a spreadsheet so that it can be updated easily.

The secret of cashflow forecasting is to keep it simple, and to work methodically and logically down the page through all the cash coming in and going out of the business.

For example, your **cash received** will come from the following:

Widget Co Limited Cashflow forecast
12 month period to 31 December 2006

	Bal BF (£000)	Jan (£000)	Feb (£000)	Mar (£000)	Apr (£000)	May (£000)	Jun (£000)	Jul (£000)	Aug (£000)	Sep (£000)	Oct (£000)	Nov (£000)	Dec (£000)	Total (£000)
Sales														
Net		50.0	50.0	75.0	75.0	100.0	125.0	125.0	125.0	125.0	125.0	125.0	100.0	1,200.0
VAT		8.8	8.8	13.1	13.1	17.5	21.9	21.9	21.9	21.9	21.9	21.9	17.5	210.0
Gross		58.8	58.8	88.1	88.1	117.5	146.9	146.9	146.9	146.9	146.9	146.9	117.5	1,410.0
Cash inflows														
Existing debtors	200.0	100.0	100.0											200.0
New sales				58.8	58.8	88.1	88.1	117.5	146.9	146.9	146.9	146.9	146.9	1,145.6
Sale of machine								29.4						29.4
Other														0.0
Total inflows		100.0	100.0	58.8	58.8	88.1	88.1	146.9	146.9	146.9	146.9	146.9	146.9	1,375.0
Cash outflows														
Existing trade creditors	150.0	75.0	75.0											150.0
New purchases				29.4	29.4	44.1	44.1	58.8	73.4	73.4	73.4	73.4	73.4	572.8
Wages		8.8	8.8	8.8	15.8	15.8	15.8	15.8	15.8	15.8	15.8	8.8	8.8	154.0
PAYE/NI	3.0	3.0	3.8	3.8	3.8	6.8	6.8	6.8	6.8	6.8	6.8	6.8	3.8	65.3
Rent				12.5			12.5			12.5			12.5	50.0
Heat, light and power		2.4	10.6	2.4	2.4	10.6	2.4	2.4	10.6	2.4	2.4	10.6	2.0	60.8
Telephones		3.5	3.5	3.5	3.5	3.5	3.5	3.5	3.5	3.5	3.5	3.5	3.5	42.3
Postage, printing, stationery		2.4	16.5	2.4	2.4	2.4	2.4	2.4	2.4	2.4	2.4	2.4	2.4	42.3
Audit					11.8									11.8
VAT	22.0	22.0			8.3			19.6			19.2			69.1
Mortgage capital	100.0	4.2	4.2	4.2	4.2	4.2	4.2	4.2	4.2	4.2	4.2	4.2	4.2	50.0
Bank interest		1.7	1.7	1.7	1.7	1.7	1.7	1.7	1.7	1.7	1.7	1.7	1.7	20.0
Corporation tax	25.0									25.0				25.0
Purchase of machine								58.8						58.8
Dividend payment										20.0				20.0
Contingency		5.0	5.0	5.0	5.0	5.0	5.0	5.0	5.0	5.0	5.0	5.0	5.0	60.0
Other														0.0
Total outflows		127.8	128.9	73.4	88.0	93.8	98.1	178.7	123.2	172.5	134.2	116.2	117.1	1,452.0
Net movement		−27.8	−28.9	−14.7	−29.2	−5.7	−10.0	−31.8	23.7	−25.6	12.7	30.7	29.7	−77.0
Balance BF	−61.0	−61.0	−88.8	−117.7	−132.4	−161.6	−167.3	−177.3	−209.1	−185.5	−211.1	−198.4	−167.7	
Balance CF		−88.8	−117.7	−132.4	−161.6	−167.3	−177.3	−209.1	−185.5	−211.1	−198.4	−167.7	−138.0	
Overdraft facility		−100.0	−100.0	−100.0	−100.0	−100.0	−100.0	−100.0	−100.0	−100.0	−100.0	−100.0	−100.0	
Headroom/(excess)		11.2	−17.7	−32.4	−61.6	−67.3	−77.3	−109.1	−85.5	−111.1	−98.4	−67.7	−38.0	

Fig. 4. Sample cashflow forecast.

- *Existing debtors* who pay during the period. Look down your list of debtors, decide who is likely to pay in which period, and fill in the boxes.

- *New sales.* Prepare a simple sales forecast by branch, line of business, contract, customer, or whatever is most appropriate for your business.

  Widget Co Ltd has forecast a turnover of £1.2 million, a 20% growth on last year, but it has also shown its seasonal pattern of sales in its forecast which are heavier in the second half of the year. Then calculate how much of these sales will be for cash (and so received immediately) and which will be on credit, where Widget Co Ltd knows that its customers take on average two months to pay. Then fill in the appropriate boxes (remembering to add VAT as your receipts will be gross).

- *Any other sources.* Will you be injecting any new funds, receiving any insurance payouts or generating any other cash from anywhere at all, like Widget Co Ltd which is planning to sell off an old machine? If so, estimate how much and when the cash will be received (don't forget VAT where it applies), and enter the figures.

You can now total all these to obtain your estimated total weekly inflows.

Outflows are calculated on exactly the same principles.

Your trade creditor (or purchase ledger) list also tells you who you owe money to for purchases and expenses. So in the same way that you forecast receipts from debtors, you can go down this list and plan when you are going to pay what to whom. Bear in mind that you will also need to continue to make purchases as you trade, so these can be forecast in the same way as you forecast sales (Widget Co Ltd is assuming purchases of 50% of sales and two months to pay) and plan in the payments (gross of VAT) for when you are going to make them.

Wages may be paid weekly or monthly so the net amounts should be shown when they will go out.

PAYE is due once a month in respect of last month's wages (so you will see that for Widget Co Ltd this rises the month after the wages figure goes up to reflect increased overtime to cater for the increased sales). VAT is normally due at the end of the month following the end of the business's quarter, so predicting the dates of both these types of payments should be straightforward.

You will need to plan payments for rent, heating, lighting, power, telephone, and your other commitments in the same way, as well as remembering to estimate how much VAT will need to be paid, and when.

The keys to successful cashflow forecasting are the following.

◆ *Know where you are starting from.* As you stand today you have a balance at the bank; you are owed money by your debtors that you are expecting to receive; and you will owe money to trade creditors, the Inland Revenue, HM Customs & Excise (now combined into one organisation, HM Revenue & Customs), and so on. Use these figures as your opening balances. If you do not have exact figures (why not?) then use your best estimates. If you have cheques sitting in the drawer that have not been sent out, add these back to your creditors and adjust your cashbook so as to show a real position.

◆ *Forecast on a cashbook basis.* This means that you post payments immediately they are made, but recognise receipts only when they have cleared the bank. The advantage of this is that it will always show a worst case position since it will always take a few days for cheques and other payments to actually hit your account and be reflected in your bank statement. So your position at bank per the bank statement will always be better than the forecast by the value of this float.

◆ *Be realistic in your estimates of timings and amounts.* Your forecast needs to take into account:
  – What level are sales/purchases running at now?
  – What changes are really likely to happen over the period?
  – What have you experienced in prior periods? (How quickly do your customers actually pay?)
  – What are your terms of trade? (What length of credit do you allow customers/are you allowed by suppliers?)
  – What are your due dates for statutory payments? (For example, the 19th of the month for PAYE.)
  – What are your periodic payments? (For example, quarterly bills for utilities and rent.)
  – What **capital expenditure (capex)** (purchases of fixed assets such as machinery) are you planning?

◆ *When in doubt be prudent.* Be pessimistic about when, and how much people are going to pay you, and when you are going to have to pay others.

◆ *Make your assumptions explicit.* If you tell your bank manager that sales are going to increase by 20% the week after next, you can then also tell them that this is because your contract with XYZ plc comes on stream. Otherwise they may just think that you are relying on the new sales fairy to wave a wand and make this happen.

Widget Co Ltd's assumptions are shown in the example on page 78.

Widget Co Ltd
Cashflow forecast
12 month period to 31 December 2006
Assumptions

Sales	Growth of 20% on the current year (2005 33.3%)
	Seasonal pattern with highest sales June to November
Cash inflows	
Existing debtors	Over two months based on debtor days of 62
New sales	Over two months based on debtor days of 62
Sale of machine	Sale of old widget reaming machine at £25k + VAT
Other	
Cash outflows	
Existing trade creditors	Over two months based on creditor days of 67
New purchases	Two months at 50% of sales (current cost of materials %) + VAT
Wages	Base payroll of £150k gross
	Overtime and temporary labour over stock building period April to Oct £70k gross, 70% net paid in month, 30% PAYE and NI paid following month
Rent	Warehouse paid quarterly
Heat, light and power	Some utilities on monthly payment plans, some quarterly (+ VAT)
Telephones	Monthly plan (+ VAT)
Postage, printing, stationery	Monthly budget for expenditure + annual catalogue produced in Feb (+ VAT)
Audit	Payable after completion of the audit in April (+ VAT)
VAT	Quarterly
Mortgage capital and interest	Monthly payment
Corporation tax	Due nine months after the year end
Purchase of machine	Purchase of new widget reaming machine at £50k (+ VAT)
Dividend payment	To be proposed based on profitable trading
Contingency	£5k per month allowed
Balance BF	Balance brought forward is − £61k per cashbook

◆ *Check that you are showing all aspects of any transaction.* Widget Co Ltd has its sales peak from June through to November so to build stock to deal with this it has budgeted for temporary extra staff and overtime from April through to October.

◆ *Experiment with sensitivities.* Flex some of your key assumptions (what if sales go up by only 10% instead of 20%, what if customers take 90 days to pay instead of 60?) to see how sensitive the forecast is to these fluctuations. Make sure that you fully reflect all aspects of any change, however. But remember to ensure you flex all the linkages; if sales go down, then purchases and wages should fall as well.

◆ *Think widely.* Check that you have allowed for all possible payments that may need to be made by comparing the type of items with last year's detailed profit and loss account.
  – Have you allowed for corporation tax, redundancy payments, pension top ups, or repairs if any of these are likely to fall due in the period?
  – Go through some old bank statements and cheque book stubs. Have you allowed for all the types of payment that you find?

◆ *Check carefully to make sure it all adds up!* Widget Co Ltd's cashflow has check totals built in at the end. These are simply sums adding up the elements of the table in different ways to ensure that nothing has been left out. An example of the principle is illustrated below, where the first 9 is calculated by adding together the values of all of the column totals, while the second is calculated by adding all of the row totals. If the two check sum totals match, you can be confident that there are unlikely to be any basic arithmetic errors in the table.

- *Tie your forecast into an integrated package.* Your cashflow forecast should link to your profit and loss forecast and balance sheet forecast and the whole package should balance. This type of integrated forecast can be set up on a set of spreadsheets, but you will need to be careful to ensure it is set up so that it balances properly. This can be complex so it may be easiest to either use one of the commercially available packages to prepare it (such as Win Forecast) or to have your accountant prepare a forecasting model for you. If you do so, it is important, however, that you own the model and operate it on an ongoing basis, as it is you and not your accountant who is responsible for understanding and managing your business's finances.

- *Finally, remember that you do not have a 100% reliable crystal ball.* Build in a margin as a round sum **contingency** to allow for the cost of things that will inevitably come crawling out of the woodwork. The more uncertain your starting point, the larger this needs to be, up to say, 10% or 20% of payments in some cases.

Part of the reason for cashflow forecasting is to ensure your lender's confidence that you are in control of your finances. Having a contingency in place is not only prudent, but if it helps ensure that you beat your forecast cash performance, it will also help to ensure that your lender's confidence in your management skills, and hence their willingness to lend you money, will increase.

The technique can also be used to review any large contract or project that the company is planning to undertake.

Whatsit Ltd is at the limits of its overdraft when it receives news that it has won a large contract, the details of which are:

Contract value:	£620K
Subcontracted labour:	£300K at £50K per month over six months
Materials:	£200K, of which £100K is required in the first month, followed by £20K per month for five months
Giving a profit of:	£120K

While the company has one month's credit from its suppliers for materials, it has to pay its labour monthly (but labour is paid gross with no **PAYE** deductions). There is no retention on the contract and the company is to bill at the end of each month for the materials delivered, labour and one sixth of the profit, and the client will pay at the end of 30 days.

The directors are jubilant, and are convinced that this is going to save the company.

Undoubtedly, it is a profitable contract. But should Whatsit Ltd take it? The answer lies in looking at the cashflow. To simplify matters, VAT has been omitted.

Projected project cashflow (£000) per month

	1	2	3	4	5	6	7	8
Receipts	–	–	170	90	90	90	90	90
Payments								
Labour	50	50	50	50	50	50	–	–
Materials	–	100	20	20	20	20	20	–
Total payments	50	150	70	70	70	70	20	
Net movement (out)/ inflow	(50)	(150)	100	20	20	20	70	90
Cumulative	(50)	(200)	(100)	(80)	(60)	(40)	30	120

The answer then, is clearly no, not as it stands. The project's early cash outflows mean that Whatsit Ltd, which is at the edge of its facility, will immediately run out of cash if it accepts the contract and starts work.

Instead, Whatsit Ltd must explore whether the proposed payment terms can be changed to speed up receipt of cash (eg an upfront payment), greater credit can be obtained from the labour and material suppliers, and/or negotiate increased facilities with its bank to enable the project to be undertaken.

Once you have prepared your forecast, use what you have produced.

◆ *Review it critically.* Having prepared it on a prudent basis, now see what scope there is for moving payments or bringing forward receipts. Compare the balance at the end of each week with the facility you have with the bank. Are you going to remain within your overdraft facility (in banking jargon to have **headroom**) or are you going to go over your overdraft limit (be in **excess**)?

- *Use it to plan.* If you are going to be in excess the way Whatsit Ltd is going to be according to its cashflow forecast on page 74, plan what you are going to do about it. Look at what payments or receipts you can change. Whatsit could for example look at:
  - offering settlement discounts to encourage debtors to pay immediately;
  - stretching its payments to its suppliers to take more credit from them;
  - reducing its level of purchases required by working down its existing stock holding before buying new supplies of materials;
  - negotiating a reduction in the capital repayments on the mortgage to reduce the contingency it is allowing;
  - put off replacing its machine until next year (or arrange to buy it on finance that spreads the payment over a number of years);
  - cancelling any dividend payments; or
  - reducing the allowance made for contingencies.

  Managing your cash tightly so as to maximise the amount retained in the business is known as **bootstrapping** as it is the business pulling itself up with its own bootstraps and generating funds with which to grow from within the business.

  You should however also speak to your bank as far in advance as possible about any expected excess to agree a temporary extra facility.

- *Use it to obtain facilities.* By working on the cashflow forecast you can use it to explain to your bank or other lender why you are going to need further facilities, how much these will be, how long it will be for, and how you are going to then pay them back.

◆ As a word of caution, however: don't run to the bank with your first draft cashflow forecast as this is likely to show a dreadful cash position (you have been pessimistic after all). Only discuss your forecast with your bank once you have had a chance to review it thoroughly to amend and adjust it for the things that you are realistically going to be able to manage to improve the position. You need to discuss a final working forecast that is challenging, but realistic and prudent, not ultra pessimistic.

◆ *Use it to monitor*. Roll the forecast **forwards**, week after week or month after month, comparing what actually happens to your forecast. Ask yourself where they differed and why. Then ask what that tells you about your estimates going forward and where you can/should amend your forecast to improve your estimates.

Where Does the Cash Come From and What Are the Issues?

WHAT ARE THE SOURCES OF BUSINESS CASH?

For any business there are essentially two sources of finance: money generated within the business itself, and money introduced into the business from outside.

How a business can be run so as to generate the maximum amounts of cash internally and use this as efficiently as possible (bootstrapping) has already been largely covered in the previous chapters where it can be seen that this is a matter of the following.

◆ Squeezing money out of working capital (or to look at it another way, making whatever cash you do have go as far as possible in funding trading) by actively managing both to:
  – minimise the investment in current assets (stock and debtors); and
  – maximise the finance available from its normal sources of trade credit
  where a technique such as consignment stocking in effect helps both sides of the equation.

◆ Retaining as much as possible of the profits from trading in the business, which is a matter of restricting the dividends paid out to shareholders (**dividend policy**) or cash drawn by the partners or owner.

The range of sources of external finance will be covered in detail in section B and divides into three broad categories.

Debt

◆ This is money that has been lent to a business by a creditor. Debt can be:

◆ Institutional, by which I mean formal lending by a financial institution set up to advance funds as a business such as banks, building societies, **venture capital** firms (in respect of some parts of their investments) and a range of businesses known as **Asset Based Lenders** (ABLs). These institutions offer a range of financing services such as overdrafts, mortgages, leasing, hire purchase, sale and leaseback, **trade finance**, factoring and invoice discounting.

◆ Non-institutional, by which I mean both:
  – loans in the normal sense such as directors' loans into the business;
  – credit provided normally in relation to a transaction or series of transactions by a third party, which is the equivalent to a loan. Examples of these would include trade credit, sums due to the Crown by way of VAT or PAYE/NI and **vendor finance** where the seller of a business allows the buyer time to pay for some or all of the purchase price over a period of time.

Grants

Grants are defined by the DTI as a 'sum of money given to individual or business for a specific project or purpose', where as long as you keep to any conditions attached to the grant you will not have to repay it as you would with a loan, nor will you have to give up any shares in your business, as you would with an equity investor.

Within grants I would include soft loans which are loans (a form of debt) but on favourable or discounted terms.

Equity

Equity is money or other assets put into a business by investors in return for their share of the profits of the business after the creditors have been paid.

At its simplest this is the personal capital put into or retained in a business by its proprietor or partners or the investment in shares and retained earnings by its shareholders.

However, it can become more complex: for example, where a business has acquired an investment from a third party such as another individual investor like a **business angel**, or an institution such as a venture capitalist, or from the public and/or institutions by way of a **listing** on a **stock exchange**. These situations may lead to different classes of shares being issued with differing rights to:

◆ control the company's affairs by voting;

◆ receive payments where some shares may be **preference shares** which have a fixed rate of dividend (akin to a rate of interest on debt) and have to be paid in priority to the ordinary shares; and even;

◆ convert into other types of shares or be repaid under certain conditions.

HOW DO YOU GO ABOUT RAISING CASH?

Raising external cash from any investor or institutional lender will involve a process, the starting point for which is a business plan.

There are many good books on business planning available (see www.howtobooks.co.uk) but essentially any business plan needs to cover:

◆ What you are going to do.

◆ How you are going to do it.

◆ Why you think you will be successful.

◆ Why you will need cash, how much you need and how long for (this is your cashflow forecast which you should first put together ignoring sources of finance. Then having established the funding requirement, you should decide what the most appropriate package of funding may be and work this in.)

◆ Why it is a good idea for them to provide the cash you are looking for, which is essentially a matter of:
  – the risks involved (and what you are doing to manage these); versus
  – the return they will get.

You also need to understand the lender's or potential investor's perspective and what they are looking for in any proposal.

Of course each lender or investor will have their own financial criteria on which to assess a proposal, but over and above this most will also have a wider ranging set of sometimes informal criteria which any proposal has to meet.

A good starting point is an old banker's acronym, CAMPARI (Character, Ability, Means, Purpose, Amount, Repayment, Insurance), capturing seven key criteria as listed below. This is one of a number of traditional checklists that bankers have for assessing any proposal (another version is known as the 7Ss but covers much the same ground). In my view any investment proposal will need to cover the points raised to the satisfaction of almost any external lender or investor.

Character

No one knowingly gives their money to a crook or a fool if they want to get it back (with a return).

♦ Will the investor or lender see you as honest? Will they trust your integrity and reliability, or have you any financial skeletons in the closet or made exaggerated claims in the past?

♦ Will they have confidence that you will keep them informed as to progress?

♦ Do they feel that you are someone they can work with over a medium to long-term period?

A track record of previous financial problems such as County Court Judgements, mortgage arrears or even insolvency proceedings (collectively known as **adverse**) is not necessarily a bar to obtaining funding. But it does tend to make it more expensive, as lenders and investors will want to build in an extra return required in light of the apparent extra risk involved in so called **sub prime** or **non-status** lending.

A track record of dishonesty can make raising finance extremely difficult, if not impossible, but even here I can think of a small number of ex-criminals who have gone on to run successful businesses which will have required financing.

Ability

However good your proposal, the lender or investor has to be confident that you can make it happen.

+ Do you and your management team clearly have the necessary skills and ability to run the business? Do you have a successful track record in this type of business?

+ Can they have confidence in your ability to manage your finances? Do you seem to be in control of your business (and its numbers)?

+ Will you be prepared get in help as and when you need it?

From a financial management point of view the more that you can demonstrate that you have future proofed your business by having and using good management information including forecasts, so that you can have finance in place before you need it, the better. No funder likes surprises. If you can foresee a requirement for cash coming then you have the time and information with which to speak to your funders about how to cover it.

The alternative is that you blunder into a cash crisis and end up writing cheques that take you over your agreed limit, which leaves the bank with the decision whether to meet the payment or to return it, something they dislike doing. One banker described this situation to me as application for overdraft by way of cheque, and it was the equivalent of the owners raising a red flag over their business saying I am not in control of my finances.

Means

How much are you worth (both as a guide to your past money

making performance and your ability to provide cash to cover any short-term problems)?

Purpose

You don't just go to the time, trouble and expense of raising or borrowing money for the sake of it. You do it because you have a plan.

◆ What is the plan and what are you intending to do with the money?

◆ How confident can the funder be that your plan is going to work? Is it a feasible idea, that appropriately matches funding against the need?

◆ Is the idea something that the lender feels is acceptable, given its own policies as a funder may not be able to become involved if the proposal conflicts with its own internal policies on:
  – ethics (as the funder may not be able to finance certain activities);
  – sector strategy (as the funder may wish to avoid certain sectors due to previous poor experiences or an assessment that they are overly risky);
  – geography (for example some building societies only wish to lend locally, as do most business angel investors, see Chapter 12, who wish to invest in businesses within easy reach);
  – concentration (where the funder already has significant exposure to a particular sector and wants to keep its risk spread across other sectors); or
  – competition (where the proposed activity is in some ways potentially in competition with some of the funder's other interests).

Amount

This really covers two areas.

◆ How much are you putting in compared with the risk you are asking the lender or other investors to take?

◆ Are you asking for enough to properly see the project through to completion?

Your plan therefore has to set out clearly what commitment you are making to the project, together with a clear picture of the further support you need (how much, how long, how it is to be paid back).

Repayment/return

Just as you do not go to the trouble of raising cash unless you have a plan that requires it, lenders and investors do not take the trouble and risk putting money into a plan unless they can see what and how they are going to:

◆ get their money back; and
◆ **earn out** of it by way of a reward for the risk taken.

As discussed above, your plan should already show how long you will need the money for and how is it to be repaid. But it also needs to show what interest a lender is going to earn, or return an investor is going to make on their money if they provide it.

The funder's job will then be to assess what risk your plan calls for them to take and whether the reward offered is commensurate with this.

Banks will typically have a matrix which gives the manager an interest charge that needs to be obtained for a given level of risk assessed as being taken by the bank.

Many investors will work on the basis of calculating the value today of the cash they expect to earn on the investment from dividends, repayments and growth in value of their shares over the period of the investment. This is done by applying an annual discount to the future streams of cash on the principle that £1 received today is worth more than £1 in a year's time, which in turn is worth more than £1 in two years' time and so on (see Chapter 11 for more details).

By applying this sort of approach to arrive at a **discounted cashflow** the investor can then calculate what this equates to as a rate of return on the proposed investment (known as the **internal rate of return** or IRR). They can then judge whether this provides a sufficiently high return for the risk involved.

Insurance

This means insurance for the lender in a somewhat colloquial sense: what assurance is there that they will get their money back? In practice for institutional lenders this translates into what sort of security is available to enable the loan to be repaid if the business is not able to make the instalments from:

- ◆ selling off the business assets;

- ◆ you, by way of calling on a personal guarantee that you have given (PG) which may also be backed up by a **charge** over your personal assets outside the business (a Supported PG);

◆ or the **Small Firms Loan Guarantee Scheme** (see Chapter 7).

Additionally, many lenders and investors will need you to take out insurance cover (eg key man life cover) as part of their insurance that their money is safe.

WHAT ARE THE ISSUES TO BE AWARE OF?

When thinking about the sources of finance for your business there are a number of issues that you will need to take into account.

Appropriateness

The need to match the type of funding (long- or short-term) to the underlying requirement has already been discussed at length.

Gearing and financial risk

The advantages in increasing the shareholders' rate of return and reducing the requirement for the owners to put up their own cash to finance the business through using borrowed funds, has to be balanced against the increased financial risk of default borne by the business.

Scalability and flexibility

Bear in mind that your finance does not simply need to support your business today, but into the future too, so ensure that your financing arrangements are flexible enough to be able to support your future plans and prospects, so that for example growth does not expose you to the risks of overtrading, or you are able to reduce your exposure if required.

Reliability and attitude to risk

Ensure that you understand to what extent you can rely on your sources of funding. Are your funders in with you for the long-term or short? What is their attitude to risk? Are they likely to support you through bad times as well as good and if not, what should you be doing about this?

Certainty

How certain is it that the finance being discussed will actually be made available in the agreed form by the investor or lender? Until you have actually signed the documentation and drawn down the funds there is always an element of uncertainty. You might be amazed by how many financing deals actually fall apart at the last minute.

Speed of funding

All finance raising exercises will take some time as a lender or investor will have a process they will wish to go through to assess the proposal before handing over any cash. This can range from a few days for a commercial **bridging loan** to three or four months for a venture capital investment. So you need to be looking forward to see what your requirements will be and to put applications in motion, allowing sufficient time for these to be completed before the need arrives.

Costs of funding

How much is your finance going to cost you?

◆ Financially, in terms of the cost of raising funds in the first place such as valuation fees, accountant's costs, and in ongoing payments such as charges and interest cost or a share in the eventual value of your business for an equity investor.

◆ In time, both to raise finance and to manage external providers after they have come on board.

- In control, with:
  - bankers requiring copies of regular management accounts and forecasts; or
  - a business angel taking an active role in the management; or
  - a venture capitalist appointing an independent director to keep an eye on their investment and driving the timing of an eventual sale of the business to give them their exit; or
  - a stock exchange requiring regular trading announcements and compliance with the appropriate levels of corporate governance for a publicly quoted company.

Tax efficiency

Generally speaking, interest is recognised as an expense of the business and is therefore deductible from profits before calculating tax. Dividends or drawings are payments to the owners of the profits made and are not tax deductible expenses of the business.

However, there has been a recent development where the HM Revenue & Customs has noticed that many venture capital investments were making a large part of the investment by way of debt (carrying tax deductible interest) rather than shares (requiring dividend payments from after tax profits). The Revenue has argued that this was an abuse of the rules and has therefore introduced a rule that where debt is provided by the main funder of a business, then the interest may not be tax deducible. The problem with this is that the rules at the time of writing seem quite unclear, for example if most of your funding comes from a bank overdraft, does this mean they are your main funder and therefore the interest is not tax deductible?

The practical position seems to be that for most purposes interest will continue to be deductible, but if you are contemplating obtaining an investment from a venture capitalist which may come as both debt and equity you will need to take appropriate tax advice.

On the other side of the coin, there are various schemes designed to encourage investment in small and medium-sized businesses such as the Enterprise Investment Scheme (EIS, see Chapter 12). So if you are seeking investors you can seek to structure the funding required to make it as tax efficient for both sides as possible.

Communication

Finally you will need to be thinking about how you can go about maintaining the confidence of your lenders or investors. Most institutional lenders or investors will have highly developed early warning systems to spot borrowers or investments that look as though they may be getting into difficulty (after all it is their job to protect their investments or loans). They will be very alive to risk and have an internal credit scoring process with which to assess their portfolio of borrowers or investments, which will then impact on:

◆ the margins they will look to earn from you given the level of risk they perceive they are taking; and

◆ their attitude towards providing further support if requested.

Having seen some of these matrixes, some of the factors that are used to flag up risk can be very sensitive and are things that the business itself may well not notice or consider particularly important. But you must appreciate that it takes lenders many,

many successful accounts earning a few per cent interest over base rate to cover a bad debt that they suffer from a business that goes down. So they will move to starting to try to exit from a relationship far sooner than most businesses ever realise.

So you will need to expend time and effort in communicating with your suppliers of outside cash, be they bankers or venture capitalists. In short you will need to manage your bank manager.

DEBT OR EQUITY SOURCE?

As will be covered in detail in Section B, the question of whether your business's cash requirements can be met by borrowing, and if so from which source, or whether you require an equity investment, will generally come down to the question of the available security. Whilst it is a bit crude, the flowchart in Figure 5 provides a rough and ready guide to the likely answer to this question.

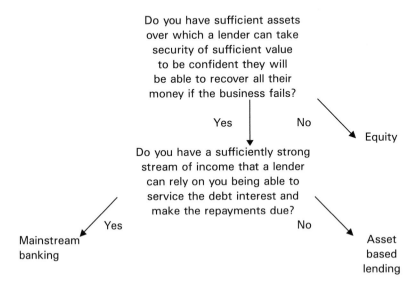

Fig. 5. Flowchart for debt *v* equity source.

Having covered the key issues the next section will look in more detail at the three broad streams of external finance available:

- debt (which will include some quasi debt sources of funding);
- grants;
- equity.

B

THE SOURCES OF EXTERNAL BUSINESS FINANCE

⑥

Debt

WHAT IS DEBT?

At its simplest, debt is simply borrowed money. Looking at a balance sheet such as Widget Co Ltd's (as shown in Chapter 2) some borrowings are easy to both see and understand. These are what could be regarded as formal borrowings, such as the overdraft and the mortgage, and are likely to be familiar to most people who have ever had a bank account or bought a house.

However, in addition to these formal borrowings, as discussed in the last section, essentially every liability on your balance sheet represents a source of cash that you have used and which you will eventually have to repay. So in addition to the obvious formal borrowings, all of the other current and long-term liabilities shown on your balance sheet, such as trade creditors and the tax man, should be regarded as sources of funding or debt to be used and managed to support your business.

Off balance sheet debt

Going even beyond this, debt can also take forms which are more complex and difficult to spot at first sight as they do not appear on the balance sheet at all. In fact some borrowings, such as the two examples below, are sometimes described as '**off balance sheet debt**'.

It is easiest to see this by taking a couple of practical examples. So, if your business needs a machine, the shareholders could either invest their own funds in order to buy it or you could borrow money with which to buy it. If you were to borrow money you will have bought an asset, so putting an asset on the balance sheet; but you will also have to show the corresponding liability for the loan.

Alternatively, you might find a finance company which will be prepared to buy the machine for you and put it into your factory. It won't be your machine, so the asset will not appear on your books but neither will you be taking out a formal loan that does so either. The finance company, however, will only have undertaken this transaction on the basis that you have signed up to an agreement that you will rent the machine over a period of time, at a cost that will cover the cost to them of the machine, plus their charges and an interest rate that is their profit on the deal. As a rental agreement stretching into the future this will not normally appear on your balance sheet as a liability.

Yet really this is still debt.

◆ The funding to buy the machine for your business's use has come from someone and it isn't the shareholders, who would otherwise have had to put up shareholders' funds to do so.

◆ Your business will be committed to making the rental payments over the next few years as if it were repayments of a loan.

◆ You are committed to a set level of payments every month or quarter the way you are with any loan (as opposed to dividends which you might choose not to pay to the shareholders if they had funded the machine) so the financial risk to the business is the same as a loan.

♦ The rental cost includes an element which is undoubtedly interest on the sum 'borrowed'.

As a second example, if you have a valuable asset such as a property and your business needs some funds, you might arrange to borrow money against this by way of a commercial mortgage at say 70% of the property's value. Again this will show up clearly on the balance sheet as cash having come into the business, matched by a liability for a new loan.

Taking this further, however, in order to raise more cash for your business than you could get through a normal mortgage, you might enter into a sale and leaseback arrangement instead. This is where you arrange to sell one of the business's assets, such as plant and machinery or property, to a finance company or investor at its full **open market value**. This enables you to release the entire value of the asset into the business as cash, but at the same time you agree to rent it back for a specified period (in some cases with an option to buy the assets back again at the end of the arrangement) so that you can continue to use the asset.

In this case what would appear on the balance sheet would again be an inflow of cash, but this time matched not by a loan but by the disposal of the asset involved.

Essentially, as in the 'rental' scenario discussed above, this type of transaction is still really a form of loan.

♦ Your business has the cash without the shareholders having to put up funds.

- Your business still has use of the asset.

- The lender has the security of the asset (it's just that they actually have ownership of it rather than the mortgage company's claim to seize it and sell it if they are not paid).

- Your business has a regular stream of payments that it needs to make monthly or quarterly that will include an element of what is clearly interest on the sums involved.

For the sake of this book, these types of financing sources, which might be described as quasi debt, such as say operating leases, are included in the section on debt as they are ways of obtaining assets for your business, are clearly not equity sources and are usually provided by very similar financial institutions to more mainstream lending.

So debt can involve:

- formal borrowings such as a loan or an overdraft;

- informal borrowings such as credit extended by a supplier;

- arrangements which provide the equivalent of a loan in terms of cash or an asset received, with a matching obligation to make payments, even if they do not appear as a liability on the balance sheet.

What you can see from the balance sheet is that debt divides into short- and long-term funding. For accounting purposes, anything due for repayment on demand (such as an overdraft), or due within the next 12 months (such as trade creditors or the next year's worth of lease instalments), will count as current liabilities on the company's balance sheet, whilst money not due in until over a year's time will count as long-term liabilities.

This chapter will therefore give a brief overview of the main sources of borrowings and types of lending available.

The following chapters will look more closely at bank borrowings, and issues such as security, before then reviewing the alternatives to banks that are now increasingly available in respect of borrowings for both investment and working capital.

WHO CAN YOUR BUSINESS BORROW FROM?

Your business can borrow from a number of different types of lender.

Yourself

You can obviously lend money to your company in a number of ways. In fact in many start-up situations it is very common for the owner of the business to do so by, for example, personally bearing expenses on behalf of the business which are only reclaimed from it later.

However, there is nothing to stop you as a director lending money to the business more formally by way of a director's loan rather than by injecting equity, if you have the funds available. This should be considered when discussing the appropriate financial structure of the business with your advisers. Obviously repayment of the loan principal is payment of a debt by the business and is therefore not taxable in your hands as income.

If you are lending money to your business, though, there is also nothing to stop you charging the business a reasonable commercial rate of interest and this interest income would be taxable.

You can also lend money to the company by way of some of the quasi debt approaches discussed above. So you could, for example, do the following.

◆ Purchase an asset that the business needs (such as a property) in your own name and rent it to the business at a commercial rate (but it may be more tax effective to do so through your pensions scheme if you have one available, see Chapter 8).

◆ Act as a sale and leaseback financier to the business by purchasing assets from it and renting them back.

If you are considering such a sale and leaseback transaction you will need to be careful of the following issues.

◆ There are restrictions imposed on the sale of substantial business assets from a company to the directors under **Section 320** of the Companies Act. These rules are designed to prevent directors looting a company's assets without the knowledge of the shareholders and so the purchase by a director of any substantial assets (in effect anything over the value of £100,000 or 10% of the balance sheet value) requires the approval of the shareholders in advance.

◆ Transfer at an undervalue, which is where an asset is sold at less than its fair value. In the event of an insolvency, the administrator or liquidator will review transactions going back over the two years leading up to the business's failure and can take action to set aside transactions at an undervalue.

Many of the above approaches will have significant tax planning implications so you should always seek advice on any proposed lending from your tax adviser.

If you are considering lending money to your business you should always ask yourself why it is required and what are the risks. If necessary, for example in a situation where the business's solvency may be an issue, take professional advice and resist the temptation to send good money after bad. After all, the business's cash requirements may still be more than you are able to afford and as an old saying popular amongst insolvency practitioners has it, 'There's no point putting enough fuel in the airplane to fly halfway across the Atlantic'.

For example, the managing director of a north-eastern business was coming up to retirement and had cleared the mortgage on his house. The business, however, got into difficulty and he decided to take out a mortgage on his matrimonial home in order to generate cash to put into the business. Unfortunately the business then failed, which of course meant he had no income from the business with which to make the mortgage repayments.

However, if you are lending to your business, don't forget that you can arrange to take security for your loan to help protect your position.

Related parties
The next group of potential lenders are related parties such as

family and friends who may be interested in advancing money by way of a loan.

Family members or friends can be a good source of funding for you. First, they already know you and your character and abilities. They may therefore be more willing to lend to you than an institution which does not know you, and are less likely to want to see a detailed business plan and sets of forecasts. They may also be more flexible and willing to lend without taking formal security, or to lend to you at lower interest rates than commercial lenders.

The disadvantages of borrowing from family and friends can be that they:

- lend you more than they can really afford so causing a high degree of stress;

- can find that they need the money back at a time when you cannot afford to pay it to them;

- may not understand the difference between a loan on which they are paid interest and an investment where they are entitled to a share in the profits of the business, or even to become involved in helping to run it.

Think carefully before accepting money from such sources as to the risks involved and the impact it might have on your relationships if it all goes wrong. For example, a retired professional invested a large proportion of his pension pot in backing a new company which was developing a new product. Eventually this business had used up all of his available cash and needed more. The individual involved persuaded his brother to put in a sizeable loan, only to find that the business went into insolvency the following month.

In particular, if your business plan has been turned down by normal commercial funders, think very carefully about why they have done so, before being tempted to use family and friends as lenders of last resort.

If you do borrow from family and friends then you should draw up a written loan agreement clearly setting out the arrangements including the rate of interest, length of the loan and the scheduled repayment dates, as well as any other conditions agreed such as a share of profits (if any), role the lender is going to have in the business (if any), as well as how any disputes may be dealt with. To minimise any possibility of subsequent problems it is probably worth having this drawn up by a solicitor.

Having a written agreement will also help you should HM Revenue & Customs ever take a look at the interest you are paying out or the interest the lender is receiving, which they will have to declare on their tax return.

Involving a pension scheme

Another related party that is sometimes overlooked is your pension scheme. A personal pension scheme is essentially a pot of money held in a trust that is controlled by the trustees of the scheme in accordance with the scheme's rules. The trustees' job is to both protect the funds received into the scheme and invest these so they grow.

As a result, pension schemes can be involved in funding a business in two ways.

◆ In some circumstances the trustees of the fund may be able to invest part of the fund by making a loan to the business at the appropriate commercial rates of return and terms for such a loan. It must be said, however, that such loans are rare.

◆ As a pot of cash and investments, personal pension schemes are usually by definition in a good position to borrow money at cheaper rates than the underlying business with its mix of assets and liabilities.

So if the business is in need of cash and the pension scheme has sufficient assets and borrowing capacity to do so, it can make sense for the scheme to borrow sufficient funds in its own right to purchase the company's property from it on a sale and leaseback basis.

Indeed if you are contemplating buying a commercial property personally, with a view to letting it to your business, then you should take advice about doing so through a pension scheme so as to obtain the maximum tax benefit available.

The ability of any pension scheme to engage in these sorts of activities is a complex area and will be dependent on the type of scheme involved, the rules of the scheme and its financial position including its capacity to borrow. To undertake any such loan you will need to take expert professional advice from an IFA experienced in this area. Finance brokers who organise such borrowings can arrange an introduction to such an adviser if required (see the Useful Contacts section at the back of the book).

Trading partners

The third general category of lenders are those people, businesses and institutions with which you are engaged in trading from day-to-day.

When suppliers provide goods and allow your business time to pay, this is in effect an interest free loan (although the supplier should have costed in the credit they will allow the company in pricing the job). The more that your business is able to borrow from suppliers with their agreement in this way, the less you have to borrow elsewhere.

Managing and maximising the financing available, through trade creditors and other sources such as the Crown in respect of PAYE/NI and VAT, has already been discussed in the need to manage your working capital covered in Section A.

The level of credit you will be able to obtain from trade suppliers is, however, increasingly becoming dependent on your business's credit rating as the role of credit insurers grows in the UK. Credit insurers are companies through which a supplier can take out a policy that you will pay your debt to them. This service is increasingly being used in connection with invoice based finance such as factoring or invoice discounting which are themselves growing in importance (see Chapter 9).

Simplistically, credit insurers work by allocating a total level of risk that they are prepared to take in respect of your business across their portfolio (say for example this was £100,000). They will then parcel this amount out to a series of credit limits (which might be ten limits of £10,000 each) to their customers who wish to trade with you until this limit is used up.

Obviously therefore, in order to maximise the credit available from your suppliers, you will want them to be able to find as much cover from insurers as possible. You therefore need to manage your credit rating so as to avoid problems by doing the following.

◆ Filing your accounts on time; late accounts are considered a significant early warning sign by most lenders.

◆ Filing profitable accounts that show a positive balance sheet and most importantly demonstrate, when the insurer prepares an SSAF (see Chapter 4) from them, a business that has been generating cash.

◆ Avoiding an adverse credit history such as County Court Judgements, loan arrears and so on.

The dangers of failing to manage the position can be significant.

A company turning over £20m failed to file its accounts on time at Companies House and the credit insurers contacted the finance director to request copies of the accounts and management information. When they did not get a reply, the credit insurers cut the company's credit limit by 50%. The effect of this on the business was that major suppliers who had previously been willing to allow credit of up to £200,000 and £300,000 in some cases immediately reduced these limits by 50%, in turn resulting in an immediate cash crisis for the company.

If you have a poor set of accounts to file and are concerned about the impact this may have on your credit rating, supply the following to the ratings agencies at the same time as the poor accounts are filed:

- an interim set of accounts for the following period that demonstrate a return to profitability; or
- a set of projections that show how this is to be achieved.

If you can do this, you can then contact the ratings agencies direct to discuss the position, although I would always recommend doing so through a professional adviser such as a member of the Society of Turnaround Professionals (www.stp-uk.org).

There are some other potential sources of finance that may fit with this category of lender, the key ones of which are as follows.

Trade or joint venture partners
Your business may have strong trading links with another business, acting for example as one of their key suppliers or developing new products for them, or be involved in a joint venture to developing or supply a particular market. As part of such arrangements there may be scope for your business to borrow money from the other party.

Dealer facilities
Where you are a franchised main dealer for a manufacturer such as a car maker, it is in the manufacturer's interests to enable you, for example, to carry a stock of their goods for use as demonstrators. Manufacturers may therefore have in-house financing arrangements to assist their dealers in carrying appropriate levels of trading and demonstrator stock.

Brewery loans

The breweries are amongst the biggest lenders to the licensed trade, offering a variety of property and trading loans as a way of tying in licensees.

Vendor finance

Where you buy a business, the seller may allow you a period of time to pay either a specific amount of the sales price (known as **deferred consideration**), or part of the price of the business may be determined by the trading performance over a period following the sale (known as an earn out). In both cases the seller is providing you with what can be a substantial amount of credit.

Banks

The obvious first source of formal finance for your business is from the high street clearing banks. Their operations are covered in more detail in the next chapter.

The advantage of the banks is that they can act as a one-stop shop for finance as they can offer:

◆ short-term working capital finance through an overdraft and longer-term finance for investment in assets through **term loans**;

◆ a reasonably full range of specialist financing products (such as leasing or factoring) through specialist in-house subsidiaries.

Banks traditionally see themselves as cashflow lenders in that they are first and foremost interested in assessing the business's ability to make repayments out of its trading cashflow. But as demonstrated in the next chapter, other than in the case of either very small loans, or in some specialist situations such as funding an MBO, the banks are in practice actually only happy to lend when they also have security in position that can be taken if required at a later point.

One point that it is worth making here is that the appetite for deals, efficiency of operations, and approach to risk or even lending into entire sectors of individual banks and other lenders will vary markedly over time. The following are examples.

- The institution decides it wants to grow its market share and therefore presses for new business.

- In some of these cases the lender has not kept up its investment in its back office functions and therefore its efficiency in handling your loan or account can suffer as these systems are unable to keep up with its growth.

- After a period of growth the lenders might become concerned about a level of potential bad debt in its book and decide to reduce its exposure to new business to concentrate on dealing with what it already has.

- In some cases the lender can simply run out of funds to put out into the market (an issue usually only for smaller private lenders) and is therefore unable to write new business.

- A lender may feel it is becoming over exposed to a particular sector (such as say, property development) or it may have caught a significant cold on a particular type of loan or in a specific industry and as a result decides to restrict or avoid further business in this area.

- The departure of a specific individual or team with particular expertise within the lender leaves the lender unable or unwilling to become involved in further lending of this type.

♦ The lender's parent decides to sell the business to a new owner or even occasionally to shut it down.

As a result we find as brokers that the lenders we deal with on a regular basis will generally change over, say, a three year cycle as the active lenders of one year are replaced by others. Knowledge of these market trends is part of the value that a good commercial finance broker can add to your business.

Because of this cyclical nature, this book will generally avoid recommending any particular lender or institution, as a source of finance's stance may be very different at the time you want to use it from the position at the time of writing.

Other financial institutions

As alternatives to the bank's one-stop shop there is a wide range of independent funders and specialist finance providers who can provide lending against specific types of asset. You may be familiar with some, eg building societies, but many, such as the factors and invoice discounters or plant and machinery sale and leaseback funders, you may not.

This type of lending is generally known as asset based lending as it is focused on a particular class of asset. Some lenders are much more focused on the asset valuations on a pawn broking basis than on the borrower's ability to pay the debt or the interest (to service the debt).

Asset based lenders

Asset based lenders have traditionally been stand-alone, independent specialist funders who would finance against any one particular class of asset. As will be discussed in Chapter 7, using a mix of such specialist lenders (such as a factor to lend against debtors, a building society to lend on the property, and an asset financier to cover the plant and machinery) can provide the ability to borrow more than could be obtained from a bank.

Over the last few years, however, many of the specialist funders have been extending their operations to become full asset financiers or asset based lenders (ABLs). So you will find that many of the invoice discounting firms have expanded the range of financing they have on offer in-house to include property lending and plant and machinery finance (and even become accredited for SFLG loans) so as to be able to provide a full package of funding across all types of asset, including stock in some cases.

This type of structured finance started with the larger players and is used extensively in many MBO/MBI transactions. It is becoming more and more mainstream, such that these ABLs are now increasingly providing a direct one-stop shop, competitive financing option to the banks. In doing so, however, these lenders are having to become more concerned with businesses' underlying cashflows and monitoring of performance and so start to act more like banks.

One symptom of this is that these lenders, which are generally factoring or invoice discounting houses, will try to limit their overall exposure to say 150% of the total debtor book value, so as to keep their lending focused on the area and type of asset where they have most experience.

As a result, as shown by comparison in Chapter 7, this means that you can generally borrow more through a structured finance 'package' from such a provider than you can from a bank. But you can still generally borrow more by using a mix of specialist funders.

Other options
Going beyond these there are also the following possibilities.

◆ **Venture capitalists**, which will often structure part of any investment funding package as debt to be repaid by the company as swiftly as possible. This approach means that many venture capital funded MBO/MBI companies are under extreme cash pressure right from the outset in order to meet the repayment schedule.

◆ **Merchant banks**, which are firms whose main activity is using their funds to participate in transactions as financial partners and providing funding to trade and industry by doing so. They tend to become involved in higher value transactions where they are able to generate minimum fees themselves of say £50,000, and where the more traditional routes of funding may not be available because of the risk or a lack of security.

From this point of view they may be looked at as really being involved in:
– cashflow-based transactions;
– specialised bridging requirements; or
– quasi equity risks;
and as a result expect to charge fees giving closer to an equity rate of return.

The public

Finally, for quoted businesses there is also the ability to borrow money directly from the public and from investing institutions through the markets by issuing **debentures**.

A debenture is a form of bond issued by a company which entitles the holder to receive a payment of interest at set intervals until the bond is redeemed by the issuer, at which point the issuer pays the holder the nominal value of the bond (or in some cases an additional amount as a premium).

As a publicly issued security your business would require professional assistance in issuing debentures in the same way as you would in listing shares for sale on the stock exchange.

KEEPING YOURSELF SAFE

While talking about the large range of lenders who you can borrow from, if your circumstances mean that you need to arrange to raise money from non-mainstream sources then you also need to be careful about how you find a lender and who it is. Particular dangers are finding that you are dealing with any of the following.

- **Loan sharks** are unregulated lenders who charge extremely high rates of interest.

- **Predatory lenders**, by which I mean lenders who may have another agenda, or unfair terms such as excessive repayment penalties or the ability to impose changes in their terms at short notice, or hidden charges.

- **Advance fee fraudsters** who will take an upfront fee to arrange financing, together with collecting cash to arrange valuations and sometimes even a monthly retainer until such time as they manage to raise finance (so how is that designed to incentivise them to succeed?), but who never deliver the funding promised.

While the cash paid out to this type of fraudster is bad enough, things can get even more serious when the victim then goes ahead with a transaction based on the understanding that they have finance in place when this is not the case. In the past two years we have come across what appear to us to be a number of examples of this problem including:

– an individual who put down a multi million pound deposit on the purchase of a commercial development property based on an offer of funding, but who was then unable to complete and not only lost his deposit but was also facing an action for costs and interest from the vendor;

– an individual who had completed on the purchase of a development property using a bridging loan at high rates of interest, and who then thought that they had arranged replacement finance, only to find that when they went to sign the completion papers for the loan they were dealing with an empty accommodation address.

A good way of finding the best loan for your business, and hopefully therefore avoiding these risks in the process, is by using the services of a **commercial asset finance broker**.

Such a broker may take a small commitment fee to enable them to ensure that you are serious about raising finance through them, but the bulk of their fee should always be based on success. You should check any brokerage's terms of business carefully on this point as the fee should be based on your successfully completing a loan; not just on the brokerage providing you with an 'in principle' offer. This is because these offers are only intended by lenders to be indicative of the terms on which they will offer a loan to you, are subject to a number of conditions and are not contractual commitments which can be easily generated by a broker from lenders and may be on terms not acceptable to you. So an unscrupulous broker could charge you a success fee for obtaining an indicative offer, that you may never actually be able to use and which may not actually meet your requirements.

Creative Business Finance Limited's terms of business for example are currently based on the following lines.

- No upfront fees.

- 1% success fee on your acceptance of an offer of funding (so it has to be an offer that you decide to take).

- A right to charge 0.25% fee if the brokerage obtains a formal contractual offer of funding (known as a sanctioned offer) that matches your requirements which you then decide not to accept, to compensate for the work they have undertaken.

- No fees to you as a customer in respect of arranging factoring or invoice discounting arrangements, as lenders all pay similar rates of commission for business that is introduced.

These general principles will also apply to brokers or other organisations who raise equity finance, although as this is generally a more difficult and risky exercise, rates of contract fees and success fees are generally higher. For example 5% plus a share in the equity raised seems common. Brokerage rates may vary significantly, however, so it is always worth shopping around. I have for example come across clients whose accountancy firms have talked about charging a 10% fee for finding and arranging finance.

However, you also need to be careful to find and use a reputable broker where you can have confidence that they will look after your interests.

We have for example come across cases where the following happened.

◆ A broker arranged a multi-million pound bridging loan for a client to buy a development property. In doing so they did not arrange for the interest to be rolled up until the bridging loan was repaid. Instead they put the client into a loan where the interest was due monthly on the basis that they would also arrange development funding which would be used to pay the loan interest as it went along and fund the build.

The broker collected his fees for arranging the bridging loan but failed to put the development finance in place. The result was that the client was unable to pay the first month's interest and was immediately liable for default rates of interest (which in bridging can run at 3% to 5% a month) and then faced a bankruptcy petition from the lender.

◆ A client found a development site and spoke to a broker to arrange financing, but it appears that the broker brought in his own property investor and bought the site to undertake the development themselves instead.

The National Association of Commercial Finance Brokers (NACFB) is the trade body for asset finance brokers and was set up in the first instance to tackle the issue of advance fee fraud. Any reputable brokerage should therefore be a member and a list of members can be found on their website www.nacfb.org.

WHAT SORT OF BORROWINGS ARE AVAILABLE?
The main lending institutions providing funds to small and medium-sized businesses are still the mainstream clearing banks. So the best place to start is with the two main products provided by the banks.

Overdraft
Much UK business funding has traditionally been by way of overdrafts as they tend to be the most flexible banking facility offered.

An overdraft is a short-term borrowing facility on a current account that will be set to an agreed limit. It is intended by banks to finance your working capital requirements, and can be drawn on and repaid on a daily basis. It is therefore very flexible as you are only borrowing what you need while you need it, and you only pay interest on the funds that you have actually needed to draw on.

Think of it as a revolving credit that should cover temporary timing differences between payments you have to make to suppliers and receipts from customers. Banks will therefore expect to see a current account swing back into credit on a regular basis and do not expect to see it used for purchasing long-term assets. As a short-term facility, an overdraft is usually repayable on demand.

The bank will also generally look to take some form of security for an overdraft by way of charges over a parcel of assets.

Caveats

Because of this approach to taking security over a range of assets (some of which, such as stock and debtors, will vary in value significantly from day-to-day), banks will take a relatively cautious view in assessing the real value of their security while specialists at lending against specific types of asset may be able to lend more. Banks will also only put a facility in place for a limited period (say a year in normal circumstances, a few months where there are problems) so that they can review the level of funding they are offering against the current security position. You therefore have little long-term certainty of funding and, of course, each renewal of facilities will cost money in the form of an arrangement fee.

Overdrafts are also time consuming for banks to manage, so expect to see banks moving more and more customers across to factoring facilities as an alternative to overdrafts.

Banks will also apply significant charges if you exceed your agreed overdraft limit.

Term loans

If you are looking to invest in long-term assets, such as plant and machinery or property, you should borrow over a period that matches the expected useful life of the asset being bought so that it repays the borrowing over its useful life.

Fixed rate loans offer you certainty over the payments you will make (but can therefore be inflexible and have repayment penalties built in).

Variable rate loans tend to be more flexible, but leave you exposed to uncertainty as interest rates change over time. If you are borrowing significant sums (say over £250,000) you may be able to buy what is in effect an insurance policy against interest rates going up in the form of a rate cap.

Looking more widely it is easiest to think of lending by the category of asset it applies to.

Property lending

Mortgages
A mortgage is essentially simply an example of a long-term loan secured against a property and all the points above apply.

Where a business has a property that is not fully lent against, remortgaging is usually the cheapest and easiest way to obtain finance.

Commercial mortgages are available from a wide variety of lenders. Clearing banks and building societies are active in this area but will tend to turn down (decline) prospective borrowers who are 'sub prime'. This means businesses with an adverse track record of County Court Judgements, loan payment defaults or insolvency proceedings, poor interest cover, or a history of losses over, say, the last three years. There are, however, a number of lenders who will cater for such sub prime borrowers, some of whom will offer loans on a **self-certification** basis where you do not have to prove your business's income or ability to meet the payments.

Bridging loans

One solution for short-term funding in respect of property is a bridging loan. Bridging loans are normally short-term loans that typically allow you to spend money that is anticipated (usually from the sale of an asset such as a property) before the cash has been received.

They can also be used to raise cash against an already owned property as emergency funding. However, while this can raise say 70% of the security value of a property within two weeks, this type of funding is extremely expensive and interest rates can often run at 1.25% to 2% a month together with substantial arrangement fees.

Banks will generally only be interested in offering closed bridges where an already agreed sale of the property or refinancing with another lender provides an established exit.

Non-bank lenders will also offer open bridges where the lenders' exit route is not put in place in advance.

Such lenders are generally quite open to sub prime borrowers as they lend on a non-status basis, which is to say they lend simply on the basis of the value of the security and without reference to your ability to pay.

Sale and leaseback

In a sale and leaseback, you sell your property to an investor realising its full open market value for cash (which in some cases may be significantly higher than a valuer may estimate it at for borrowing purposes). You then take out a lease on the property, typically of 15 or 25 years on normal institutional terms (such as upwards only rent reviews every five years). The new owner then holds this as an investment property and will be looking for the rent charged to provide a reasonable current market **yield** against the price paid for the property, which in current market terms could be anything from 7.5% to 10% of the capital value.

As the property is to be held as an investment, sale and leaseback is usually only applicable to larger properties (say over £500,000 in value). The investors will be concerned to ensure not just the value of the bricks and mortar, but the strength of the rental covenant being acquired which means your business's likely ability to pay the agreed rent for the period of the lease.

Plant and machinery lending

Hire purchase
Hire purchase involves you in agreeing to purchase an asset by making payments in instalments over a set period.

Hire purchase agreements vary widely in their terms, offering fixed or variable interest rates, and you need to check the rates carefully (particularly where there is an interest free period, as rates for the balance of the term are likely to be high).

Some hire purchase agreements are structured with low ongoing payments and a large (balloon) final payment in settlement at the end.

In general, while you will be responsible for maintaining and insuring the asset from day one, legal ownership will remain with the finance company until the last instalment is paid, but for tax purposes you may be able to claim capital allowances.

Leasing

With leases, the finance company always retains ownership of the asset. There are three basic types of lease.

- **Finance leases** are usually used for major items of plant and equipment where the finance company buys the asset and the business pays a long-term rental that covers the capital cost, interest and charges, and is responsible for insurance and maintenance. Once the capital is repaid there may be an option to purchase the equipment outright or to continue to rent it indefinitely for a small fee (peppercorn rent).

- **Operating leases** are typically used for smaller items such as photocopiers, where the equipment is rented for a specified period and the finance company is responsible for servicing and maintaining the equipment.

- **Contract hire** is a type of operating lease where the renter is responsible for day-to-day maintenance and servicing (for example this approach is often used for motor cars).

You may need to pay an initial deposit on setting up a lease. From a tax point of view, while the rental can usually be treated as a cost, as you do not own the asset, you cannot usually claim capital allowances on it. There is a proposal currently that the tax treatment of leases will be brought into line with what would happen if you had borrowed the money as a loan and bought the asset, which would mean that you could claim capital allowances. However, these are only proposals at the moment and look as though they would only apply to leases of over five years, so the practical impact is likely to be minimal.

You also cannot generally use the asset as security for other borrowings as it does not belong to you.

If you already own valuable plant then using a sale and leaseback arrangement can be a way of raising cash for your business.

Working capital funding

Factoring/invoice discounting
This is allowing your company to raise money against its outstanding debtors by assigning the outstanding invoices to the lender who will advance you, say, 80% of the approved invoices immediately.

In factoring, the lender takes over management of the sales ledger and actively chases in payment, which can in itself be an advantage if the company's credit control has been poor. In some cases factors will allow a CHOCs arrangement for key accounts (client handles own customers) whereby the company retains control of the contact with the customer.

Invoice discounting is usually only available to businesses with turnovers of greater than £1m and a positive balance sheet, and differs from factoring in that the company continues to run its own sales ledger and collect in the debtors. As the company is continuing to do the work, it is therefore possible to have confidential invoice discounting (CID) which means that the customers will not be aware of the arrangement.

Some invoice discounters will take stock into account and are then able to offer higher levels of advance against invoices (sometimes exceeding 100% of the debtor book).

As the lender takes over the debtors as security, these are then not available for a bank to secure its overdraft. So completion of a factoring deal usually involves paying off any existing overdraft out of the proceeds of factoring the ledger being taken over.

The issues you need to consider are these.

- With factoring you will lose control of how your customers are chased for payment. With invoice discounting, since you continue to run your own sales ledger this is not an issue.

- Your facility will be based on a percentage advance against approved invoices. The actual advance you receive as a percentage of your total debtors can be significantly less than this headline percentage as the factor may disallow debts over three months old, overseas debts; or may set **concentration** limits where individual customers' debts cannot be more than a set percentage of your sales ledger. You need to look at the nature of your debts and ensure that you will not run into such problems with your factor.

- Factoring issues arising in respect of age or collectability impact on an individual debt on an item by item basis. With invoice discounting you prepare a monthly return and so such issues impact in a single monthly adjustment to your facility.

- Some debts are difficult to factor. There are only a limited number of factors who will deal with contractual debt involving stage payments (such as construction contracts).

- As the advance is tied directly to invoicing, factoring is well suited to fast growing companies as the financing automatically expands as the business grows, reducing the danger of overtrading.

- However, as the facility is tied to sales volume, if sales fall, so does the funding available (which may be just the moment that you need finance the most).

- Once you have this type of facility in place, it can be extremely difficult to get to a position where you can exit the arrangement.

- There is still a stigma attached to factoring in some circles as it has been seen as financing of last resort. However, as banks have moved more customers to this form of financing, this stigma is disappearing (and of course is avoided with confidential invoice discounting).

- Factoring and invoice discounting are often perceived as expensive. However, when comparing costs against bank facilities it is important to compare against the total cost of equivalent bank facilities including interest, management charges etc, to achieve a fair comparison.

Trade finance

This covers a variety of funding arrangements, the most common of which is in funding the importation of goods manufactured overseas. In cases where you are holding orders from customers that cover either all or a substantial part of the value of a container of goods that you wish to import, there are funders who will step in and finance the acquisition, transportation and clearing of goods through Customs on your behalf. They will then look to be paid from the proceeds of sale of goods. So some of these financiers will work hand-in-hand with a factoring or invoice discounting company so that the moment the goods are cleared, a sales invoice can be raised to your customer and factors, or discounted so that the advance can be used to pay the trade finance company's charges.

Some of these funders are prepared to finance a wide range of risks (at a price) such as the following.

◆ Funding transactions which are not backed up by a confirmed customer order, such as the purchase of a quantity of fashionable consumer electronic equipment in the period leading up to Christmas, where the funder took the view that even without an existing customer order, they could rely on the goods being sold. However, in this case the funder took the precaution that the goods were held in their warehouses and were only released as they were sold, so that the lender could ensure their borrowing was repaid.

◆ Some lenders will also consider purchasing goods and raw materials on behalf of a company in difficulty which is therefore unable to make purchases on its own behalf, and then selling these into the company as required at a mark-up.

There are also specialist products available for specific sectors, for example a facility designed to provide motor and machinery dealers with the finance with which to buy and deal in stock. As a somewhat specialised service with a perceived high degree of risk in the underlying security, these types of arrangements can be expensive, but can still make sense if they allow you to undertake a profitable transaction which you would not otherwise be able to fund.

Away from the normal financial lending institutions, as seen for example in the automotive industry, manufacturers may provide their dealers with favourable stock financing terms or arrangements.

Block discounting

Where you have a long-term stream of income such as rental from property or machinery that is rented out, you may be able to borrow what is in effect an advance against this future income through **block discounting**. This is a specialist market where each deal is very much a one-off, so you are likely to need to use an independent broker to explore this if it is appropriate.

Other products

Finally there are some other lending products which do not rely on security and therefore are not tied to any particular class of assets.

Mezzanine finance

This is funding supplied by banks and a number of specialist providers which falls between normal secured debt and an equity interest in the business entitled to a full share of the profits. It is therefore applicable to situations where all possible sources of normal secured lending have been used, but where a business's owners do not want to bring in further equity investors which would dilute their existing share of ownership of the business.

Mezzanine funders may therefore look at situations where a business has a strong potential cashflow, particularly where this is linked to ownership of potentially valuable intellectual property rights over which the funder may seek a specific charge.

As a high risk loan without traditional security, mezzanine finance is both expensive and rare, only usually being available for requirements in the millions as the providers have to tailor each arrangement to the specific circumstances of the borrower and will also need to undertake a detailed review of the proposal (a **due diligence** investigation) in the same way as a potential equity investor.

Wageroller
Wageroller is a newly developed product targeted at small and medium-sized businesses which are relatively strong credit risks, but which may have for example a seasonal cash requirement, or difficulty in raising working capital finance because for instance they are involved in contracting work which is difficult to factor. Wageroller provides a facility whereby up to two months' worth of the business's gross payroll is paid by the finance company, using a payroll bureau to make the necessary calculations if required, and is then repaid by the business on a rolling basis.

The finance company does not take any security for this service, so can be used by businesses without disturbing existing overdraft or factoring/invoice discounting arrangements. It should be looked at as essentially a rolling unsecured bridging loan to cover two months' wages. Interest rates are higher than normal bank overdraft levels with an initial minimum period of three months, and there is a monthly administration charge, but once put in place the business can reuse the facility at will. For further details contact finance@creativefinance.co.uk

SOURCES OF ADVICE
Given the number of sources of finance available you may want to seek advice as to which is most appropriate for your business. There are number of sources that you might consult. The main ones are listed below.

Your bank manager

Your bank manager will obviously be experienced in finance and will have experience of advising many businesses of your size. The disadvantages are, however, that they will only be selling the bank's own products (for which they will probably be incentivised by the bank), and of course they are unlikely ever to have actually been in the position of running a small or medium-sized or entrepreneurial business themselves, so this may not be the best option.

Your accountant

Your accountant is a good choice to a degree as they should know your business and understand your objectives. However, when it comes to raising finance for your business their experience may vary, as will the amount of time that they devote to keeping in touch with the market. They may therefore not be particularly up to date with individual lenders' preferences, or aware of new products coming onto the market that might provide you with what you need. Whilst they can be very helpful in giving you advice as to the general type of finance you need, they can be poor at actually finding you the right deal. In some cases they can even be actually harmful, such as where they adopt a shotgun approach, firing out details of your requirements to every lender in the market, which can actually damage your chances of getting a reasonable offer, or where they are inexperienced at managing the process through to a conclusion. They will also tend to charge by the hour and so their fees are usually not success based.

Business Link

Your local Business Link is intended to act as a signposting organisation directing you to appropriate advisers in all areas including finance. However, due to the way that they had been run in the past some Business Links have a poor reputation and so some advisers are reluctant to work with them. Furthermore, given the hoops through which you have to jump to become a Business Link accredited adviser, many firms providing financial advice, and in particular those with a strong reputation who attract a good volume of work in any event, simply do not bother.

Brokers

A broker is a specialist in raising finance and so will have a good knowledge of what is in the market, particularly in how to combine different pots of lending from different funders into a sensible package; and experience in project management to get a deal through to completion. The disadvantages of using brokers are that they will be sales orientated and will be focused on the type of finance that they raise, so their ability to give you more general advice about the right type of finance for your business may be limited. As this is an unregulated area of business where anyone can call themselves a broker, you should also read the warnings about unscrupulous brokers in this chapter and you should always check that the broker is a member of the trade association, the National Association of Commercial Finance Brokers, and preferably that the bulk of their charges are on a success fee basis.

The best combination for most businesses is therefore probably a mix of advice from your accountant who understands your business and can advise you on the type of finance you need, and working with a good broker who understands the market and how to place and complete the deal.

ISLAMIC FINANCE

Finally, the Islamic world, like everywhere else, has its traders and businesses that require financing and so has developed a financial industry. However since under Islamic law (*Sharia*) the charging of interest (*riba*) is forbidden (*haram*), Islamic banks and finance institutions operate quite differently from mainstream UK lenders.

As there are now Islamic banks operating in the UK which provide finance to customers irrespective of religion, this section gives a very brief layman's outline based on my understanding of how Islamic finance operates.

Since the charging of interest is forbidden, Islamic financial institutions have had to find an alternative way of being rewarded for providing funds. As a result some Islamic finance arrangements seem to be based around the idea of shared ownership of an asset to be financed between the borrower and lender with shared profit, instead of interest and shared risk. The result of this approach can seem to be more one of a partnership between the lender and the borrower than a traditional UK banking arrangement.

The three main financial instruments to be aware of are the following.

◆ *Ijara*, which is equivalent to a leasing or hire purchase arrangement where the funder buys the assets involved, (typically motor vehicles or machinery) and the borrower makes regular payments for its use and, in some variations, obtains ownership of the assets at the end of the period.

◆ *Murabaha*, which is a form of trade finance where the funder buys the goods (typically raw materials on behalf of a manufacturer) and then sells these to the manufacturer at a mark-up on cost to give a service charge, which in some variations can be paid by instalments.

◆ *Musharaka* is a form of joint venture that is equivalent to a partnership in that investors share the profits in proportion to their investment in the venture. However, they also share the risks in the same proportion and have unlimited personal liability.

The Islamic approach to law recognises that circumstances change over time, and that therefore guidance under the *Sharia* will need to be provided to cover new situations and issues as they arise. Financial products and services are no exception to this and so Islamic financial institutions will have a group of *Sharia* advisers or a *Sharia* board whose job it is to ensure that any new products or arrangements comply with *Sharia* requirements in that they are not in conflict with the teachings of the Koran or precedents. Internationally the Islamic Financial Services Board has been set up to seek to standardise Islamic approaches to finance.

KEY POINTS

◆ Think of debt in the widest sense as funding that doesn't require you to give away an interest in the business.

◆ Debt can be off balance sheet, such as rental arrangements, sale and leaseback as well as formal loans.

◆ Match funding appropriately:
  – short-term/flexible funding for working capital;
  – long-term stable funding for investment.

◆ You have a choice of funders.

◆ You have a choice of types of borrowing.

◆ If borrowing from family or friends:
   − think carefully whether this is wise;
   − set out the deal properly in writing to avoid disputes.

◆ Use a reputable broker, working with your accountant, to arrange finance for you.

◆ As interest is *haram* under Islamic *Sharia* law, Islamic financial institutions provide alternative forms of finance which avoid the use of interest.

7

Borrowing from Banks

The starting point for most businesses looking to raise finance is bank borrowing. This is also a useful point to start with in discussing debt finance in general as the banks offer most types of lending services either directly or through their specialist subsidiaries. Discussing how the banks work therefore illustrates in general how the business of borrowing works in the UK, what the issues are, how things are changing and what this means for your business.

This then acts as background with which to compare the offerings available from alternative suppliers, discussed over the next two chapters.

MANAGING YOUR BANK MANAGER

The first thing to remember when dealing with a bank is that banks are businesses like any other, albeit large ones. They have their structures and processes, their shareholders, a requirement to be profitable, their products and policies, their employees' career paths and office politics.

The second thing to remember is that bank managers are employees like any other. They have their place in the organisation's structure chart, they have their levels of authority, their reporting deadlines, their processes and bank policies to comply with, their targets, bonus schemes, annual objectives and own bosses to think about.

So if you understand how the bank is managing your bank manager and what they are being tasked to do and rewarded for, then you can arrange to manage your bank manager so that you get what you want out of the relationship.

The face of the bank that is most familiar is the high street branch network; however, this is only one aspect of the banks' operations and for business borrowing purposes most of the banks have segmented their market into three distinct business units, based largely on customer size, and a typical split is now:

Level	Businesses with turnover*	Characteristics
Retail	up to £1m	Basic banking and off the peg banking products serviced through the local branch network which will also be dealing with personal lending. Individual managers may specialise in business relationships, but managers will typically be being expected to handle several hundred accounts each so there will be little contact between business and bank manager. In order to keep costs down, most lending decisions will be made purely based on an automated credit scoring approach rather than by the banker forming a view. In fact many bankers complain that their discretionary lending limits (the amount they are empowered to lend on their own authority) are very limited these days.
Commercial	£1m to £20m	Solely business focused banking offering a range of business focused products. Lending will be less driven by automated procedures and more based on a traditional approach of:

- managers agreeing ('sanctioning')
  lending within their own discretionary
  limits; and/or
- a process of credit committee
  approval of proposals passed in by
  the manager.

As a result, lending may be more flexible than in the retail sector.

Some sectors such as agribusiness may be served by specialist teams of managers.

Managers will handle a smaller number of clients (but still in some cases say 50–100) and will be expected to meet with their clients on a reasonably regular basis.

Corporate	£20m +	Large/complex borrowing requirements which may involve multi bank and tailored solutions.

* The criteria may also be based on level or complexity of debt.

The exact dividing points and how rigorously these are enforced will differ from bank to bank.

Within each of these units, customers will be given a credit rating based on a range of factors, from the strength of the balance sheet and robustness of the profitability, to the strength of the management team and robustness of the financial controls and forecasting. Often the length of the existing relationship will be taken into account as banks see their customers as streams of revenue stretching into the future and tend to want to stick with customers who have stuck with them in the past, as they feel it is likely that the customer will continue to do so. A customer with a record of frequent switching to chase the lowest interest rate or service charges (a 'rate tart') on the other hand obviously has no loyalty to the bank, and the bank has much less long-term interest in the relationship.

This internal credit rating by the bank is absolutely crucial as this matrix determines how the bank views and manages the relationship and governs, for example:

◆ whether the bank should consider lending more under any circumstances;

◆ what interest rates to charge;

◆ whether to require formal security; and even

◆ whether the bank should be looking to retain the relationship or should be seeking an exit.

At its crudest each of the above business units of the bank will have:

◆ a good book; and

◆ a doubtful book (sometimes further divided into doubtful and bad books) which may be referred to as 'intensive care', 'specialised lending services' or 'business support'.

Staying in the bank's 'good book'

The good book represents the bulk of the bank's customers that the bank is happy with in terms of performance and the bank's perceived risk. These customers will be dealt with by the appropriate local manager. The bank will have some requirements for information such as annual accounts and forecasts, but these will not generally be too onerous for most businesses. The bank may also be relaxed about taking security, may be predisposed to lend on the basis of an appropriate request and the margin sought on borrowings will be at the lower end of the bank's scale.

If your business's credit score starts to fall, you will start to drift towards the doubtful book and you will notice the bank's approach hardening as you pass down through their matrix. Seeking loans will be harder, interest rates will be higher, security and personal guarantees will be sought and the bank will be looking for more regular information. Eventually, if your business is dealt with by the commercial level of the bank, the relationship will be passed across to the business support arm of the bank, which will have its own managers and reporting structures that you will need to deal with and will be looking to either return the relationship to the good book or to exit.

This is a particular issue if you have a change in your relationship manager. Human nature being what it is, your relationship is at maximum risk during the first three to six months of a new manager's appointment. They will tend to take a hard look at the portfolio they have inherited to identify and weed out problem accounts while these can be blamed on the previous incumbent and before they become items that have arisen on the new manager's watch.

You therefore want to ensure that your business remains firmly in the bank's good book. Remember that:

> Maximised credit score = minimal reporting +
> maximum ease of borrowing

You do so largely by communicating with and managing your relationship with your bank manager. Remember they are employees with a boss that they have to satisfy. They will have targets to meet and reports to file, so the last thing you want to do is flag your business up as an exception in their reporting or adversely affect their input into your credit rating by being a problem for your manager.

Your relationship with your bank manager is usually one of your business's key relationships. I am always surprised by the number of business people who have given little or no thought to actively managing this relationship.

Your job is to make it as easy as possible for them to lend to you, which means making your internal credit scoring as high as possible.

Creating a quiet life

That means managing, first and foremost, the provision of financial information which will impact on their assessment of your business and therefore on the subjective aspects of your score. The critical steps that you should take are therefore the following.

◆ Report on time – for example if your bank manager has asked for quarterly management accounts this may well because they have an internal reporting calendar to comply with, so assuming the requirement is for these within a reasonable period after the quarter, delivering on time makes their life easier, demonstrates financial reporting is in place and avoids the absence of accounts being flagged up as a warning sign of potential problems.

◆ Report fully – agree the package of information that you are going to supply to the bank manager and ensure that you supply it.

- Report accurately – check what you are sending in to the bank manager to avoid problems. Faxing a set of accounts across to the bank that had accidentally failed to include the month's sales caused difficulties for one business.

- Know your numbers – make sure that you are familiar with any numbers provided to the bank manager and can answer at least general questions about what they contain. One business was plunged into an immediate crisis when the bank manager asked the managing director why the forecast cash position showed a £1m greater overdraft requirement than had been advised a month before, only for the latter to respond: 'does it?'

- Demonstrate the strength of your financial controls and management information – ensure that you are providing a full package of management information, which should include a budget for the year, comparisons of your actual performance with the budget, and information explaining the differences that have arisen between the budgeted performance and the actual performance (known as variances).

- Avoid surprises – which more than anything means ensuring that when it comes to preparing your annual accounts these are in line with the management accounts you have been presenting during the year, and on which the bank manager has been completing internal reports. If there are major differences this will immediately raise concerns about the accuracy and adequacy of your management controls. Remember the bank is relying upon you to manage the finances and accounting of your business, they cannot do it for you, and if the accounts produce a major surprise at a year-end this will undermine their confidence in the strength of your management.

◆ Report in time – in addition to reporting about historical performance, you should also be using forecasts to look forwards so that if you are going to need cash, you can flag this requirement up early enough in advance. Don't forget, your bank manager will have a process they will need to go through within the bank in order to approve any increase in borrowings. Issuing a payment which you are unable to meet because you have not applied for an overdraft ('application for overdraft by way of cheque') not only counts as a surprise to the bank (see above), but worse tells them that you are not in control of your cash.

Being a high value account

The more valuable your business is to the bank, the more you would expect it to want to keep your business by providing you with what you want. In terms of managing your relationship this means making yourself of high value to your bank manager who you need to think of as being the bank's salesperson. The bank is a business like any other and it needs to generate revenue by selling you services. Your bank manager will therefore be incentivised by the bank to win the types of business that the bank wants, but it is a mistake to think that the bank is particularly interested in lending you money.

Whilst banks obviously do earn money from making loans by way of both charges and interest, bank managers may not be targeted on growing their loan book. This is because the bank may make more money at less risk by selling other services such as insurance, where obviously they don't run the risk of suffering bad debts. Similarly banks make much of their money out of transmission charges, so your bank manager will be very interested in talking to you about overseas trade as this can provide opportunities for the bank to earn significant sums in payment transmission and exchange charges.

If you therefore find your bank manager acting in their dealings with you more like an insurance salesman than you might expect, this is simply likely to be because of the targets they are looking to meet.

Your bank manager will also undoubtedly have a personal target for a number of new banking relationships to be achieved over the year. Given that most business owners seem to perceive banks as being interested only in lending, it may come as a surprise that banks are often very interested in finding customers whose accounts will remain in credit, because this will provide the bank with cash to lend out to other customers. They may also have targets for the number of introductions they have to make to other arms of the bank, such as factoring or leasing leads.

So if you are able to introduce potential prospects the bank manager will be keen to look after you.

Keeping your account swinging

Bear in mind that the thing that your bank manager sees day-to-day is how your current account is being operated. They will be looking for signs that show whether it is operating safely from the bank's point of view, or indicating that there is a potential problem.

The graphs in Figures 6 and 7 give examples of what might be described as good and bad account behaviours. Although as a bank will be looking at its lending to you, if they physically prepare such graphs the scale will tend to be inverted as they are measuring their exposure to you.

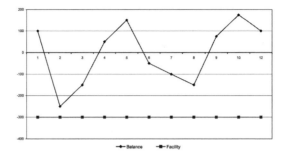

Fig. 6. Good bank account behaviour.

The account in Figure 6 is showing the behaviour a bank would expect to see on an overdraft facility in that the account is swinging back into credit on a regular basis. Since banks regard overdrafts as temporary facilities which are designed to meet short-term timing requirements arising out of working capital needs, banks do expect to see the account swinging back regularly into credit as the business realises profits from its transactions.

The company also has a reasonable degree of headroom before it runs up against its current overdraft facility of £300,000.

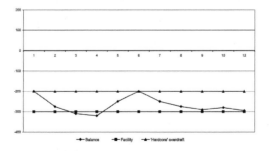

Fig. 7. Poor bank account behaviour.

The account in Figure 7 by contrast is showing a number of worrying signs.

◆ The company has a £200,000 level of **hardcore** overdraft borrowing that is never being repaid, indicating that the overdraft has become part of the long-term funding business. The bank will often suspect, particularly in the absence of any management accounts, that this is as a result of losses having been incurred.

◆ The company has had 'excesses' where its overdraft has exceeded the agreed facility of £300,000.

◆ The degree of swing in the company's account has reduced to a very small level, indicating that the company has been trying to manage its payments to creditors to keep within the facility. This shows the bank that the company has a cashflow problem and may be suffering disruption and difficulties as this becomes evident to its suppliers.

Together these signs will be causing the bank concern and are likely to lead to a reduction in the company's credit rating.

Approach to funding requirements

If you do need to ask your bank manager for an increase in borrowings you should do so on the basis of providing a cashflow forecast, including details of the assumptions underlying the numbers you are presenting so that you can give them the fundamental data they are going to need to consider your request.

◆ How much? What size of loan do you need? Is the bank the only source of funding or are you putting some cash in as well? Are you asking for enough to meet the whole requirement?

- Why? What is causing the requirement for cash? What do you need to do with the money you are borrowing?

- How long? What period does the loan need to be for?

- How will the borrowing be repaid? What will be the source of cash that will enable repayment?

The number of businesses which approach their bankers to borrow money without having given any thought that they might need to answer the questions above never ceases to amaze me.

Don't forget also that your bank manager will have to make a judgement about the case for their business (the bank) to take the risk of making the advance. The typical banker's CAMPARI checklist has already been given in Chapter 5, which you will see covers a wide range of financial and business issues on which your lender will need to feel comfortable. If you are looking to borrow money because your business is in difficulty you will need to prepare your case carefully and some guidance on this is given in my book *Turning a Business Around.*

However, how much you can borrow usually comes down in the end to the level of security available to support the borrowings.

WHAT CAN YOU BORROW?

Loans such as a mortgage are known as secured debt as the loan is backed by a charge over assets that can be sold to recover the lending if the borrower defaults.

Loans which are not covered this way are known as unsecured lending.

Since banks earn a limited margin in terms of interest on any money that they lend your business they tend to be risk averse. They therefore will seek to lend only where there is sufficient security cover available (although at the outset they may not always put formal charges in place over these assets).

While you may be able to find some unsecured lending this will tend to either be at a very limited level, or from non-bank sources such as the Wageroller and mezzanine finance products described in Chapter 6.

Most normal bank lending therefore rests on two legs:

◆ Can the client afford to make the payments?
◆ How do I get my money back if it all goes wrong?

You can see the sort of process in action if you've ever applied for a mortgage to buy a house. If you do so there are two things the lender will generally want to satisfy themselves about.

◆ How much you earn, and to a degree what your outgoings are, so they can see that your income (or to be more precise your personal cashflow) is enough to allow you to make the payments.

◆ What the value of the property is compared with the loan, so that if you cannot make the payments and they had to take possession of the house (their security), they would be able to sell it for enough to recover the loan.

The position in respect of a business borrowing from a bank is exactly the same. The bank will want to see the company's forecast cashflows are sufficient to enable it to make the payments and it will also want to see that the assets over which it can take charges are sufficient to cover its borrowings.

The difference from an individual taking out a mortgage to purchase a house (which is a specific loan, for a specific amount, secured against a specific asset and to be repaid over a set schedule) is that a company may be arranging an overdraft the level of which may vary from time to time, the funds from which will be used for a variety of purposes and the company will have a variety of assets which might be offered by way of security.

Debentures

The way that this situation is dealt with is that instead of a single charge given over a single asset, a bank will seek to take a standard bank debenture. This would give it a mix of what are known as fixed and floating charges over the whole of the business's assets from physical items such as property, plant and machinery, and stock, through financial assets such as money due in from debtors, and even intangible assets such as the business's goodwill.

This type of debenture will give the bank the right to appoint a receiver over all of the business's assets in the event that you default on their loans. The receiver will have the right to sell those assets, which in practice means your business, in order to generate cash with which to repay the lending.

Security statements

The steps required to calculate the basic security statement which underlies the banks' and any other secured lenders' approach to lending are to:

- obtain an up to date balance sheet (a statement of assets and liabilities);
- restate assets at current values;
- reorder the assets and liabilities according to their relative priorities;
- apply appropriate recovery estimates.

Widget Co Ltd's balance sheet is shown in Chapter 2.

The company, which employs five staff, has net assets, so you might think that the bank would feel secure. However, to check, we need to produce an estimated security position statement by applying the steps set out above.

Restate assets at current values
Realistically, for the purposes of most discussions with banks, this usually needs only to be done for land and buildings where the book value based on the property's original purchase price may be wildly different from actual current value. In Widget Co Ltd's case the property is recorded in the books at its cost of many years ago of £100k (book value). However, as the property is currently worth £200k on an Open Market Value (OMV) basis this is the value that will need to be used in looking at the security position.

If, however, plant and equipment have a significant value then it may also be worth requesting a desktop valuation of its realisable value from chattel agents.

Where plant and machinery are held under hire purchase or a lease, it is not actually the company's property. Nevertheless, if the value of the plant exceeds the outstanding hire purchase or lease liability, then this surplus value (equity) is owned by the company and has a value, as in theory a receiver could pay off the HP, sell the assets and realise the difference in cash. So where there is such equity this needs to be shown as an asset in a security calculation.

If the outstanding HP is greater than the value of the assets, the net value of the plant and machinery available to the bank should be shown as nil. Any apparent deficit suffered by the HP company would be added to other trade creditors.

Reorder assets and liabilities according to the relative priorities

A normal UK bank debenture will give the bank fixed and floating charges. Assets must therefore be divided into these two categories.

- Those subject to the lender's **fixed charge** (generally land and buildings for a bank) which are assets that the company can therefore not sell without the bank's agreement.

- All the other assets, which will be covered by the bank's floating charge and which the company is free to buy and sell on a day-to-day basis.

If it has to call on its security, the bank will be paid out first from the net proceeds of sale of the assets subject to its **fixed charge** before any of these funds are available for other creditors.

What will effectively be covered by a fixed charge is a matter both of how the charge is drafted (and therefore what it claims to have a fixed charge over), and the current status of case law which will determine whether such a claim will be successful.

If a bank has a fixed and floating charge, and its fixed charge is ineffective, then the asset will be swept into the group of assets covered by its floating charge.

Fixed assets and fixed charges
This case law approach can unfortunately make the position appear complex. You also must be careful not to confuse the accounting term 'fixed assets' with what is meant by assets subject to a fixed charge.

For example, a bank's debenture will probably state that plant and machinery (which are fixed assets in accounting terms) are covered by a fixed charge. This will not generally be effective and therefore plant and machinery will instead be caught by the bank's floating charge. If, however, the bank has taken a chattel mortgage over specific listed and identified items of plant and machinery, then these items should be included under the fixed charge.

For many years debtors (a current asset in accounting terms) were regarded as effectively covered by bank's fixed charges; however, as a result of recent cases called Brumark and Spectrum Paints, debts are now only covered by a bank's floating charge.

Creditors
The proceeds of sale of the assets subject to the bank's **floating charge** are used to first settle certain creditors (known as the **preferential creditors**). Under the Enterprise Act with effect from

September 2003 these are now broadly limited to **employees'
arrears of wages** of up to £800 per month for the **last four months**
(but not redundancy).

Only once the preferential creditors have been paid is any surplus
cash paid to the bank under its floating charge.

Also, only once the bank's lending has been settled are any funds
then available for all the other creditors such as trade suppliers,
landlords, other sums due to employees, the Crown and so on,
(collectively known as the **unsecured creditors**). This has generally
meant that there has been very little left for unsecured creditors in
insolvencies. Under the Enterprise Act therefore, where a floating
charge has been created after 15 September 2003, a portion of the
cash generated from floating charge assets will be retained in a
ring fenced fund for the benefit of the unsecured creditors.

As set out above therefore, creditors fall into one of four general
categories for deciding where they rank in priority to be paid,
which are in order:

- secured creditors with fixed charges;
- preferential creditors;
- secured creditors with floating charges;
- unsecured creditors.

Where you have more than one secured lender (and remember if
you have a director's loan there is no reason why you should not
have taken security for it) their priority is determined by the
following three rules.

* *An effective fixed charge over an asset beats a floating charge.* Different lenders may have charges over the same asset, but if one is an effective fixed charge, this will trump either a straightforward floating charge or an attempted fixed charge which is only in practice working as a floating charge. So for example, factors and invoice discounters can take effective fixed charges over debtors, but following Brumark and Spectrum Paints, banks' fixed charges are no longer effective and will only operate as floating charges. So a factor or invoice discounter's fixed charge on debts should beat a bank's.

* *An earlier charge beats a later one.* Charges have to be registered at Companies House to be effective and priority runs in order of registration.

* *But secured lenders can vary their relative priorities* by agreement between themselves.

As secured lenders are in a better position than other creditors, debt that is secured is sometimes known as 'senior debt'.

Apply appropriate recovery estimates

Having established current open market or book values for the assets as appropriate, for an estimated security position (also known by its insolvency terminology as a statement of affairs) these values would then be discounted to reflect the values that can realistically be expected to be achieved if the business fails.

These will usually be estimated on:

* a going concern sale, where the business may be traded on in receivership or administration and sold as a trading entity; and

- a gone basis, reflecting a liquidation and break-up of the business.

Some typical rules of thumb that are applied by the investigating accountants who prepare these sorts of analysis for the banks on businesses in difficulty are shown below.

Asset	Discounted values	Comment
Land and buildings	70%–85%	Banks' favourite form of security but which may need to be discounted by the need to achieve a swift sale as part of a going concern realisation, or sale as a vacant property following a liquidation.
Debtors	75%–50%	If there are significant balances due in over three months, these will be fully discounted when valuing security.
		Overall insolvency practitioners' experience is that collection of a company's debts tends to be hit by the company's failure as customers see this as an opportunity to avoid payment. Where a business is sold as a going concern this can often help in collection, but even so 75% recovery is likely to be a realistic maximum.
		Banks treat debts in respect of stage payments on long-term contracts (such as in the construction industry) very cautiously. This is due to the potential for counter claims by customers in the event of non-completion of work by a failed company. They may therefore have a much lower estimated realisable value of say 10%–25%.
Plant and machinery		Varies significantly depending on the nature of the plant, the ease with which it can be recovered/sold and how active a second-hand market there is.
		Given its rapid obsolescence, computer equipment, for example, has a low realisable value.

Finished goods stock	Nil to 50%	Depending on the nature of the stock. Pencils would be easily realisable at near normal price. Complex specialist equipment, however, might be difficult to sell without a meaningful warranty to support it.
Work in progress	Usually nil	Unless it can be sold to someone who can finish it off. In construction, the key will be: can the contracts be transferred to another company to complete?
Raw materials	Often nil	Varies depending on the nature of the stock. However, suppliers will often have reservation of title claims over unprocessed supplies which will need to be resolved to obtain a complete picture.

The result of applying this approach to Widget Co Ltd's balance sheet is a security position statement that might show:

Widget Co Ltd
Estimated security position

	Net book value	Open market value	Going concern basis	Gone basis	Notes
Assets subject to a fixed charge					
Property	100	200	170	140	85%/70% of OMV
Less due to bank			−159	−159	Cash balance set off
Surplus/(deficit) to bank			11	−19	
Assets subject to a floating charge					
Plant and machinery	50	75	53	38	70%/50% recovery
Debtors	200		150	100	75%/50% recovery
Stock	90		9	0	10%/0% value
Less preferential creditors					
Employee claims			−5	−5	Arrears of wages and holiday pay
Available for floating charge holder			207	133	
Bank surplus (deficit)			11	−19	
Bank surplus/(deficit)			218	114	Available for unsecured creditors

Obviously this shows that the values that can be obtained through selling off the assets (including the recovery of the outstanding debtor book that can be expected) on a gone or break-up basis, say in a liquidation, are less than might be expected if the business and all its assets can be sold on as a package on a going concern basis, say in a receivership or an administration.

So on a going concern basis the bank clearly has substantial cover as the statement is showing a surplus of £218k. However, while the statement also shows a surplus on a gone basis, this statement is drawn up without taking into account the costs of any insolvency procedure that might be required to recover the money which would have to be met from the business's assets. Since these can easily escalate into tens of thousands, the apparent surplus of £114k on a gone basis gives less cover than you might think.

If you were a director of Widget Co Ltd it's also worth noting that this statement has only covered the bank's position (and the employees' preferential claims). Even though there is a surplus as regards the bank, this statement is already showing that there is a deficit on a gone basis to the £200k of unsecured trade and Crown creditors remaining on the balance sheet before any crystallising claims such as employees' redundancy, customers' warranty claims, or landlords' claims for dilapidations or the balance of the lease term.

This should be a matter of concern, both in terms of keeping an eye on your potential personal liabilities for the company's debts under insolvency legislation, and more directly your personal exposure should you have given a personal guarantee in respect of any of these items (such as a property lease) where the creditor can therefore look to you to make up any loss that they suffer.

SECURITY FROM OUTSIDE THE BUSINESS

So far we have looked only at the security available to a lender from the assets within the business. But security can also be provided from sources outside the business.

Personal guarantees

Where a borrower is a limited liability company, lenders will often look to take personal guarantees (PGs) from directors or shareholders to support repayment. By giving such a personal guarantee, you are promising that if your company cannot repay whatever has been guaranteed, then you will do so personally.

There are three general reasons for requesting personal guarantees.

- Most commonly, where there is insufficient security available within the company itself in terms of the value of assets that can be pledged to the lender, so the lender wants to look to the owner's personal assets outside of the business in order to meet their requirements for security cover.

- To ensure that the directors/shareholders remain focused on and committed to the business and are not simply able to walk away if it runs into difficulty while the lender's funding remains outstanding.

- To act in effect as a warranty to ensure that the lender is able to rely on the facts that have been given to them. For example, the terms of a sale and lease back of a company's machinery will often include a requirement for the directors to give personal guarantees that:

- the plant and machinery involved in the transaction does actually belong to the company; and

- the directors will ensure that none of the machinery is subsequently disposed of without the agreement of the financing company.

While the use of personal guarantees is most common in respect of loans by banks and other financiers, they are also sought by other suppliers with a medium-term exposure to risks of non-payment by the company such as leasing companies and landlords.

The advice in respect of personal guarantees is simply to avoid them wherever possible and, if you have to give them, to seek to minimise the risk you are taking on.

If you have to give a personal guarantee then always ensure that you understand the circumstances under which it can be called, and in practice you (and your spouse if there is to be a charge on your matrimonial home as discussed below) will be advised by the lender to obtain legal advice.

To manage the risk you should try to ensure the following.

- Have the guarantee **limited** to a specific amount (eg up to £25,000 of the company's overdraft) rather than **unlimited** which would mean that you are liable for the whole of the company's borrowings from the lender.

- Have the length of the guarantee limited to a specific period or until a defined event.

- Avoid giving a **supported** guarantee (where the guarantee is backed up by charges over specific assets such as a charge on your home) and instead give an **unsupported** guarantee, not tied to any particular asset that can be seized.

- Speak to your insurance broker about obtaining insurance cover for your personal guarantee risk.

A personal guarantee is, however, not a simple substitute for normal security over a business's assets, as banks and other lenders do not like having to rely on personal guarantees for a number of reasons:

- they can be costly, difficult and time-consuming to pursue;
- pursuing a claim against someone's home can lead to bad publicity;
- most importantly they can be difficult to actually take effectively as the law is complex and can change.

For example, if a personal guarantee is to be supported by a charge against property co-owned with your spouse, they will have to confirm to the lender that they have received independent legal advice as to the nature of the charge being taken and its implications, or confirm to the lender that they have opted not to do so.

Challenges to personal guarantees
There have been successful challenges to personal guarantees backed up by the matrimonial home by a spouse, where the spouse has claimed that they didn't know what they were signing. Lenders therefore will now insist on the spouse taking or electing to waive the taking of advice so that they can defeat any subsequent challenge to the guarantee by the spouse on the grounds that they did not understand what they were agreeing to.

Recent cases involving personal guarantees have centred around the legal position that a guarantee given in respect of a loan is only effective for that specific loan, or another loan that was being contemplated at the same time.

In one case a borrower gave a guarantee in respect of a loan which was later refinanced with a new loan from the same lender. The court held that despite the new loan simply replacing the original, the personal guarantee was no longer effective. This means that to ensure they can rely on any personal guarantee, lenders in practice may need to ensure that they get a new personal guarantee signed each time the borrowing changes, as they may not necessarily be able to rely on old guarantees.

Confusingly, another case in progress at the same time suggests exactly the opposite, so each of these cases will need to be settled through the appeal process in order to actually decide the law.

Financial guarantors

Where your business has a financial investor in its equity such as a venture capitalist, it may be that the investor may be willing to act as a guarantor for borrowings if needed, as an alternative to being required to introduce further funds itself.

Small Firms Loan Guarantee (SFLG)

If bank borrowing is so dependent on the assets available to provide security, what happens if you have a viable business plan which requires a loan, but do not have the security required? In some circumstances all is not lost. The DTI, in cooperation with a number of participating lenders, operates a scheme designed to meet these types of cases called the Small Firms Loan Guarantee

(SFLG), whereby the government will provide the lender with a guarantee against default by the borrower.

To qualify for this scheme your business must be less than five years old and have a turnover of less than £5.6m. Under the scheme the government provides the lender with a guarantee for 75% of the loan amount in respect of loans of up to £250,000 and terms of up to ten years which can be used for most purposes, although there are some business sectors which are not eligible.

The cost to the borrower of this guarantee is a payment to the DTI of a premium of 2% of the outstanding loan, in addition obviously to the lender's own charges and interest.

The scheme has been reviewed recently in order to increase the level of take-up, which has resulted in the removal of a lot of bureaucracy which had meant many lenders were reluctant to get involved in referring cases across to the DTI for approval. Under the new arrangements the participating lenders, which include both banks and asset based lenders, are allocated a level of guarantee which they are able to administer themselves.

WHAT IS CHANGING IN THE LENDING MARKET

Having looked at the basic question of security, to then understand how much your business can borrow it helps to be aware of what is happening with bank lending, and why banks are moving customers away from overdraft borrowings and on to factoring or invoice discounting and other forms of lending, to the extent that some commentators are predicting the death of the overdraft as a means of financing businesses.

Bank lending is always based on a mixture of cashflow and the security available. Banks are moving away from old fashioned overdraft lending because of two main problems:

- risk; and
- cost.

Traditionally a bank's overdraft lending has been secured by a fixed charge on the company's debtor book, which gave the bank first call on the cash collected in from a business's customers if it failed. This comfort has disappeared following rulings in the Brumark and Spectrum cases, although the removal of PAYE and VAT's preferential status has mitigated this problem for the banks.

Banks' problem – your opportunity

There is a more fundamental problem for banks with this type of lending in that they will set the overdraft limit at infrequent intervals. When taken out, a £100k overdraft might be well secured against £200k of debtors. But who knows what the security will be worth tomorrow, next week, three months later, or if the business fails and the bank has to rely on its security?

The point being that the level of overdraft will move up and down at the same time as the level of debtors (the bank's supporting security) is also changing. There is always a risk that the bank can become exposed if the business is in difficulties as the security reduces, fewer sales leading to fewer debtors, while the overdraft increases. Therefore to ensure that they are well covered by their security, banks are conservative in the **loan to value** (LTV) amounts they will advance. Even so, it is still difficult to manage exposure, which means this type of lending is inherently risky.

To manage this risk the bank therefore needs to employ people with sufficient skills and experience to look at company accounts and speak to businesses to monitor their performance, and these people cost money.

By contrast, an invoice discounter or factor only ever advances against invoices that are issued. As a result it automatically matches its exposure in funds advanced to the level of security available. This makes an invoice discounter or factor's lending much less risky and the automatic nature of the cover makes it less costly to manage.

This problem may be exacerbated for banks over the next few years as the results of an international agreement known as Basle 2 start to make themselves felt. This agreement is designed to improve the stability of banks by setting the level of capital that they need to have in order to support the loans that they make. This is a technical subject and opinion is divided on how much impact it will have on UK banking, but the principle is that the higher the level of risk in their loan book, the greater the capital the bank will need to retain to support it. The implication therefore is that banks may be even less willing to lend money that is perceived as being high risk, or if they do, the rates charged will be higher.

The bank's problem is, however, your opportunity, as the range of asset based funders available now means that you have a real choice of independent specialist funders. You can therefore look at mixing and matching your funding to provide a package of lending better tailored to your business's needs.

HOW MUCH YOU CAN BORROW FROM DIFFERENT SOURCES

Since the borrowing you are able to achieve will normally be driven by the available security, the finance you can raise by way of loans against your business's assets will comprise a package of borrowings against its:

- ◆ property by way of commercial mortgage or sale and leaseback;
- ◆ plant and machinery by way of sale and leaseback; and
- ◆ debtors (and sometimes stock) by way of a factoring or invoice discounting facility.

The easiest way to see how bank lending works and how other sources may differ is by working through Widget Co Ltd's options.

For clarity I am ignoring any further finding that might be available based on other security such as an SFLG backed loan.

Borrowing from bank

Widget Co Ltd is currently borrowing from a mainstream clearing bank. Given its assets, the maximum levels of borrowings likely to be available from this source without additional security being given such as a PG are as shown below.

What this statement clearly shows is how the bank's funding package is clearly structured around the property and the debtor book, supporting a mortgage and overdraft respectively.

Unlike the estimated security position shown earlier in this chapter this statement assumes that all of the company's debtors

Widget Co Ltd	Book value	Open market value	LTV	£000	
Property	100	200	60%	120	Mortgage
Plant and machinery					
Cost	150				
Depreciation to date	−100				
Net	50	75			
Debtors	200	200	50%	100	Overdraft
Stock					
Raw materials	30	5			
WIP	15	0			
Finished goods	45	20			
	90				
Total funding available				220	

are good. However, you will see that the loan to value percentages applying to the values of property and debtors mean that the levels of loans that these support are less than the estimated recovery from the assets shown in the security statement. By applying these loan to value percentages the bank is therefore intending to ensure that any loan it makes can always be recovered if necessary, given the values that tend to be achieved in insolvencies.

It is worth pointing out at this stage that the banks will in theory lend at higher loan to value ratios against property than I am showing here, in some cases publicising that they will go up to 80%. I have used 60%, as my experience in practice is that banks are more conservative in reality and like to build themselves in that extra bit of safety, for example to cover themselves should there be a shortfall on the overdraft side of the lending package. Of course if you have convinced your bank manager that you are an excellent risk you may be able to obtain that higher level of advance.

You will see that there is no lending shown against either stock or plant and machinery. Of course, depending on the type of plant and machinery the bank may be able to provide some finance against this asset separately through its leasing business. So if we assumed that say £50,000 might be raised this way, this would give a total funding available of say £270,000.

This compares to actual current borrowing of £61,000 on the company's overdraft compared with a suggested maximum limit of £100,000, and a current mortgage of £100,000 against a suggested maximum level of £120,000. Given that according to last year's accounts the outstanding mortgage was £150,000 this might suggest that the bank may have either:

◆ taken the view that across both the debtor book and the property there was sufficient security to keep them covered; or

◆ have asked for a personal guarantee as additional security in respect of the mortgage borrowings.

This may also explain why the company has arranged to pay £50,000 off its mortgage over the year, which brings it within the bank's normal lending criteria.

Borrowing from a range of asset based lenders

As an alternative to bank borrowing, the company could look at borrowing from a range of individual asset based lenders, each specialising in a different type of lending as a way of increasing the funding available to it.

In this case the borrowings available might be:

Widget Co Ltd	Book value	Open market value	LTV	£000
Property	100	200	75%	150
Plant and machinery				
Cost	150			
Depreciation to date	− 100			
Net	50	75	100%	75
Debtors	0	200	75%	150
Stock				
Raw materials	30	5		
WIP	15	0		
Finished goods	45	20	100%	20
Total funding available				395

Working down the balance sheet you can see that two things are happening in comparison with what would be available from the bank. First, the company is able to borrow against more of its assets and secondly, the level of borrowing it is able to achieve against those assets is also higher. The result of this is an increased level of funding available.

In this case the company has gone to a specialist property lender which is able to concentrate solely on its risk in lending against the property and is therefore not worried about ensuring there is some security left in the property to cover an element of the overdraft as well. This lender has therefore been able to provide a mortgage of 75% loan to value (although up to 85% may be available in some cases), as opposed to the 60% available from the company's bank, a difference in this case of £30,000. In fact if the property had been worth more than £500,000 it might have been possible for the company to go for a sale and leaseback, and could have raised over 100% of the property's estimated OMV (see Chapter 8 for the reasons why this might be the case).

The company has also entered into a sale and leaseback arrangement in respect of its plant and machinery which has allowed it to realise their full value.

By going for factoring of its debtors the company has obtained an advance of 75% against the book (and by shopping around amongst the independent non-bank factoring companies might even have been able to obtain 80% or 85%). However, having done so the company would not generally be able to get an overdraft from its bankers as the debtors would no longer be available as security with which to support it.

Taking stock into account
The statement is also showing that the company has obtained an advance against stock although normally this would not be seen as a separate item. Many of the factoring and invoice discounting lenders are now prepared to take stock into account in order to give an enhanced level of **drawdown** against debtors. So the £20,000 stock advance would actually appear as an increased level of funding against debtors by the factor, which in this case would result in an actual drawdown of say £170,000 against a debtor book of £200,000, or an effective advance of 85%.

Borrowing from structured finance lenders
Finally the company could also try replacing the bank with an asset based lender, providing a full package of lending across the different classes of asset known as a '**structured loan**'.

In principle the lending available from this source looks to be the equivalent to what can be obtained from a mix of funders as above.

Widget Co Ltd	Book value	Open market value	LTV	£000
Property	100	200	75%	150
Plant and machinery				
Cost	150			
Depreciation to date	−100			
Net	50	75	100%	75
Debtors	0	200	75%	150
Stock				
Raw materials	30	5		
WIP	15	0		
Finished goods	45	20	100%	20
	90			
Total funding available				395
Limitation on total funding available				300

The difference here, however, is that since most of these **package lenders**' core business is invoice discounting, they tend to have a policy that while they will lend across all different classes of assets, they like to keep their overall lending tied to the level of the debtor book. While these lenders will obviously vary the degree to which they do so and the degree to which they will make exceptions, they will tend to operate a policy of having an overall limit on lending to any one particular business as being no more than a set percentage of the debtor book.

In this case the lenders' restriction is to 150% of the value of debtors, which obviously reduces the total lending available to £300,000.

Conclusions
Widget Co Ltd therefore has the following indicative options when it comes to borrowing:

Source	Likely availability
	£000
Bank	270
Mixed	395
Package lender	300

Clearly if the company wants to maximise its ability to borrow, using a mix of funders offers it the best chance of achieving this objective. The disadvantage of this approach, however, is that the company then has a large number of lenders with which to deal. During normal operations this may not be a problem, but if the company were to get into difficulties it would need to deal with its many lenders in order to get support, each of whom may have a different agenda.

In contrast, both bank and the package lender offer solutions where the business will apparently only have one lender to deal with. Of these, the package lender on these figures offers the company the prospect of a higher level of advance. But it may also offer another advantage over the bank in that it really is a single lender solution.

Remember that in order to get to an **availability** of £270,000 we have had to assume that the bank can provide £50,000 of funding against the plant and machinery through its leasing subsidiary. In practice if the business gets into difficulty, each arm of the bank will tend to look out for its own position. This means that whilst you thought you were dealing with a package of lending provided by a single bank, and whilst some banks do make an effort to avoid this happening, when it comes to the requirement for support to get you through a difficult period you can find that the bank, its leasing company (and its factors if they are involved) are each looking after their own narrow interests rather than the big picture.

BUSINESS BORROWING ABILITY READY RECKONER

To allow you to estimate how much your business can actually borrow from these different sources, the brokerage Creative Business Finance's ready reckoner is given in Figure 8. By completing this with estimates as to the value of your business's assets, you can calculate how much you are likely to be able to borrow from a mainstream bank or from asset based lenders.

Remember, however, that you always need to match your borrowings to your business's circumstances since as discussed in Section A, excessive borrowings (overgearing) can lead to business failure. You should therefore take advice from your accountant or other professional advisers as to your financing requirements and strategy.

WHAT TO LOOK OUT FOR WHEN BORROWING

Whatever the source of funding you choose, the total amount available should not be your only criterion. The five key issues to consider in respect of any loan are as follows.

Price

By this I mean the cost of taking out the loan. This will generally comprise two elements: interest and charges, and when comparing financing packages it is important to take an overall view of both. You may, for example, find that a lender is being flexible on interest rates only to load other charges.

CreativeBusinessFinance
www.creativefinance.co.uk

BUSINESS BORROWING ABILITY READY RECKONER

To calculate a business's indicative borrowing ability, complete the form below using:

- the basis of valuation noted to calculate the security value of the assets; and
- the percentages shown to calculate the likely borrowings available.

Your actual borrowing ability will be determined by a number of factors and the table below can act as a general guide only.

	Estimated open market value	Bank	Mix of specialist lenders	Package lender
Property	£	£ 60%	£ 75–85%	£ 75%
Plant and machinery	£	£ Usually nil although may advance if significant	£ 75%–100%, less existing HP/ leasing liabilities to be settled	£ 75%–100%, less existing HP/ leasing liabilities to be settled
Debtors	£ Debts under three months old	£ 50%	£ 75%	£ 85%
Finished goods stock	£	£ Nil	£ Can be used to top up advance against debtors to say 100%	£ Can be used to top up advance against debtors to say 100%
Total		£	£	£
Restriction			£ Limited to say 1.5 times debtor book	
Net available		£	£	£

Reproduced with the permission of Creative Business Finance Ltd

Fig. 8. Business borrowing ability ready reckoner.

One example of this was a bridging lender that was offering interest rates of 0.5% a month lower than the competition. What was not mentioned until you went through the small print of the offer was that they then charged an exit fee at the end of any loan which was the equivalent of 0.5% per month of the life of the loan!

Interest rates will often be quoted on the basis of a percentage over one of two figures so make sure that you know which rate is being used. The two rates are either:

◆ base rate which is the rate set by the Bank of England; or

◆ LIBOR (London Inter Bank Offered Rate) which tends to be slightly higher than base.

Rates quoted may be either of the following.

◆ Variable, in that the interest charge payable on the loan will move up and down in line with any movements in the underlying base rate.

◆ Fixed, in that the interest rate remains fixed for a specified period irrespective of any movement in base rates during this time. This has the advantage that the level of your payments is fixed for the period, which can help you in planning your finances. It also protects you from any increase in base rates. The disadvantages are that you will tend to pay a small premium in rate over current variable rates for the benefit of fixing. It also means that you will forgo the potential benefit of having a cheaper rate should interest rates go down. There are also usually penalties if you wish to terminate the loan early.

Variable rates may also be discounted for an initial period so that a reduced interest cost is borne in the early years.

For larger loans banks will offer clients the ability to hedge their risk, by for example purchasing a cap which acts as an insurance policy against movements in interest rates.

With a cap, a company is protected against the effect of increases in interest rates above the level of the cap in that in the example in Figure 9 10% is the maximum rate that the company will ever pay. Obviously the company will have to pay a premium for this policy, but this can be mitigated by taking out a matching floor (sometimes also known as a cap and collar, see Figure 9) where the company agrees a minimum interest rate that it will always pay. Then if rates go down the company will not get the full benefit because the lender will enjoy the difference between the floor (of 5% in the situation above) and the actual rate.

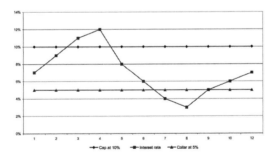

Figure 9. Interest rate cap and collar.

These techniques have in the past only been available to large corporate borrowers raising millions of pounds, but are increasingly becoming available to smaller businesses borrowing sums of, say, £250,000 and up.

Charges will include both arrangement fees for setting up the loan and ongoing charges that will arise through the life of the agreement, such as ongoing transaction based bank charges. It is important therefore to try to ensure you have a view of the likely total cost of the facilities over the period, so as to compare different facilities on a like for like basis.

While talking about charges, it is worth noting that UK banks are supposed to offer small business customers a choice between free banking or receiving interest on accounts in credit. It does appear, however, that banks do not push the free banking option very hard, so if you are paying bank charges it may be worth asking your bank manager whether these can be avoided.

In addition to the lender's own charges there may be other costs to take into account such as:

◆ SFLG scheme premium if applicable;

◆ valuation costs, where a lender will require an independent valuation of assets to be taken as security which will need to be paid for.

Term

Term means the length of time you will have over which to repay the loan. This may range from say six months for a bridging loan, to five to ten years for a general purpose business term loan, through to 25 to 30 years for a commercial mortgage.

If you take out an overdraft your bank will provide you with a facility letter setting out the period that this facility will be in place. Remember, however, that an overdraft is always repayable on demand, so while a facility letter gives you some comfort that the facilities will be available for the specified period, this is not a guarantee.

Security and conditions

First consider what security the lender is requiring for the loan, specific fixed or general floating charges, or both? Are they asking for a personal guarantee? Can you obtain the same borrowings from another source while giving away less of your available security, so keeping more in reserve for future borrowings if required?

Secondly, it will cover any conditions that the lender attaches to the loan, known as covenants. For example, if you take out a mortgage in order to buy a commercial property to let to your business, the lender may attach covenants to the loan that you have to supply the lender with copies of the business's annual accounts and that these must show the business:

◆ making a profit; and
◆ having a positive balance sheet.

For a trading business loan the covenants might cover provision of monthly management accounts, targeted levels of profitability and liquidity ratios to be maintained.

If you then breach these covenants you are in default on your agreement and this then gives the lender the right to exercise their security if they wish to. Of course in most circumstances the lender will not do so, but these act as both part of their early warning system for spotting problems and to clear the decks for action if required by giving the lender the right to take action.

Thirdly, the lender may also insist that you take out insurance cover such as a key man policy, which would pay out in the event of your death or serious illness, and that you note their interest on the policy so that it will pay out to them to cover the debt due.

As already discussed, your bank manager will be keen to sell this type of insurance (as one once said to me when discussing lending: 'Remember, no banker ever lost money selling insurance') so they will want to sell you the bank's own tied policy. You should be able to shop around, however, and may well find a cheaper rate elsewhere.

Flexibility

One of the great advantages of term loans can be their certainty, in that you know you have a specific payment to make each month or quarter comprising a mix of capital and interest. But this certainty comes with a disadvantage, in that you normally have to make that payment each month or quarter, whatever your circumstances.

If you do run into difficulties there is nothing to stop you approaching your lender to explore whether the loan can be varied, for example by:

◆ being rescheduled to be repaid over a longer period so that the regular payments are reduced;

◆ switching to a period of interest only payments;

- or even by having a complete repayment holiday for a short period.

Some lenders, particularly in the secondary or tertiary markets where the lenders know that they will be dealing with borrowers who may require greater flexibility in their arrangements, will already have built some of these options into their products. So it is worth examining how much flexibility will already be built into your loan.

On the other hand, you may want to arrange to repay some or all of your loan earlier than scheduled, or terminate the arrangement so as to move to a different lender.

In this case you need to know the following.

- What early repayment penalties exist and how long will these apply? Penalties will generally apply to the initial period of most fixed rate or discounted rate loans as the lender needs you to remain as a borrower for a set period in order to either match the fixing of their own funds that they have had to do to provide you with the facility, or to make enough return at full rates of interest to compensate them for the initial discount. For example a typical repayment penalty regime on a second tier commercial mortgage provider might be a 5% penalty in the first year, reducing by 1% a year.

- What notice you will need to give? Typically on a factoring arrangement for example, you will be required to give a minimum of three months' notice to the lender, although factors will sometimes try to negotiate such terminations between themselves, and the existing factor will agree to waive notice for payment of a penalty (which the new factor may help provide the company with some assistance to pay).

Are there any other constraints which will affect your ability to change? For example most factoring agreements are for a minimum contractual period of a year, during which time you cannot give notice, and some even specify that notice can only be given on the anniversary of the arrangement.

Cash impact

This is where you need to compare the actual cash movements that the funding will provide.

- *Cash in*: are you going to receive the whole of the agreed amount or will you only receive it net of the costs of arranging the loan, or even in the case of some bridging loans, net of the interest charges for the whole of the loan period which some lenders will deduct up front; and

- *Cash out*: where you need to be sure that the loan is affordable and where the actual cash being paid out by your business on its monthly or quarterly payments on a loan of the same amount at the same interest rate can differ widely as a result of:
    - the length of term taken, so for example a normal capital repayment loan of £100,000 at 10% interest would cost £1,322 per month over ten years, but over 15 years the monthly cash out at the same interest rate would be £1,075, a cash saving of £247 per month. The loan repayment table included at the end of the book sets out the monthly instalments you will pay on loans of five to 25 years in length at interest rates of 6% to 20%, which can allow you to see how much you can reduce your cash outgoings by increasing the period of the loan;

- initial discounted periods, as discussed above;
- interest only periods, where for example some commercial mortgage funders will now allow you to make payments of interest only over the first three years so that you do not have to make any payment in respect of the capital element;
- or even no ongoing payments at all, as on some bridging loans it is possible, for example, to roll up all payments of both capital and interest until the end of the loan.

As a general rule, whenever considering affordability it is best to build in affordability and flexibility for yourself by borrowing long but paying short. This means arranging your borrowing over a longer period than you think you require (say 15 years when you think you can afford to pay back over ten), so as to reduce the regular payments that you are committed to, as in the example above. This means that if times get harder, you are not held to the higher level of payments that you thought you could afford to make, and when times are good, you can make higher payments and aim to clear the loan in the ten years you really envisaged, if not earlier. Obviously when using this strategy you need to check the repayment penalty position very carefully so as not to get caught out.

MONEY LAUNDERING

Most professional advisers and all lenders are now caught by the laws covering money laundering and the tracing of the proceeds of crime. These rules will introduce a degree of bureaucracy into any financial transaction you undertake.

The two main requirements that all such professionals and institutions need to adhere to and which will affect you are as follows.

Identify their clients

They will need to see original documents as evidence of your identity and address. They will therefore look to take copies of one form of identity for each of the following categories:

- Category A – identity, can be your passport or a photocard type driving licence;

- Category B – address, can be a personally addressed utility bill from within the last three months (but not a mobile phone bill), a bank statement or HM Revenue & Customs correspondence.

Shop their clients

They are now under a duty to report any suspicions they may have of money laundering, or that funds are the proceeds of crime, under which the government includes any evidence that might suggest tax avoidance. Such professionals face long prison sentences if they do not report anything that comes to their attention and can also be jailed if they tip you off that they have made such a report. So if you operate a cash business and your financial position would suggest to your advisers that you may have been working cash in hand to avoid VAT or tax, you need to be aware that they are now under a duty to file a report.

Other paperwork

There may be further paperwork that you will need to deal with in respect of raising funds depending on these factors.

- The type of funds you are raising: for example now that some mortgages are regulated, advisers will have to comply with the Financial Services Authority's requirements to know your client. This means that they will need to complete a fact find on your personal financial circumstances in order to be able to advise you.

◆ The type of advisers with which you are dealing: for example, if you need to instruct an accountant to help you, they will be governed by their institute's rules. This means that they will have to issue you with a formal letter of engagement setting out the terms on which they will act for you.

KEY POINTS

◆ Manage your bank manager to get what you want.

◆ Remember lending rests on two legs: affordability (can you make the payments) and security (how does the lender get their money back if you cannot make the payments).

◆ Don't give personal guarantees if you can avoid it, and if you do, keep them as limited as possible.

◆ With the rise of asset based lenders there are now real alternatives to bank finance.

◆ Build yourself in flexibility by borrowing long and paying short (but check for repayment penalties).

8

Borrowing on or for Fixed Assets

Fixed assets are those items such as property and plant and machinery which your business acquires with the expectation of retaining and using over a period of years. As such they can be regarded as a business's investments rather than working capital. Therefore funding for these long-term assets needs to be on a long-term basis.

It is important to note that the type of funding follows the use that the business is going to make of the assets, not the type of assets themselves. For example, a plant and machinery dealer will buy a piece of machinery, but this will be to sell it on in the short-term. It will therefore not become a fixed asset on their balance sheet, but will form part of their working capital as it is their stock. Their funding for this machinery will need to be flexible funding based on short-term requirements where the relevant assets will be changing from day to day. The security taken will need to be of a floating charge nature that allows the dealer to buy and sell the item without running to get the lender's permission each time.

Contrast this with a manufacturer that buys the machine from the dealer. They may expect to keep it for a lengthy period, say three to five years; they can offer a fixed charge over the specific machine as specific security for a specific loan or other financing arrangement used to purchase it.

FINANCING FIXED ASSETS

While you can sometimes raise funding against intangible fixed assets such as goodwill or intellectual property (see mezzanine finance in Chapter 6 for example), or be able to borrow against the value of investments held in other companies, the principal fixed assets which you may need to fund are:

- property; or
- plant and machinery.

While talking about financing such assets it is important to remember that this can be a two-way street in that you may look to raise finance in order to buy such assets; but you may also use the value of such assets that you already own to raise finance for other purposes, such as further investment or to fund working capital requirements.

PROPERTY FINANCE

Some businesses, such as a hotel or a shop, may be based around ownership of a particular property which you may therefore need to buy in order to run the business. Other businesses may not be tied to a particular property, but may still want to acquire or expand the premises in which they operate.

If you want to own rather than rent, but do not have sufficient funds available to buy such a property outright, you will need to borrow money with which to do so, either through your business or through your pension scheme. The normal route to financing will be via a long-term commercial mortgage.

Occasionally your circumstances may mean that you will need to use short-term funding through a bridging loan to finance a purchase.

Pros and cons of buying commercial property

Buying a business property is a major step for any business and needs to be carefully considered. Many businesses see that their likely mortgage payments (on which the interest element will be tax deductible) will often be similar to the level of rental payments for a similar property. They therefore think it makes sense to buy a property, so as to ensure control of their site and not be subject to rent increases or landlord's restrictions, while obtaining the advantage of any increase in the building's capital value which might include any future planning gain involved in conversion of the site for housing use.

There are, however, many potential disadvantages of buying a property, as the other side of increased stability is a lack of flexibility. While you could possibly sublet any unused space in buying a property, you will have had to tie up a large amount of your capital in a substantial deposit on the building; funds which you might subsequently want to have available for other use in your business. You will also have a large loan which will need to be serviced over a long period. Also, if your business changes, expands, contracts or needs to relocate, it can be far harder to do so as the owner of a property that needs to find a buyer or a tenant for the business, as opposed to exiting a lease at an agreed break point.

Also many commercial properties increase in value at a much slower rate than domestic properties so the prospects of a capital gain may be much less than you expect, while since you are now responsible for the costs of maintenance of the property, any reduction in the property's value will directly affect your balance sheet. Do not forget as well that if you take out a variable rate mortgage you will be exposed to increases in interest rates, which can change over short periods of time in comparison to rent reviews which will generally only happen on a five-year cycle.

Existing and developing ownership

Alternatively, you may already own a commercial property and wish to use these services to raise some cash. If you need to maximise the cash raised you can also consider a sale and leaseback arrangement.

In addition there are specialist funding products available for property development and these are covered in detail in Chapter 15.

COMMERCIAL MORTGAGES

A wide variety of banks, building societies, asset based lenders and insurance companies provide mortgages against commercial property. The monthly magazine *Business Money* gives tables showing the rates and advances available from the main lenders across a variety of sectors and is therefore an excellent starting point for identifying what is likely to be available for your business. These can be the building that you use in the business (known as owner occupied), or investment properties that are rented out.

This type of finance should be readily available in most situations. The issues that the lenders will look at, as with lending to an individual on a domestic mortgage, concern:

- the property's value; and
- the loan's affordability for the borrower.

Finance professionals tend to divide lenders in many areas of business into tiers. In the case of commercial mortgages for example, banks and building societies will be regarded as the top tier or primary lenders. Strong borrowers with a record of profitability, good cashflow, a healthy balance sheet and no problems with their credit history (known as adverse) such as County Court Judgements (CCJs) will tend to be able to obtain offers from the primary lenders at low rates.

Below these there are a range of secondary lenders, typically smaller operators who have a particular specialism or product. Finally there is the tertiary tier of lenders who may deal with cases with significant levels of adverse, or issues about profitability or lack of accounts.

As deals become more difficult, borrowers have to go down the tree to the secondary and then the tertiary tiers where rates become higher to compensate for the increased levels of perceived risk.

Property value

The amount of money you will be able to borrow will be determined first and foremost by the value of the property. While many providers advertise higher levels of loan to value, advances from banks are usually in the range 60% to 70% of Open Market Value (OMV) based on the security of a first fixed charge, where the lender's charge has priority over any other secured lenders. Through a brokerage you may be able to raise 70% to 75% from specialist secondary lenders, with some on occasions going to

85%, although in practice advances of this level are available only to borrowers with a 'clean' five year credit history.

The property value used will normally be the current Open Market Value. When you own the building and are looking to take out a mortgage to raise cash, be realistic about how much the property is likely to be worth. If you have an unrealistic figure in mind you are simply going to be disappointed as the lender will always require an independent valuation before confirming any offer of funds. If the valuer reports a lower figure for the property than you have given in your application (downvaluing) then the lender will reduce the proposed advance accordingly. Where the property is rented out the lender and the valuer will be concerned about the rental income stream.

When buying a commercial property mortgage lenders will usually lend based on the lower of either the valuation or the purchase price, as they take the view that the actual sale price is always the real value of the property, whatever a valuer might say. This can lead to problems in circumstances where you are genuinely able to buy a property at a discounted rate or depressed value, perhaps as part of a larger deal. In some of these situations it can make sense to take out a short-term bridging loan as discussed below, and arrange to refinance again in, say, six months, since once you have owned a property for over six months many more mainstream lenders will then be able to lend based on a valuation rather than the purchase price.

Key issues that can affect valuations, and in practice therefore the speed and ease of raising mortgages as well as the sum available, include the following.

- Whether there are any environmental or contamination issues with the property. These can include items built into the property, such as asbestos often found in older industrial units, or underground oil tanks which may be seen as a threat to groundwater, and can be surprisingly expensive to fill in and seal.

  Contamination issues can obviously also arise from the work that has been carried out on a site. Where heavy industry has been involved the risk may be easy to see, but some can come as a surprise. One site had been used after the Second World War for dismantling aircraft, with the result that part of the site was found to be contaminated with low levels of radiation from the luminous paint used on the cockpit dials. In another case, a paddock in West Midlands was described as fireproof as a result of a history of use in scrapping railway carriages with asbestos brake linings.

  If such issues (particularly asbestos) occur, at the very least you will be looking at a requirement for a specialist survey to assess the risk and cost involved. This is important as these issues can be real risks to you as a buyer (and to the lender in terms of the value of their security) as the existing owner can be held responsible for the costs of decontamination by the local authorities. So in the worst case you may have to meet the cost of clearing up someone else's mess.

- Whether there are any party wall issues.

- The area – some lenders such as the smaller building societies will only wish to lend in their local area.

- The type of property and its uses where lenders will differ in the types of properties they will lend against. For licensed premises the breweries offer a range of specialist deals, while there are also specialist lenders in respect of agricultural land.

- The tenure of the property, which can be freehold or leasehold so long as the lease has sufficient length of time to run, which for most lenders means that the remaining term of the lease has to be a specified number of years longer than the term of the loan.

Many smaller commercial properties such as rented shops are only held on short leases which mainstream lenders do not therefore regard as providing any meaningful security. But even here some specialist lenders do claim to operate.

- Whether any part of the property is to be used as a domestic residence for you or members of your family, as is common for example with many pubs and shops. Under the new mortgage regulations, loans which take a first charge over domestic properties are now regulated by the Financial Services Authority (FSA) and borrowers therefore need to have had advice from an appropriately regulated person such as an Independent Financial Adviser (IFA).

This requirement is limited to properties where over 40% of the area is used for domestic purposes and, as the total area for this purpose can include external spaces such as car parks, in practice many pubs can escape this issue.

This regulation can also crop up as an issue on other types of commercial loan if you give a personal guarantee which is supported by a first charge on your home.

Loans supported by second charges over your home are not covered by this legislation.

Affordability

Unlike bridging, which is discussed below, most commercial mortgage lending is status lending, which means that it is based on assessing the borrower's likely ability to make payments in future. Lenders will therefore want to check whether you appear to be able to afford both to service the loan, which means to pay its interest, and to repay the capital borrowed.

Their starting point is to look at your last three years' accounts to check whether you have had both reasonable trading results and reasonable stability over this period. They will therefore be looking to see whether you have had:

◆ an overall profit in total over the three years;

◆ an upwards or downwards trend in the profit or loss over the period; and

◆ any catastrophic trading results in any one year.

If your business demonstrates a reasonable level of stable profits over this length of time the lender will be looking to move to the next step, which is to check that the level of profit is sufficient to cover the payments required. To do so the lender will usually arrange to add back into your profit and loss account a number of items such as depreciation charge, any interest charge on loans that will be replaced by the mortgage that is being taken out, and sometimes part of the directors' remuneration, so as to assess the business's underlying ability to generate cash with which to make the payments, and the ratio of this cash to the likely payment level. If you are applying for a loan through a broker they will normally request detailed information about your business's costs in order to prepare a credit application (sometimes simply known as a 'credit') to put into lenders with this type of analysis already done.

Businesses with adverse histories

It may be, however, that your results show an overall loss over the period, or insufficient profits to meet mainstream lenders' normal affordability criteria, or a catastrophic loss in a recent period, or perhaps you simply do not have accounts going back far enough to give the required history as you may be a start-up or relatively new business. While this means you are unlikely to be able to borrow from the mainstream primary lenders, such as banks and building societies, there are reputable second-tier lenders who will provide commercial mortgages on a self-certification basis of £50,000 to £2,000,000. This means that rather than the lender establishing that you are likely to be able to make payments by comparing your results with their standard criteria, you and normally your accountant will be required to sign a form confirming that you believe you will be able to make the payments. Since this is obviously a riskier proposition than lending to a business which has a clear track record of profitability, rates for such loans tend to be higher than more mainstream borrowings, but at present only by say 2% a year.

These lenders will also accept clients with significant levels of adverse credit who are assessed on a case-by-case basis. Again, to cover the increased level of perceived risk these lenders will load the interest rate, but at present often only by say 1% a year.

So, while at the time of writing a strong borrower with a good credit rating might be able to arrange a commercial mortgage at say 1.5% over base rate, a business with no accounts that would have to borrow on a self-certification basis might pay 3.5% over base rate, rising to say 4.5% over base rate if it also has a history of CCJs or defaults on loans.

Since this type of secondary lender expects that borrowers then go on to generate reasonable profits, and will look to refinance at lower rates with more mainstream lenders, they will also often have early repayment penalties built into their contracts. A typical example might be a 5% repayment penalty in the first year, falling by 1% a year.

Since borrowers dealing with these type of lenders often need quite flexible facilities, some of the lenders offer a variety of terms which can assist in budgeting for payments, including:

◆ fixed or variable rates of interest;

◆ initial interest only periods of up to three years to keep the first payments to the minimum;

◆ loan periods from ten to 30 years;

◆ the value of loan can be increased (assuming there is sufficient security and all payments have been met) once the arrangement has been in place for six months.

You can use a broker to obtain a no obligation, initial offer in principle of funding subject to valuation, usually within 24 hours. So if you are looking at raising finance you can obtain this type of offer by contacting your finance broker, or by photocopying the form in Figure 10, which is supplied by Creative Business Finance, and faxing a completed copy to the number shown.

Buy to let portfolios

Buying properties in order to rent them out has become a mainstream activity over the past few years, helped by the ever increasing availability of specialist buy to let loans based on the rental income that can be obtained from a property, even if it is not currently let.

The same principles apply as for normal commercial mortgages other than the following.

- On valuations, the valuer will be interested in establishing the market rent of the property, particularly if it is currently vacant.

- On affordability, lenders will be looking for either the existing rental income or the valuer's estimate of market rental rates to give typically 125% cover of the loan payments at either the expected or a specified flat rate of interest on the loan.

Loans available run up to 25 years with a rate fixed for up to three years.

You may, however, have a portfolio of investment properties, which can be either commercial or domestic buildings that are let out to tenants. These may have been acquired at different points and using different lenders. Whilst this may mean that you have obtained good individual loans, typically on a buy to let basis for domestic properties, it can often mean that you have a fragmented approach to financing your portfolio. This can often then limit your ability to borrow more money against your existing holdings with which to expand your portfolio.

Creative BusinessFinance
www.creativefinance.co.uk

Commercial Mortgage Enquiry Form
For a free commercial mortgage quotation please complete and return the form below

Name of company **or** names of individual applicant(s) _____

Is the applicant a limited liability company?   Yes ☐   No ☐

Nature of trade/business   _____

Does the applicant or a related person (spouse, common law
partner, parent, sibling, child, grandchild, grandparent) dwell
or intend to dwell at part of the property being offered as security?   Yes ☐ No ☐

If so, does this exceed 40% of the total security area?   Yes ☐ No ☐

Loan required (up to 79% of property value)   Amount (£) _____   Years
(10–30)

Purpose of loan

Income evidence to be provided for commercial mortgage (please tick)
2 years audited accounts ☐   Management accounts ☐   Rental income for ☐
investment property

Employment income ☐   Self declaration and ☐   Self declaration and ☐
accountant's certificate   projections (new start-ups)

Primary security
Property address   _____
Description of property
Tenure   Freehold ☐   Leasehold (and years remaining) ☐ ☐

Purchase price (original or current if buying)_____

If owned   Date bought_____ Current value_____

Existing mortgage   Lender_____ O/standing bal_____

Adverse information
Any existing CCJs?   Yes ☐   No ☐

– If yes, unsatisfied CCJs in past 2 years?   Number ☐   Value ____

Previous bankruptcy?   Yes ☐   No ☐

– If yes, date discharged?   _____

IVA or CVA?   None ☐   Current and
satisfactory
____

– If IVA or CVA completed, over   1 year ago ☐   2 years ago ☐

Highest arrears in past year?   Months ____   Value ____

Your contact details
Name and telephone No   _____

Email   _____

Signature   _____

Date   _____

When complete, please fax back to 0870 220 8587

Fig. 10. Commercial mortgage enquiry form.

It can therefore make sense to try to consolidate your borrowings with a single lender, as some of the specialists in this field can provide you with a pre-approved line of funding, using the security available across the whole of your existing portfolio at up to 85% loan to value, to provide you with a forward buying facility with which to acquire properties. The lenders providing this type of service can cover portfolios of up to and above £5m, either for individual clients or limited liability companies, with no limitation on the number of properties involved.

The information the broker will need to explore whether there is scope for generating this type of facility is summarised in the form in Figure 11.

BRIDGING

Bridging loans are short-term loans, typically six to 12 months maximum with a three month minimum period, secured against property (although there are now some funders who are starting to offer a bridging facility against plant and machinery).

The advantages of bridging loans are that:

♦ they are generally quick to put in place, taking a week or two if all goes well, and do not tie you in long-term to a particular funder; and

♦ they tend to be based on the property's value and not simply its purchase price.

As a relatively flexible source of finance they therefore tend to be used to help arrange transactions such as buying sites for

Creative Business Finance
www.creativefinance.co.uk

Property Portfolio Finance Enquiry Form

For a free estimate of finance available from your property portfolio please complete and return the form below

Introducer name	
Introducer contact details	
Client name	

Residential

Property address (including postcode)	Property type/ description	Current open market value	Current monthly rental income	Purchase or refinance	Date of purchase	Current mortgage	Tenancy type

Commercial

Property address including postcode	Property type/ description	Current open market value	Current lease income (indicate annual/monthly)	Purchase price	Date of purchase	Current mortgage	Commercial/ industrial/ lease outstanding

Adverse	Please given details of any CCJs, arrears, defaults or any insolvency proceedings past, present or pending

When complete please fax back to 0870 220 8587   Please use continuation sheets as necessary Page......of......

Fig. 11. Property portfolio enquiry form.

property developments, helping to achieve business purchases or raising short-term business cash.

In one example, a business sale included property which was valued at £1.5m, but which for a number of reasons was included in the sale contract at £1m. This meant that the buyers could only obtain £700,000 in funding against the property from mainstream commercial mortgage lenders who operated on the basis of lending at the lower of purchase price or valuation, which obviously would leave them with a large requirement for equity investment to fill the gap. However, they took out a bridging loan against the property instead, which was based on 70% of the valuation of £1.5m, enabling them to raise more than the £1m purchase price. Six months later they were then able to replace this with a normal commercial mortgage as, on refinancing, the lenders were prepared to look at valuation.

As discussed below, however, bridging loans are expensive so you should always be looking from the outset at how you are intending to repay the bridge, either by selling the asset or refinancing it, (known as 'takeout' finance). You should never go into a bridge without having your exit planned. If anyone you are dealing with appears to be advising you to take out a bridge without having both this and the funding of the ongoing interest charges covered you should seek another adviser immediately.

Bridging loans can be as follows.

♦ Based on first charges over the property, where loans of 75% (or even occasionally 80% using specialist top up facilities) of

OMV are usually available, falling to 65% where given on a second charge basis.

- 'Closed', where the arrangements for the take-out by way of a remortgaging or a sale are in place at the outset, or 'open' where they are not.

- 'Status', where the lender has satisfied themselves that the borrower can repay the loan, or 'non-status' where the borrower is simply operating on a pawn broking basis, that is if the borrower defaults the lender can recover their money by the sale of the property. Advances in bridging therefore tend to be driven almost exclusively by the property's valuation.

So for lenders, the key criteria and issues in lending are:

- valuation of the property by a professional valuer on the lender's panel;

- the quality of the property;

- the borrower's ability to service the borrowings; and

- the viability of the proposed exit.

The mainstream banks will offer closed bridges on a status basis. For open bridges and non-status loans there are a limited number of serious players in the commercial property bridging market, mainly lending up to £2m. Larger bridging loans can be arranged, particularly in relation to potential property development sites where we have seen £10m bridges being offered, but this is an area where specialist advice is required in placing the proposal.

Bridging is, however, expensive money. As well as valuation, broker, and legal costs you can expect to pay a lender's arrangement fee of 2% to 3%, and discounted interest rates currently of between 1.25% and 2.5% per month. Interest is either collected upfront by way of a deduction of the total interest charge for the facility period from the initial drawdown, monthly or weekly in advance, or very rarely rolled up into a bullet payment at the end of the arrangement.

Against this, being interest only, bridging loans can in some circumstances have short-term cashflow advantages over a normal commercial mortgage where regular payments would include an element of loan capital.

Paying for bridging

The interest rates quoted above are the discounted rates for prompt payment and it is normal for the full rates to be almost double these. It is crucial that you are aware of this as in the event of default on a payment (such as failing to pay exactly on the due day), you will lose the right to pay interest at the discounted rate and will be charged at the full rate.

In the event of default, you should expect all lenders to take swift and robust action to secure their lending by way of appointing receivers to sell the property. In addition you will find that the lender will reserve the right to charge administration costs incurred in dealing with any default.

If you take out a bridge where the interest is deducted from the advance on drawdown this has the advantage that you do not need to find the cash to make payments during the period of the loan. Against this, it reduces the funds you actually raise by entering into the bridge. Do not forget that at the end of the period you will need to find the cash to repay the gross amount advanced, not the net received.

The alternative is to take out a bridge on a pay as you go basis, in which case you must ensure that you have sufficient funds to make all the payments on time to avoid the increased interest costs and charges that arise on default. The results of taking out a bridge without having this funding in place can be potentially disastrous.

As defaults are an area in which lenders can make extremely high returns, and can recover these by appointing receivers to sell your property, you should take care that you are dealing with a reputable lender. While bridgers will generally be robust in their approach and expect to act swiftly in both lending and recovering, you should be cautious about dealing with lenders who appear to be willing to lend very aggressively, or who are completely unconcerned about your ability to pay the interest or to repay the loan at the end of the term. You should also check the terms of any loan carefully to ensure that:

◆ the rate and/or the basis of charges (for example the percentage over bank base rate) will remain set for the whole of the facility period and cannot be varied by the lender once you are signed up; and

◆ that there are no unexpected exit fees.

While a broker will charge you for arranging a facility (typically 1%, deducted from the advance drawn down), using a reputable asset finance broker will assist you in finding a reputable bridging lender.

If you are considering using bridging funding to raise cash for property development, you should be aware that there are specialist funding products for property development (see Chapter 15).

As this is an area of small specialist lenders, it is one where there is always a lot of change in what is on offer. At the time of writing for example, some lenders are developing alternative and hybrid products such as a two-year super bridge and a one-year bridge that automatically converts to a normal 15-year term loan at the end of the period assuming that the account has been operated correctly.

The information required to obtain quotes for a bridging loan is set out in the form in Figure 12.

SALE AND LEASEBACK

A property sale and leaseback is a technique for releasing the full value of your property into cash by selling it to an investor, while agreeing to rent the property back from them on some form of normal institutional lease. The new owner will then hold this as an investment and will therefore be looking for the rent charged to provide a reasonable current market rate of income, usually referred to as a yield and calculated as a percentage of the price paid.

CreativeBusinessFinance
www.creativefinance.co.uk

Property Bridging Finance Enquiry Form
For a free estimate of bridging finance available please complete and return the form below

Applicant

Individual

Name	
Private address	

Company

Name	
Company number	
Registered office	
Director name	
Director private address	
Contact number	
Email address	

Subject property

Full address and post code of property. Please include title number if available

Property description

Valuation

Valuation of property	
Basis of valuation (eg open market value, bricks and mortar value)	
Is this an estimate or has a professional valuation been obtained?	

If professional valuation, please attach copy

Loan

Amount sought	
Period required	
Completion date sought	

When complete, please fax back to 0870 220 8587

Fig. 12. Property bridging finance enquiry form.

$$\text{Yield (\%)} = \frac{\text{Rental income per year}}{\text{Money invested in buying the property}}$$

To make the costs of undertaking such a deal worthwhile, many investors tend to be interested in larger commercial transactions, as a guide say over £500,000 in value.

Having said that they are a technique for releasing cash from a property that you own, of course you don't have to have actually owned it very long, a split second can sometimes be enough. A simultaneous ('back-to-back') sale and leaseback, where you agree a sale to an investor at the same time as buying the property from the seller, can therefore be used as a means of acquiring the use of a property without having to find the cash for the say 30% deposit that would be needed if you were going to buy in the normal way using a commercial mortgage that raised 70% of the property value. They are often very useful, for example in **management buy outs (MBOs)** or **buy ins (MBIs)**, where there is a need to make the cash available to buy and invest in the business go as far as possible, and where this technique avoids having precious capital tied up in bricks and mortar.

Moreover, when valuing a property for lending purposes, surveyors have to work on the basis that a lender may have to rely on their estimate in order to get their money back in case of default. If the valuer gives a valuation that is too high they may be at risk of being sued so they will naturally tend, within reason, to err on the side of caution as they have their PII (professional indemnity insurance) policies to consider.

In some cases therefore actual sales price achieved in a sale and leaseback can be well in excess of the surveyor's opinion as to open market value and the value attributed to the property in the business sale, resulting in an injection of working capital into the company that the buyer has formed through which to make the purchase, either at the outset or later on.

For example, a management team bought out a manufacturing company, including its premises, which were valued for lending purposes by most valuers at £1.2m before the buy out team, which was looking to maximise their borrowing, found a valuer who would give £1.5m as his opinion. Less than a year later the buy out was in need of cash and sought a sale and leaseback with a target price for the property of £2m. They actually achieved a price of £2.3m, resulting in a net injection of cash into the business of over £1m after costs and redemption of the existing mortgage.

The value that can be achieved through a sale and leaseback will be based on the value of the property to an investor which is essentially a matter of:

$$\text{yield} \times \text{rent} = \text{value}$$

However, this simplistic calculation will be affected by three main issues.

◆ The local market for commercial property underpins any valuation, as the investor will be concerned with what happens if their tenant defaults. For example, a manufacturing MBI arranged a sale and leaseback at £1.5m to raise cash much like the example discussed above. Only in this case, having paid off the bank loan, the directors then decided they still did not have enough cash to take the business forward as it was and put the company into administration within weeks of completing the deal. Fortunately for the landlord, the directors then bought the business back and continued to operate from the premises.

A valuer will therefore be looking at the local level of demand for this type of property, so as to assess the local market rent and ease of finding a replacement tenant, as well as any alternative use that the site may reasonably have, such as for property development which might give it an underlying hope value.

- In investing in a property based on a lease which may run for 25 years, the investor is taking a risk in that it may find that at some point in the future its rent may not be paid. The investor will therefore be concerned with the strength of the tenant's covenant. Renting a property to, say, a large established company with a strong credit rating and a reasonable expectation that it will be around for 25 years obviously appears to present a lower risk of default than renting to a new MBI with a high degree of other borrowings (highly geared or leveraged) that give it a high degree of financial risk.

The higher the level of risk being taken by the investor, the higher the level of yield that they will therefore be looking to achieve.

- The lease terms which will be negotiable to a degree will also have an impact. Investors will typically be looking for a normal institutional form of lease. This might for example, mean a period of 15 to 25 years, with upwards only rent reviews every five years.

You might, however, want or need to negotiate other terms which are more advantageous to you such as:

– rent reviews which are not upwards only;
– rights of access for third parties such as other lenders as discussed below.

Obviously again, the more you look for terms that are advantageous to you and onerous for the landlord, the higher yield or rent the landlord will want.

Depending on the degree of risk involved you may therefore find a landlord looking to achieve a yield of between 7.5% and 10%.

Investors in sale and leasebacks are often individuals or property companies and not the type of financial institutions that provide mortgages. To reach these investors you can employ a number of different people to try to put a sale and leaseback in place.

♦ Normal commercial estate agents will act to sell your property for you, and may charge between 1% and 2% for finding a buyer. They will often require marketing costs to be paid up front. Their level of experience of arranging and negotiating sales and leasebacks will vary as will their ability to find an appropriate investor.

♦ There are a limited number of specialist matchmakers whose business involves building up panels of potential investors and managing transactions through to completion, sometimes in conjunction with firms of commercial estate agents. These brokers will typically charge more than an estate agency, say 3%, but this is on a success fee only basis with no marketing costs, and you are also buying their expertise and experience in this particular area.

◆ Finally, there are some internet based property broking web sites on which you can list your property and the terms you are seeking. This approach is usually cheaper than estate agents, at 0.75%, and enables you to hit an emailing list of many thousands of potential investors, which should allow you to quickly find out whether there is appetite for your deal. These are, however, simply marketing and introduction services and will not provide you with any support in negotiating and completing the deal.

When thinking about a sale and leaseback some key issues that you may need to consider are the following.

◆ As a result of the sale you will obviously lose the ownership of the property and the potential future development value it may have, so this is not a step to be taken lightly. There have occasionally been sale and leaseback arrangements which had a buyback option built in, but these are rare.

◆ The potential interaction of any proposed sale and leaseback with the position of other secured lenders which can often lead to problems in completing a deal. For example, a company looking to complete a transaction ran into problems over both its plant and machinery finance and its invoice discounting arrangements which included an advance against stock. The plant and machinery lender's terms included a provision that in the event of default or the failure of the business, the lender had a right of access to the property for up to six months in order to be able to arrange and complete a sale of the equipment covered by its charge, while the invoice discounter had a similar provision in respect of stock.

While the company owned the property these clauses were not an issue, but for a landlord with a defaulting tenant, any restriction for up to six months on its ability to obtain vacant possession in order to market and re-let the property was a major problem.

In the event a negotiated solution was found which involved reducing the lender's access period to three months and the company placing part of the sale proceeds into a three-month rent deposit.

◆ Finally there may be tax issues to take into account. Obviously the rental that you will be paying for the property will be a tax deductible expense of your business going forward, but more importantly the sale itself may crystallise a capital gain (or conceivably a loss). You should always take tax advice at an early stage in the transaction as there may be steps you can take to either mitigate the liability or, for example by changing your business's year end, to significantly defer the payment of any tax due.

PENSION PURCHASE

For some businesses it may be possible and appropriate for the pensions scheme to raise a mortgage and to purchase the premises from the company by way of a sale and leaseback, much as described above. This injects funds into the company from the realisation of the property while the property is under the control of a known party. In some cases the pension scheme may be able to borrow more cheaply than the company can.

To be able to undertake this sort of transaction, the pension scheme must have the appropriate structure and borrowing powers. You must seek specialist advice and assistance from an Independent Financial Adviser (IFA) experienced in this area.

PLANT AND MACHINERY FINANCE

As with borrowing against property, plant and machinery finance can involve either:

- funding the acquisition of new machinery; or
- raising funds by refinancing against your existing kit.

The main types of funding available for purchasing new equipment have already been covered in Chapter 6 and are the following.

- **Hire purchase,** where you buy the asset by making payments in instalments over a set period which may include a final larger bullet or balloon payment at which point ownership passes to you from the finance company.

- **Leases,** where ownership always remains with the finance company.

These types of arrangement are readily available from a wide variety of financial institutions and to get the best deal you will need to shop around. Your starting point can therefore be as follows.

- The seller, as they may have existing arrangements with a finance house whereby they are able to arrange funding. This can be expensive, but in some cases sellers who are looking to move their products, such as car dealers, may be able to offer advantageous financing deals such as 0% interest.

♦ Your bank, which will have a full range of products available through its specialist in-house subsidiary.

These days, though, given the numbers of lenders, you should always consider searching on the internet where you will be able to find many providers and compare their current offerings.

RAISING CASH FROM PLANT AND MACHINERY

Refinancing plant and machinery is an increasingly popular way of raising trading funds for businesses, as banks traditionally do not ascribe significant security value to such assets for lending purposes.

Financing in this area is by way of a sale and leaseback of the assets and is driven by asset valuation.

To be financeable, plant and machinery in general has to be clearly identifiable, of significant size (so no small tools), have a significant remaining working life, and be readily removable and realisable. Machinery that is too specialised or built into a property to the extent that it would be difficult to remove will attract low valuations and be difficult to finance. Similarly, it is traditionally difficult to arrange this type of finance for IT equipment due to the steep depreciation and low residual values attaching to it.

There are three main sources of this type of refinance funding.

♦ The banks' in-house asset finance subsidiaries. However, as these have a significant captive market of bank introduced leads they tend to be less quick to move on externally introduced opportunities and less flexible on deal structure. In practice, other than as part of arranging the finance for MBO/MBIs, it is our experience that most bank owned asset financers are not interested in refinancing transactions.

◆ Structured finance providers, where the larger invoice discounters are adding on plant and machinery and/or property finance capabilities in order to be able to provide companies with a full refinancing package. These lenders tend to be interested in larger deals and only those that involve a debtor financing element.

◆ A limited number of stand alone asset financiers, who are the specialists in undertaking stand alone plant and machinery refinancing deals.

A sale and leaseback will typically be over three to five years. Interest rates vary dependent on the business circumstances, but might typically be a flat rate percentage in the range 10%–15% although there are lenders dealing at the high risk end of the market who are charging bridging levels of rates equivalent to 20% +.

Arranging to refinance plant and equipment is a relatively straightforward process that begins with a valuation of the equipment.

You therefore need to prepare a list of the available machinery giving the basic details set out in the form on page 220. Your broker should then be able to obtain a desktop valuation from the lender which will give an indication of how much can be raised.

CreativeBusinessFinance
www.creativefinance.co.uk

Free Initial Estimate of Funding Available

To obtain a free initial estimate of the level of funding that might be available to you through a sale and leaseback of your plant and machinery assets, please complete and return the following machinery refinance summary.

Plant and machinery refinance summary

Client:..

Date:..

Number of sheets............... /.................

Ref				
Item				
Make				
Model				
Serial No				
Age				
Date acquired				
Bought new or used				
Cost when new				
Usage (mileage, impressions, etc)				
Finance owed				
Condition				

When complete, please fax back to 0870 220 8587

Fig. 13. Initial estimate of funding available.

The valuation process

Lenders vary in their approach to valuation and therefore their advance, so it is worth having your broker explore the options. Some lenders seek what could be described as a surveyor's valuation of what the equipment is likely to be worth if sold, and will then normally lend up to 70% of this figure although one lender is now having its valuers obtain insurance cover to certify their valuations and as a result is now able to lend 100% of valuation. Others will seek a more specific dealer valuation as to what could readily be obtained in today's market, which tends to be lower, but will lend closer to 100%. In one case the first type of valuation gave a figure of £100,000, sufficient to suggest a loan of £70,000, while the second type of value came out at closer to £10,000 where even a 100% loan to value clearly was nowhere near the first lender's figure.

This is a marketplace with only a handful of main players so it is important not to spoil your prospects. Businesses will often contact a number of brokers to try to find them a deal in the belief that this competition will help. In practice it tends to work against you as by the time the lender has had the same deal referred into them from half a dozen brokers, the tendency is to feel either there's something wrong with the deal, or that the client is desperate and the price can be adjusted accordingly.

It is also an area where a number of the lenders' terms are negotiable and, whilst brokers will charge for arranging such finance, they are likely to be able to get you a better deal than you would be able to get yourself by going direct to the lender.

Having established the level of equity available, the lender may seek permission to undertake credit reference searches on the company and its directors before issuing an indicative offer of terms.

If these are acceptable, the company will need to commission a formal valuation of the equipment from one of the valuers on the lender's panel. Once this is received by the lender, they can then issue a formal offer and the proposal is authorised by its credit committee. It is then up to the company to accept the offer and on completion of the paperwork it can draw down the funding.

The following are part of any transaction.

◆ All HP or other finance (such as peppercorn rentals) will have to be cleared on any currently financed assets to be included in a sale.

◆ A letter of priority will have to be obtained from any existing fixed or floating chargeholder such as your bank, so that the finance company can ensure it has clear rights to the asset.

◆ An agreement will be needed with any landlord for rights of access to allow the finance company to collect and/or sell assets from site, as well, as in some cases, an agreement as to the limitation of the landlord's rights to distrain on plant and machinery for unpaid rent.

Lenders may also seek specific assurances as to business performance (for example that **Crown debt** is up to date, or an agreed schedule of repayments is being adhered to).

Lenders will also want at a minimum, directors' warranties that the assets to be financed belong to the company and, once financed, will not then be sold without the lender's consent.

Lenders vary in their requirement for Personal Guarantees (PGs) from directors. Some deals are done without, other lenders insist on a limited PG of say up to 25% of the sum lent to ensure that the directors adequately maintain and protect the financed assets.

KEY POINTS

◆ Match long-term funding to long-term assets.

◆ Finance is a two-way street:
  – you can raise it to buy assets;
  – you can also use owned assets to raise cash.

◆ Commercial property mortgages are much like domestic ones and are governed by:
  – property value; and
  – affordability (your ability to afford the loan repayments).

◆ If you cannot provide accounts or you have a history of losses or adverse credit history, you should still be able to obtain a mortgage (for example on a self-certification basis), but you will pay an interest rate premium for doing so.

◆ Bridging is an expensive way of raising short-term cash where you need expert advice.

◆ Sale and leaseback can raise you over 100% of a surveyor's estimate of the property's value for lending purposes, but once it's gone, it's gone.

◆ Financing the acquisition of new plant and machinery is a very wide market where you will need to shop around.

◆ Refinancing plant and machinery is a very small market where you should take advice and care not to spoil the market for your particular deal.

9

Borrowing for Working Capital

Borrowings for working capital are used to provide short-term, flexible funding to meet your business's day-to-day financing needs. Traditionally in the UK this requirement has been met through bank overdraft facilities, broadly secured by a charge over the company's book debts or a personal guarantee from the directors. But as covered in Chapter 7, banks are increasingly reluctant to provide this type of facility, preferring to move borrowers on to debtor based factoring or invoice discounting arrangements and these lenders are in turn also increasingly adding an element of stock financing to their products.

There has always been a degree of stock finance available through trade finance houses, but this has been tailored mainly to funding imports and exports. Some of these lenders are now expanding their operations into more straightforward stock finance. Stand alone stock loans are also becoming available from the banks, but only at the £1m + level due to the management costs involved.

As will be apparent, many of these forms of finance are therefore becoming interrelated, as the different elements are all linked to the business's working capital cycle.

This chapter therefore covers:

- debtor based finance which includes factoring, invoice discounting and block discounting;
- trade and stock finance;

◆ how you may be able to become your business's own stock funder.

FACTORING AND INVOICE DISCOUNTING

Factoring and invoice discounting are both forms of finance that allow you to raise money directly against your outstanding debtors.

The easiest way to visualise this is to imagine that you can 'sell' your unpaid invoices to the lender at their full face value. This lender will then pay you for these in two instalments:

◆ an initial payment of the majority of the value (the advance, which is usually between 65% and 85%);

◆ with the remaining balance being paid, less the lender's charges, once your customer has paid the invoice.

The impact of this is to short circuit the bulk of the normal debtor stage of the working capital clock and so accelerate your cash receipts up to the level of the advance percentage as illustrated in Figure 14.

Since the type of debt that can be discounted can include both goods supplied and services, this type of financing is often used very successfully by businesses such as temporary employment agencies, where the business will need to pay the employees out working on contracts on a weekly, fortnightly or monthly basis, but where its customers may not pay for these staff for up to two months from the date of invoicing. By factoring or discounting the invoices with a lender the business can obtain cash in on invoicing to match the work done and to pay the staff.

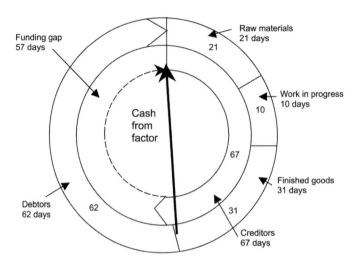

Fig. 14. The working capital clock.

Of course the lender does not actually purchase your debt, but will take a first fixed charge over it as security for the advance. As a result, your debtors are then not available for your bank to use to secure an overdraft facility. Completion of a factoring or invoice discounting deal therefore usually involves paying off your overdraft out of the initial advance received.

While stock finance is discussed later in this chapter, it is worth noting at this stage that some invoice discounters will also take finished goods stock into account and can then offer higher levels of advance against invoices (sometimes exceeding 100% of your debtor book).

Factoring or invoice discounting?

In both forms of finance the lender will provide you with funding known as an advance against the value of the cash due in to you from your debtors. As you forward them new sales invoices and they receive your debtors' payments on a daily basis the total advance they are prepared to give you will change from day-to-day. Deducting the previous day's outstanding advance from the total advance they are prepared to make today gives you your availability, which is the amount of cash you can ask the lender to send to you (or draw down).

While they both involve borrowing directly against the security value of your debtors, factoring and invoice discounting have important differences in how they operate. The most important are as follows.

Visibility and control

In factoring, in addition to advancing you money, the lender also takes over management of your sales ledger and credit control and provides a service in actively chasing in the customers' payments on your behalf, which can in itself be an advantage if your credit control has been poor. You will also have to place a notice on your invoices that the debt has been assigned to the factor and that your customers should pay the factor direct.

This means, however, that your customers will quickly become aware that you are factoring. They will see the notice and will be contacted directly by the lender about their bills, so factoring is normally a very public form of financing.

As this can cause some businesses concern as to how their key customers are handled, in some cases factors will allow a CHOCs arrangement for key accounts (client handles own customers) whereby you retain control of the contact with the customer. Some have also gone on to develop confidential factoring facilities.

Invoice discounting is usually only available to businesses with turnovers of greater than £1m with a positive balance sheet. It differs from factoring in that you continue to run your own sales ledger and collect in your own debtors. As you are continuing to do the work you obviously retain control of the process and it is therefore also possible to have confidential invoice discounting (CID) which means that your customers will not be aware of the arrangement.

Live and delayed adjustment

As a factor is advancing on individual invoices and is running your sales ledger, any adjustments to the amount of lending they are prepared to advance is immediately tied to the individual invoice movements.

With invoice discounting the lender does not run your ledger and instead requires you to provide a monthly reconciliation of the account on which any adjustments are made to cover the impact of, for example, disallowing older debts. As a result you can find yourself suffering a significant adjustment to the funds available as a single hit, rather than having a daily series of smaller movements which, while they may amount to the same value in terms of cash, may be more difficult to deal with. This difference is likely to disappear over time as one lender has just introduced a service which automatically updates their records daily by linking in directly to your accounting system which avoids large month-end movements. I would expect other lenders to follow suit over the next few years.

Further differences

Factoring and invoice discounting also differ in that as the invoice discounter is not directly in contact with the ledger on a day-to-day basis, this is perceived as being a riskier form of finance to offer than factoring. Discounters therefore tend to only want to provide facilities to larger businesses, typically with turnovers in excess of £1m, and to businesses with a positive net worth on the balance sheet.

Some of the key differences between factoring and invoice discounting are summarised below:

	Factoring	Invoice discounting
Visibility	Normally public	Normally confidential
Debt collection	Part of the package	You do your own
Adjustments to availability	Live	Monthly on reconciliation
Application	Most businesses with factorable debt	Businesses with turnovers of over £1m and a positive balance sheet

Factorable debt

Not all debt can be factored or discounted, however (and to avoid unnecessary duplication the generic terms factor and factoring will be used to cover both types of funding from here on except where there is a specific difference in how they operate).

As with most commercial debt funding the driving factor for how much can be borrowed is the value of the asset, in this case your debtors, as security. Some debt is impossible to factor as a lender cannot rely on it as security. This includes the following.

♦ Items sold on a sale or return basis, as the customer can always return the goods and cancel the debt on which the lender has already advanced. For a debt to be factorable there must be a clean sale.

♦ Even so, any debt which exists on a pay when paid basis as happens, for example, where a customer may be holding a consignment of stock, will not be factorable as the lender cannot necessarily determine a specific point at which the invoice raised will become due and payable, if indeed it ever does.

◆ The debt must be due from another business (a business to business or B2B sale) as factors are not interested in or set up to collect debts due from consumers (B2C sales). Factors are also wary of sales to government bodies, but some will fund against sales to local authorities or quasi governmental and public sector organisations.

◆ The other business must be a genuine third-party as factors will all discount any intercompany trading within a group.

◆ To the extent that a debt is due from a business that is also a supplier to the business the lender faces the risk that the customer will set off (contra) any sums that are due to them as suppliers against the debt due to the business. Any such debts will be excluded from the funding arrangement, or a reserve placed on the account which restricts the drawdown available so as to cover this risk for the factor.

Even having excluded the above, some business debts are still difficult to factor due to their nature, or circumstances which affect a factor's ability to collect in your debts to repay their lending in the event that your business fails, such as the following.

◆ Contractual debt for the provision of a service over a long period which involves stage payments such as:
  – engineering contracts where a payment of a third with order, a third on delivery and a third on commissioning is not unusual;
  – construction contracts which may last for many months are a particular problem, as they are normally based on a process of monthly applications which are estimates of the value of the job completed to date rather than invoices for a definite

amount. In construction contracts the application has to be agreed with the customer's architect or surveyors before the final agreed sum becomes payable, normally within two weeks. The bulk of the construction company's debtor book therefore usually consists of applications which will turn into a debt, but where the value of the debt is uncertain.

Contractual debt is always difficult to factor; if the supplier fails part way through delivery of a contract, its customer will normally seek to offset the costs of replacing the business and any associated disruption costs (which particularly in the construction industry can be quite creative), against the debt outstanding. As a result there are only a limited number of factors who will provide funding against this type of debt and this is usually at lower levels of advance (say 50% against a more normal level of 75% to 85%, together with a requirement for personal guarantees) as they have less certainty as to both the collectability of any debt and in the case of applications, its actual real value.

- ◆ Some contracts, for example for the supply of materials to a manufacturer for use on its production line, may include liquidated damage clauses. These are intended to provide a mechanism whereby the customer can be compensated for any interruption its production suffers if your business fails to supply it with widgets as agreed. These clauses create problems for factors as in the event your business fails, they give rise to the basis for your customers to offset a claim against the sums due to you on which a factor has lent.

- ◆ Sales which require extensive after sales service or warranties (such as bespoke computer software) may not be fundable as again the customer may seek to offset a claim relating to the loss of this support or the costs of replacing it against any debt due which the factor would be looking to collect.

- Sales to overseas customers can be a problem as the factor's ability and cost to collect will obviously vary from country to country. Some factors, such as the banks, are members of international groups and are therefore able to consider funding ledgers with a relatively high degree of international exposure (of say up to 50%), although even here this will involve an assessment of the spread of the ledger on a region by region or country by country basis. Most of the independent sector are, however, focused on UK based debt only.

- Sales to a single or very low number of customers can lead to a problem with what is known as concentration. To avoid having all their eggs in one or very few baskets, factors generally like to see their risk spread across a number of debtors with any individual customer making up no more than 20%–25% of the borrower's debtor book. However, this is an area where factors differ greatly in their policies.

In one case a company went into a discounting agreement with a concentration limit of 25% on any one debtor. Unfortunately it acted as a contract manufacturer for only six customers of which it was usually only working for one or two at a time. As a result, at the end of the first month when it submitted its reconciliations showing the bulk of its debtor book with only two customers, almost 50% of its book was **disallowed**.

In these situations the lender may allow temporary overpayments, but these will usually come at an additional cost.

The starting point for any lender in setting up a factoring facility is therefore an audit of the debtor book, which may be undertaken by in-house staff or subcontracted out to a firm of accountants. To avoid undertaking unnecessary work, factors will often seek to charge for this audit on the basis that the cost will be refunded if you go ahead with the deal. In doing so, they are often testing how serious you are about proceeding with an invoice discounting or factoring relationship. Some will take a view on this and may not make a charge, assuming that they conclude you are serious.

As well as checking for evidence of any of the issues noted above such as concentration, overseas exposure, and any contractual debt or liquidated damages clauses, the auditors will be looking at the quality of the debtor book for security purposes and in particular those listed below.

Aging

Since factors are lending against the security of debts they only want to lend against debts which they are confident will be paid. Where a debt has been outstanding for say three months, almost all factors will conclude that they cannot rely on this debt being paid and will therefore disallow it from their facility. So the auditor will look at the spread of your debtor's aging. Does your book include large older balances which would be disallowed by the factor? If so why have these arisen and what is the risk that more will arise in future?

Your accounting system will produce an aged debtors' schedule but this can often be produced on the basis of either the age of the debt since the invoice:

- was issued; or
- fell due for payment.

The age limit to which factors will fund can be 90 days either from the point the invoice was issued or from which it fell due, but they generally prefer the first approach as it avoids any risk of a hidden build up of old debt in the ledger, or of lending against debt that is not immediately recoverable.

In one case a company was selling off its surplus Christmas stock at the end of February. In order to do so they agreed with the customer that the invoice was not payable until the following November. The invoice discounter was allowing debt up to 90 days after the due date. However, this was on the expectation that the company's normal credit terms were 30 days. When the funder realised that some debts were effectively nine months old before they actually fell due for payment, this led to a significant increase in the reserves placed against the company's facility and therefore a reduction in the funds available from drawdown.

Contras

In some cases you may be buying from and selling to the same organisation, in which case your customer may have an amount due to them which they may be able to offset against any debt due to you. Factors will therefore disallow debt from their facility in respect of any such potential contras. The auditor will therefore look to match any supplier balances against customer balances.

Credit notes

Factors are wary of the risk that your debtor book can be diluted by the raising of credit notes so that they find themselves having advanced against invoices that are no longer there. The auditor will therefore look at your history of raising credit notes, including the numbers raised, values and reasons, so as to assess the risk.

Bad debt record

What has the company's experience been of suffering bad debts? What levels have they run at and for what reasons?

Customer strength

The factor will obviously take an interest in the credit worthiness of your customers, as in the event that the factor needs to rely on their security they will be looking to these customers for payment.

Terms of trade

The auditor will want to see your terms of business, and your paper trail from opening accounts and receiving an order, through to dispatching the goods, obtaining proof of delivery and invoicing, to ensure that you have appropriate agreements in place and systems that they can rely on to support the debts against which they are lending.

Customer's tools

If you hold a customer's tools, you can expect some difficult conversations with auditors as to whether this is a good or bad thing in respect of securing payments from customers. Some take the view that this can give rise to customers having a counterclaim, while others take the view that holding a customer's tools usually gives you a hold over the customer in order to ensure payment.

Advances, charges and terms

The level of advance that you can expect will vary from lender to lender, but in general the banks' factoring arms have a high degree of captive business introduced through their banking colleagues and therefore tend to be more conservative than the independents. As a guide, you might expect the bank factors to advance say 60% to 85% against a normal book, whilst the independent firms may range between 75% and 90%. They will in addition consider providing top-up facilities against stock or agreed temporary overpayments of say up to 100% to cover specific items such as a peak requirement at a VAT quarter, or exit penalties imposed by another lender.

These advances are all at nominal levels, as all factors will only advance against approved debt, which is to say your total debtor book less the debt that has been disallowed as a result of:

♦ aging when normally debt of over 90 days will be disallowed; and

♦ reserves placed against the accounts to cover any:
  – supplier contras;
  – balances in excess of agreed concentration limits;
  – intercompany trading; or
  – individual debtors that the lender won't fund for whatever reason, such as overseas debtors.

As a result of this disallowed debt, your effective advance (ie the funds available that you can actually draw down from the factor) will often be significantly lower than the percentage advance you have agreed with the lender. And be warned that in situations where a business is in difficulty, one way of managing a factor's exposure is for the factor to take a more aggressive stance in disallowing debt or placing either specific or general reserves on account so that the percentage they have advanced against the total book reduces. I have, for example, worked with companies where as a result of this sort of approach by the factor's operations department the effective advance has dropped to as low as 20%.

The costs of factoring will include two main elements.

◆ A service charge which for factoring can run at 0.5% to 1% of turnover. Factoring tends to be more expensive than invoice discounting as the charges include the cost of providing the sales ledger function of the facility, and the number of customers and the number of invoices being issued will therefore come into the equation for determining the costs. These charges are very visible and one of the reasons why factoring has a reputation for being expensive. However, when you're comparing the cost of factoring with other sources of finance you will need to take into account any savings you may be making by outsourcing your credit control function. When comparing factoring with the cost of normal bank facilities, be sure to take into account any management charges that your bank is imposing.

◆ Interest costs, which will be quoted at a rate over base and which should therefore be directly comparable with interest rates from other types of lending.

There are, however, some other costs to take into account which include:

◆ any initial audit cost as discussed above;

◆ a take-on fee to cover the administrative costs of setting up the arrangement;

- credit insurance costs where the lender may insist that you obtain insurance cover on some or all of your debtors;

- transaction costs such as telegraphic transfer fees (TTs).

Since it is difficult for a business going into factoring for the first time, or even looking to switch factors, to make a judgment as to the quality of service they are really going to receive, it's understandable that many will fall back on simply seeking the cheapest quote. This is often a mistake as the following may apply to the cheapest quote.

- It is often not the cheapest in the long run due to hidden charges such as TT costs. Some lenders appear to be in the habit of quoting low rates to customers on the basis that they will make up revenue on extras. Others try to give more of an all-in price, which will tend to be higher, but in the long run will give you fewer nasty surprises; so ensure you are comparing like with like. When looking at quotes make sure you know what is and is not included.

- It may reduce the flexibility of the arrangement. It is also true to say that, as with many things in life, you get what you pay for. If, for example, you negotiate a low rate of charges with your lender, you cannot expect a high degree of flexibility over advances if you are seeking an overpayment.

- It may actually cost you money in interest charges if they are inefficient at collecting, resulting in your borrowing money for longer than you need to, as illustrated below (ignoring VAT), where a higher sum charged is compensated for by better services and therefore a lower interest cost.

	Funder A	Funder B
Turnover	£1,000,000	£1,000,000
Service charge	0.85%	0.75%
	£8,500	£7,500
Debtor days	45	65
Average debtor balance	£123,288	£178,082
Funds out at 75%	£92,466	£133,562
Interest rate	5.00%	5.00%
Interest charge	£4,623	£6,678
Total cost	£13,123	£14,178

Most importantly when considering costs you will need to ensure that you are comparing like with like as factoring can be on a different basis.

♦ *A recourse basis*, where in the event that a customer does not pay, the lender can recover the funds they have advanced to you from your current availability, leaving you exposed to the impact of the bad debt.

♦ *A non-recourse basis*, where if a customer fails to pay a debt where there are no grounds for dispute; this is the factor's problem not yours.

Obviously in non-recourse factoring the lender is taking a much greater risk, or will be bearing an expense in insuring the debt, which will be reflected in the price of the service.

What you will usually find is that the factor will advise you of a credit insured limit for each customer, which will be the figure up to which non-recourse applies. So if you have three customers who do not pay, the result would be as shown:

Customer	Debt due	Credit insured limit	Impact of failure to pay on your facility
A	£10,000	£15,000	The factor's 'insurance policy' pays you out for the debt so you suffer no reduction in facility and the factor then pursues recovery in the normal way.
B	£10,000	£5,000	The factor's insurance policy pays you out to cover the first £5,000 so that there is no loss of facility in respect of this, but the factor will claw back the advance made in respect of the further £5,000 in excess of the credit insured limit. The factor will then look to recover the full amount from the debtor and if they do so they will restore the funds to your account.
C	£10,000	£0	The factor will deduct the entirety of the advance made against the £10,000 debt which will reduce the funds available to you.

The factoring and invoice discounting market

This has been a rapidly expanding market over the last few years with between 50 to 60 active factors and invoice discounters operating at the time of writing. There is therefore a wide variety of lenders falling into three main categories.

◆ The main clearing banks' own and branded firms which obtain much of their work by their in-house bank referrals, although some work hard to produce strong solutions for clients and as a result are successful competitors in the market.

◆ Large independents who may well be owned by smaller banks or other financial institutions. These often provide both factoring and invoice discounting facilities as well as now being able to provide packages of structured finance combining an number of asset based elements, including property and plant and machinery loans as well as stock and debtor finance. They are therefore sometimes known generically as asset based lenders or ABLs.

◆ Smaller players, generally focused on factoring, but who may well have developed particular niches such as construction debt, architects' practices, government debt, or care homes, which can require particular expertise in lending.

For reasons that have already been covered, many businesses have found themselves moved on to factoring or invoice discounting by their banks and as a result have transferred over to their bank's in-house firm. There is therefore quite a degree of churn in the market where businesses realise that having lost their requirement for a banking relationship to maintain an overdraft, they are in fact free to seek a better deal elsewhere. This typically involves moving to an independent which, not having a tied stream of enquiries have to try harder, typically offering better advance rates and more flexibility.

If you are seeking to transfer from one factor to another you need to be aware that there is a protocol agreed between the firms and that the new lender will seek an inter-factor reference from the old lender. The particular issues that they will be looking for are any suggestion of either of the two great sins of factoring.

Pre-invoicing

The fresh air invoice, where cash has been raised against an invoice where no goods have in fact been supplied, is the most obvious fraud that factoring arrangements (and more particularly confidential invoice discounting where the lender is not in contact with your debtors) are open to. The lender will guard against them by holding regular debtor audits and contacting your customers to verify invoices. Any suggestion in a reference that this has taken place can be sufficient to sink a deal.

Diversion of cash

In a factoring arrangement the customer will be instructed to pay debts direct to the factor. On occasions customers will still make payments to the company direct. Where this happens it is your responsibility to pay the cash over to the factors as otherwise you are still borrowing funds in respect of an invoice which is no longer outstanding. If you do not make such a payment you are actually diverting cash that is due to the lender. Again, invoice discounting arrangements, where you are responsible for collecting in the cash and then paying it into a trust account for the benefit of the lender, are much more open to this form of abuse.

Penalties

If you are seeking to transfer before the end of your current contract, as discussed below, you are likely to be liable for penalties. In these situations there may be a deal that can be negotiated between the incoming and outgoing factors to mitigate these, or if not, the new factor will typically seek to provide some assistance through either an enhanced initial drawdown, or in some cases a sharing of the cost of penalties in order to win your business.

Issues to consider when choosing a factor

This chapter will hopefully have given you a better idea of some of the things to consider when choosing a factor or invoice discounter. Obviously you will need to decide first whether this type of debtor based finance is appropriate for your business, and if so whether you are better off with factoring or invoice discounting.

◆ With factoring you will lose control of how your customers are chased for payment unless you opt for a CHOCs arrangement. With invoice discounting this is under your control.

- Your facility will be based on a percentage advance against approved invoices. The actual (effective) advance you receive as a percentage of your total debtors can be significantly less than this nominal headline percentage as the factor may disallow debts over three months old, sales to suppliers, overseas debts, or may set concentration limits where individual customer's debts cannot be more than a set percentage of your sales ledger or credit limit per customer. You need to look at the nature of your debts and ensure that you will not run into such problems. As the levels of reserves only change monthly in invoice discounting, based on your reconciliation of the account, this can lead to some big swings in your availability.

- As the advance is tied directly to invoicing, debt based finance is well suited to fast growing companies as the financing automatically expands as the business grows, reducing the danger of overtrading.

- However, as the facility is tied to sales volume, if sales fall, so does the funding available (which may be just the moment that you need finance the most).

- Once you have this type of facility in place, it can be extremely difficult to get to a position where you can exit the arrangement.

- There is still a stigma attached to factoring in some circles as it has been seen as financing of last resort. However, as banks have moved more customers to this form of financing (and it becomes a normal part of almost every MBO/MBI transaction), this stigma is disappearing (and of course is avoided with confidential invoice discounting).

- Finally, what happens if you get into difficulty? As already discussed you may find that the factor will look to manage its risk by reducing its effective advance, sometimes to a level which can lead to the strangulation of the business.

In these circumstances invoice discounters will look to move your account onto a factoring arrangement as a way of giving them a much closer understanding of the exact profile of your debtors and hold much more detail about the outstanding book in case they have to undertake a collect out.

Most invoice discounting and factoring arrangements have built in a scale of charges to cover collect out situations where they have to recover their money from a business's debtors following its failure. In practice this means that the lender's exposure is often limited, because they have successfully restricted drawdown prior to a failure. This then gives them scope to recover their collect out charges which can be highly remunerative.

Some key questions that you need to ask in respect of any particular provider's offer follow below.

◆ Given that the credit control function is part of what you are paying for in a factoring deal, and its efficiency is a key determinant of the total cost to you or the deal, make sure you understand what level of service you are buying. Are all debtors to be chased or just a top slice? How effective is the chasing? How good are they at collecting debts?

Be sure to take references and obtain their statistics. Ask to meet the operations team who will be handling your account, as the sales person you are dealing with now will usually not be involved in the relationship going forwards.

Not all lenders are as efficient as others. For example, some lenders are still not set up to collect data on your sales on a same day basis electronically. They rely on you to post/fax a schedule of sales against which you can then draw down, thus building a delay (and uncertainty when the post goes astray) into the process.

◆ Does the lender suit the nature of your business and for example its level of debtor concentration or overseas sales? How flexible are they and what other lending are they providing you with? Will they provide you with an enhanced level of advance against finished goods stock as part of the debtor funding package?

◆ What additional security are they asking for in terms of personal guarantees?

◆ How competitive is the cost and what does it include? How does it compare with other offers you have received?

◆ What are you committing to? What is the minimum contract length (usually 12 months although one lender has an 'easy in, easy out' facility designed for situations where you may only want or need a short-term arrangement) and any notice period thereafter (often another three months). What are the termination provisions and any exit penalties if you need to get out early? What level of minimum charges are built in which may mean you end up paying charges even if you do not draw down cash?

◆ How easy will it be to operate? Ask to see copies of the statements that you will receive on your account. Ensure that these are fully explained to you so that you understand how to follow them once the arrangement is up and running. Try working out how easy it will be to establish how much cash you will be able to draw down day-to-day, as some statements are almost impossible to follow.

The information that Creative Business Finance Limited seek when arranging an introduction to an appropriate funder is set out in Figure 15.

Creative Business Finance
www.creativefinance.co.uk

Debtor Finance Enquiry Form
For free advice as to the appropriate debtor funder for your business please complete and return the form below

Your business
Company name　　　　　　＿＿＿＿＿＿＿＿＿＿＿＿＿＿＿＿＿
Nature of business　　　　　＿＿＿＿＿＿＿＿＿＿＿＿＿＿＿＿＿
Annual turnover (£000)　　　＿＿＿＿＿＿＿＿＿＿＿＿＿＿＿＿＿

Your debtor book
Total debtor value　　　　　　＿＿＿＿＿＿＿＿＿＿＿＿＿＿＿＿＿
£　Over three months old　　　＿＿＿＿＿＿＿＿＿＿＿＿＿＿＿＿＿
£　To overseas customers　　　＿＿＿＿＿＿＿＿＿＿＿＿＿＿＿＿＿
£　To suppliers　　　　　　　＿＿＿＿＿＿＿＿＿＿＿＿＿＿＿＿＿
£　Stage payments　　　　　　＿＿＿＿＿＿＿＿＿＿＿＿＿＿＿＿＿

Your existing facility (if applicable)
Lender　　　　　　　　　　　＿＿＿＿＿＿＿＿＿＿＿＿＿＿＿＿＿
Type (eg factoring)　　　　　　＿＿＿＿＿＿＿＿＿＿＿＿＿＿＿＿＿
Current advance (£000)　　　　＿＿＿＿＿＿＿＿＿＿＿＿＿＿＿＿＿
Advance against stock　　　　　＿＿＿＿＿＿＿＿＿＿＿＿＿＿＿＿＿
Current interest rate and service
charges　　　　　　　　　　　＿＿＿＿＿＿＿＿＿＿＿＿＿＿＿＿＿
Any particular concerns or problems
with your current facility (or use
current lender service assessment
below)　　　　　　　　　　　＿＿＿＿＿＿＿＿＿＿＿＿＿＿＿＿＿

Optional current funder service assessment

Please tick appropriate box	Yes, I'm happy	No, I'm not
• Easy to understand statements, so that I know where I am		
• Free from hidden charges that have made it more expensive than I was expecting		
• An actual cash advance that matches the level that I was promised at the outset		
• Easy and efficient communication with the lender's operations and a good working relationship		
• A good competitive rate without an onerous monthly minimum charge		
• An advance against stock as well as debtors, to maximise the funds available		
• Efficient and effective collection of debts by my factor, that doesn't upset my customers		

When complete, please fax back to 0870 220 8587

Fig. 15. Debtor finance enquiry form.

Block discounting

As forms of debtor based finance, both factoring and invoice discounting are only available where goods or a service have been supplied and can therefore be invoiced. However, they cannot be used to raise funds against future contractual income as despite being certain in terms of timing and value, this has yet to become a debt that is actually due and payable.

Where you have a long-term stream of contractual income such as a rental income from property or machinery, you may be able to borrow what is in effect an advance against this future income through what is known as block discounting. This is a specialist market where each deal is very much a one-off, tailored to the particular nature of the asset and contracts involved, so you are likely to need to use an independent finance broker to investigate such funds.

FUNDING STOCK AND TRADING

Introduction

Funding stock and purchases has always been difficult as lenders have found it difficult to take effective security on which they can rely, and to value any such security as follows.

- The level of a business's stock will move up and down markedly in many businesses, so knowing how much stock is likely to be physically there when the lender needs to rely on it is difficult.

- If the stock is valuable, easily moveable and easily sellable, this is a particular problem as it is likely to be gone by the time the lender needs to call on it. But if it is not valuable, difficult to move and/or sell how much value is it as security?

♦ In addition to tracking the quantity of stock, tracking its value is also difficult, as book values of stock are likely to be wildly different from its actual realisable value:

- despite being on the books, much of the raw materials stock may turn out to be covered by suppliers' reservation of title clauses and so may not actually belong to the borrower until paid for in full;

- there is generally no market for any uncompleted work in progress after a business's failure;

- without a company to supply after sales service and warranty support, will the finished goods stock actually be saleable?

♦ In the event of an insolvency there is also a risk that the HM Revenue & Customs, may have distrained stock for unpaid taxes or the landlord may have done so for unpaid rent.

As a result true stock financing is rare, but there are some options available from a limited number of lenders, the key ones of which are:

♦ stock finance as part of an invoice discounting facility;
♦ stand alone stock finance;
♦ machinery dealer finance;
♦ trade finance;
♦ letters of credit and loans against imports;
♦ personal funding (eg through Fleximortgage).

Stock finance as part of an invoice discounting facility
As has been covered in the previous section, many of the factoring and invoice discounting firms will now advance funds against finished goods stock as part of their facility. In practice the advance is made by way of an overpayment against the debtor book, so for example, taking the percentage level of advance up

from a nominal 85% to say a nominal 100%, but whatever the value of stock involved, the lender will still regard the debtor book as the core of their security.

To advance against stock, all lenders will, in the same way as the factor or invoice discounter will with debtors, need to become comfortable with the value of their security. This means they will need to undertake a detailed audit of the stock and will require you to run a detailed stock reporting system on a live basis to provide regular reports on quantity, value and movement of stock.

As the HM Revenue & Customs have the ability to distrain against stock for outstanding PAYE/NI or VAT balances, while your landlord has similar abilities in respect of rent arrears, the lender will also want a regular statement of your position in respect of Crown debt and rent payments. In order to be able to realise the stock should they ever need to, the lender may also wish to enter into an access and **priority agreement** with the landlord.

Stand alone stock finance

Having explained all the difficulties involved in lending against stock, it may come as a surprise to find that there are a number of lenders who are developing a range of stock financing products.

As a developing area it is difficult to give definitive guidance at the time of writing, but in addition to invoice discounting based facilities as described above there are for example the following options.

- Smaller end lenders offering initial facilities in the order of £30k, with some larger sums being available once a trading relationship is established.

- Short-term loans against stock which are in practice bridging arrangements and are costed accordingly at rates of up to 2% per month.

- Larger loans available, for example through banks in respect of stock balances where the value is in excess of say £5m, and therefore where the level of advance starts to make the costs of regular monthly monitoring and audits a more reasonable prospect.

- Term loans where a bank will sometimes convert part of a hardcore overdraft facility, that may have arisen in relation to a build up of stock in the business, into a term loan to be repaid over a number of years that is then described as a stock loan.

In addition to these arrangements some of the trade finance companies discussed below will offer finance by way of supplier undertakings. Crudely this can in effect mean that they use their ability to obtain credit to purchase goods that you need from your suppliers on your behalf, and then sell these on to you at a margin as part of a financing arrangement. This type of facility can be very useful where, for example, a business has a large and profitable contract to undertake, but it lacks the working capital to finance the required purchases, or where a business is in temporary cashflow difficulty and is therefore unable to obtain credit itself from its suppliers for the goods it needs. Each such arrangement will need to be tailored to the company's particular circumstances and as a tailored solution will be costed accordingly.

Machinery dealer finance

The difficulty of borrowing against stock is a particular problem for businesses across the wholesaling, retailing, and dealing sectors where stock may be the main asset of a company.

Some industries have evolved particular arrangements to deal with this issue, such as motor trade main dealers where the manufacturers will often provide the local franchise with formal stocking arrangements.

In other cases finance companies have developed services designed to cater for particular niches. One key service exists, for example, for experienced dealers in machinery who can demonstrate a successful track record in spotting and converting opportunities at a good margin. This type of business generally requires a revolving facility secured against the equipment currently in stock, which allows the stock to be sold on and funds to be reused to purchase further items for resale. Since the security involved is an ever-changing level of stock this is an area where banks have often been reluctant to provide appropriate facilities.

As a result, independent finance companies can now provide facilities of up to £2.5m in the first instance to fund the buying in of assets to sell on. These can provide flexible funding that can be drawn down as required of up to 100% of the cost of the asset together with duty and VAT. This obviously provides the appropriate solution, but as a specialised product providing funding for areas where the banks are reluctant to do so because of the security risk, the cost of such borrowings will be high.

Trade finance

This type of funding brings us on to trade finance, which should be seen as the financing of a particular transaction or series of transactions, rather than as a loan to the business. Trade finance houses therefore provide cash to finance transactions that you have set up. A typical example might involve funding the importation of a container of goods from overseas for resale here.

The funding available ranges from:

◆ the funder purchasing the goods themselves, arranging and financing transport and customs clearance, only reselling the goods to you immediately before you sell them on; to

◆ the funder guaranteeing payment to the supplier but not actually having to remit funds.

The funder's principal requirement when lending in such situations is the ability to clearly see the route through to the recovery of its funds. They will typically therefore look to:

◆ fund finished goods (although some will occasionally finance the purchasing of components for assembly prior to sale);

◆ support transactions with a high gross profit margin;

◆ see that a significant majority of the goods (sufficient to repay the borrowing) have been pre-sold;

◆ have terms that do not include any element of sale return;

◆ have creditworthy customers.

Critically for a trade finance house the success of the specific transaction being funded is what really provides them with their security. Therefore to be able to lend they have to be completely confident that they will be able to recover their money from a successful sale of the goods, which can affect their ability to fund. On the other hand, since they are looking at specifics of the transaction and are simply concerned with whether it may or may not be successful, they will also be very flexible about the type of transaction to look at and they will not necessarily be concerned:

- if your business is in financial difficulties;
- if the goods are being purchased from the UK or overseas;
- if the goods are being sold to the UK or overseas; or
- never even land in the UK.

So for example, in one case a trade finance house was happy to fund the purchase of a large quantity of electronic consumer goods for delivery in the autumn, even though the importer had not presold the consignment. This was because the finance company took the view that it could rely on the goods selling in the run-up to Christmas.

Advances and rates will be tailored to the specifics of the deal involved and type of financial support required. Some lenders will insist on factoring your debtors as part of such an arrangement, so that they can be paid out immediately on sale of the goods and a typical arrangement might therefore look as summarised in Figure 16.

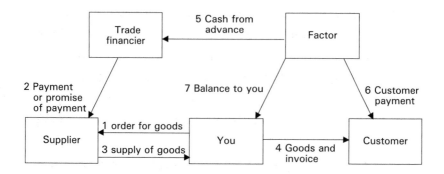

Fig. 16. A simplified trade finance arrangement with a factoring house.

Letters of credit and loans against imports

Where buying from an overseas supplier you may be asked to provide a **letter of credit** (LC). This is essentially a promise by your bank to pay the supplier for the goods upon production of the relevant paperwork, which is normally the documentation showing that the goods have been shipped. There are two main advantages of this to your supplier.

♦ First they do not have to rely on you for payment, but can trust your bank.

♦ Secondly, they can present the letter of credit to their own bankers as an irrevocable promise to pay for the goods once delivered, and use this as security on which to borrow from their own bank in order to manufacture the goods for sale, a process known as discounting an LC.

Where your bank issues a letter of credit this has the same effect as though they had promised to issue a cheque on your behalf and they will therefore take this liability (sometimes referred to as blocked funds) into account when considering how much overdraft facility to allow you.

So if you would normally have sufficient security to support a £1m overdraft, but you have issued letters of credit for £250,000 through your bank, the bank will normally only allow you an overdraft facility of £750,000 so as to maintain their total exposure to your business at under £1m, even though they may not have to pay out on the LCs for some months.

Once the supplier has provided the relevant paperwork and been paid out on the LC this cost will then be deducted from your bank account. Banks will sometimes offer a loan against imports (LAI) facility for say 120 days, which means that from the date of payment of the LC it will be 120 days before the cost is deducted from your bank account. This is designed to enable you to sell the goods and recover the cash from your customers in order to be able to meet the payment of the LC.

Obviously, where you are using trade finance your suppliers may wish to be paid using LCs from your trade finance house. If this is the case you need to be very careful as to how much you will be charged as shown in the following example.

The company imported goods from the Far East and provided its suppliers with an LC payable on shipping of the goods (generally three months) which the suppliers then discounted with their own bankers to fund the production of the goods. The company then paid off the LC within 45 days by selling the goods on once they had arrived in the UK and cleared customs. To fund a new line of business requiring £2m of LCs it sought quotations from two trade finance houses for which the charges were:

	Funder A	**Funder B**
Flat charge for funding		
the transaction	3%	Nil
Monthly LC interest rate	1.75%	2%
Calculation of interest	Daily from date	From moment LC
charge	that the LC is	raised, calculated
	paid out	monthly for each
		month or part month

Most of the other terms and administrative charges to cover the costs of issuing the required documentation were similar.

The difference in the interest costs the business would face from the two lenders differed markedly, however:

	Funder A	**Funder B**
Total interest cost	Flat fee 3% + 2.6%	Three months since LC
	(45 days at 1.75%	raised plus two months
	pm) = 5.6% or	to cover the 45 day
	£112,000	shipment and sale period
		gives 5 months at 2%
		per month = 10% or
		£200,000

Lender A also came up with a number of suggestions as to how the company could structure the transaction to avoid having to pay any interest, such as by issuing the supplier with a longer term LC so the lender did not have to pay out for 45 days after shipment, so eliminating the 2.6% interest charge.

Personal funding (eg through Fleximortgage)

As an alternative to seeking stock finance from institutions, if you own a business and have a significant level of personal equity in your domestic property, you can think about using a domestic mortgage such as a Fleximortgage to raise cash to enable you to act as your own stock financiers.

This involves borrowing money at domestic mortgage rates to purchase the stock personally for the business giving options to:

- only feed it in as required, thereby retaining ownership and control of the stock; or

- place the stock into the business, but take a charge over the business's assets by way of security and again to charge a fee to the business for provision of this facility; while

- charging a commercial rate of interest for such high risk lending, which since domestic mortgage rates are generally amongst the lowest borrowing costs can enable you to turn a personal profit on this activity.

A Fleximortgage allows for easy drawdown/repayment of cash against the value of your property without penalties (up to certain limits and usually only if you have a good credit history). Giving advice on and arranging for borrowing against domestic property on a first charge is now regulated through the Financial Services Authority (FSA) hence mortgages are now known as '**regulated loans**'. You will therefore need to obtain advice from an appropriately regulated adviser if this is something you want to explore.

KEY POINTS

- Factoring and invoice discounting are becoming mainstream parts of business finance as banks shy away from overdraft funding.

- As finance based on your levels of debtors, the cash available will directly tie into your trading performance, but not all debt will be fundable so you may not be able to generate as much cash from this route as you might hope.

- Factoring and invoice discounting differ in that factoring provides collection services as well as funding, whilst invoice discounting can be on a confidential basis.

- There is a large market of active invoice discounters and factors which gives you the freedom to choose the funder that suits you, but the choice between different funders can be complex as:
  - you need to understand how the characteristics of your business, from the nature of its sales to the location and nature of its customers, may affect how much different lenders are willing to advance;
  - the approach of presenting costs can vary widely; and
  - you need to be able to make a judgement as to how efficient a lender will be.

- A reputable commercial finance broker with a good current knowledge of the marketplace can be useful in helping you to find the best lender for your circumstances.

- Stock is generally difficult to finance:
  - it can form part of an invoice discounting or factoring facility by way of an overpayment;
  - for larger situations there are now some stand alone stock finance facilities available;
  - trade finance houses can be used to fund the individual transactions such as the importation of goods for sale.

10

Grants

The DTI defines a grant as a 'sum of money given to an individual or business for a specific project or purpose'. While grants may not cover the total costs of the project or purpose, the advantages of this type of funding are that as long as you keep to any conditions attached to it you will not have to repay it as you would with a loan, nor will you have to give up any shares in your business, as you would with an equity investor.

Grants are generally given to assist with business development. They will therefore be linked to a specific area of activity such as training, new product development, or investment in plant and equipment.

THE PRACTICAL ISSUES

This may sound too good to be true and in practice obtaining grants can be a long, time consuming and frustrating process, with no guarantee of success, that involves the following.

Finding out what grants are available for your business

This can be difficult as there is a wide variety of grants available across the country (with over 4,500 grants and financial programmes available to UK organisations according to www.j4b.co.uk, see below). They are funded by a wide range of organisations including:

- local authorities
- Regional Development Agencies;

- central government;
- European Union bodies; as well as
- non-government organisations such as the Prince's Trust; and
- quangos such as the National Endowment for Science Technology and the Arts (NESTA) or the Carbon Trust.

Each of these will have its own application procedures. The grants are given for a variety of purposes, as they are usually designed to assist in achieving some economic development or regeneration policy which then helps to determine the criteria you have to meet in order to apply. These can include:

- the size of your business – some may only be available for small or medium-sized businesses (SMEs);

- the industry you are in – some may be designed to help a specific industry, or a general grant may exclude businesses in some specific sectors; and

- your location, for example many European union grants are only available in specified geographical areas requiring economic regeneration;

- the use to which the funds are to be put.

Meeting the criteria

Finding out whether you meet the criteria for the grant that you are applying for, as discussed below, may be complex.

Applying in advance

Apply before you start the project or incur the expenditure. Most grants are not retrospective and you have to apply for your proposed project in advance. This can result in delays in getting your project underway if you have to put it on hold while you go through the grant process.

In practice in the SME sector many suppliers of business services have become adept at taking advantage of whatever grants are available in their sector, and will offer to try to obtain these on your behalf in order to help pay for the costs of their services. So for example, a marketing or training consultancy may quote you a rate for a project as part of the tendering process, but do so on the basis that they will expect to be able to obtain grant funding to part pay for it.

Matching funding

Very few grants will provide 100% of the cash required for a project, and you will therefore need to both arrange the matching funding to provide the balance, and be able to prove to the grant provider that this is in place. This matching funding can be cash introduced into the business by the owner or a new investor, come from the company's own cash reserves, or be money that has been borrowed for the purpose.

For some smaller grants and support you may be allowed to count the cost of your time that is contributed towards the project as part of the matching funding. From what I have seen in the small business arena, this approach is wide open to abuse. For example, a firm providing advisory and support work which is part paid through government grants could inflate the total value of the project claimed for such that the grant applied for (which in theory is providing only say 50% of the costs) actually covers the majority of the true costs, so reducing the cash that the client has to pay as their share; with the balance of the project's nominal cost then being made up by this 'time contribution element'.

Finding cash for other elements

You may have to find cash to pay for the elements of your project which are not covered by the grant, where, for example, a grant to help develop a business website might have no element to assist in buying a computer on which to host it.

Again in practice many of the businesses providing services to the SME sector which are used to playing the grant game will be adept at managing the process of applying for a grant so as to obtain maximum advantage.

Pre-funding

Find out if you can obtain cash prior to expenditure. Many grants provide repayment to you of part of an expense or investment that you have to make and cannot be retrospective.

Remember that even once you've been awarded a grant in theory, you still actually have to be paid it. This payment might be at regular intervals throughout a project, or may be in arrears once you have submitted proof of the expenditure. You therefore will need to look at your project's cashflows to ensure that you are able to finance the project until the grant cash actually comes through to you.

Other issues

- Arranging a public or private sector partner as applicable, since many grants are available only to such public/private partnerships.

- Finding out when the application has to be made. Some funds are only available for part of the year and others may have deadlines which have to be hit. Remember that most grant funding bodies will be bureaucratic institutions that are managed on the basis of paperwork, which will have to be in on time and in triplicate.

◆ Completing the application process, which you will generally find includes attempting to estimate how many jobs will be created, or staff helped to obtain NVQs or other qualifications, as a significant part of both the form and the selection criteria.

◆ Awaiting approval of your application and payment of the funds required which may take some time. A locally administered grant should take no more than a few weeks; however, an application for national funds may take months, while applications for European funding can take anything up to a year.

Remember that many grants are either run as competitions or may in practice be competitive, as the number of businesses are all applying for a limited pot of funding. You therefore cannot rely on automatically getting any grant and you need to consider whether your project is viable if the grant doesn't come through.

Almost all grants will come with strict terms and conditions which will include a requirement to provide extensive information as to the impact of the grants which can, for example, require you to provide details of numbers of employees and qualifications gained as a result of the grants. The danger with grants is that if you breach the conditions they are usually repayable immediately, although at least no interest is charged.

This leads on to the other danger: in order to get a grant you may have to commit your business to meet specific criteria which may cause a subsequent problem. For example, an electronics business MBO had obtained a significant grant which specified the number of jobs this grant had to have secured. When the industry had a downturn and its competitors laid off staff to reduce costs, the company was unable to do so as this would immediately trigger repayment of the grant in full. As a result, the company staggered on without reducing its cost base until eventually it failed and all the jobs were lost.

WHAT DO GRANTS COVER?

Business Link's *Grants and Support Directory* (see below) starts from an extensive checklist that asks you to identify the type of support you are looking for.

Taking a broader view, grants are made available by funding bodies in order to help them achieve their objectives and at present in the UK break down into a number of main areas (some of which obviously overlap).

- Training across many areas, most notably in IT skills or any training which would lead to a qualification such as an NVQ (see the Learning and Skills Council www.lsc.gov.uk).

- Research and development, together with the implementation of innovation and then taking products to market, where there is a wide variety of awards available, including for example the DTI's SMART award scheme and support from NESTA.

- Economic regeneration, where for example, businesses based in assisted areas can be provided with assistance through the Selective Finance for Investment in England scheme, providing up to 50% of relevant capital expenditure (which has largely replaced Regional Selective Assistance grants, see www.dti.gov.uk/regionalinvestment) if this helps to stimulate local employment urban regeneration or regional development, while there may also be support for example for small rural businesses.

◆ Ecological improvements or extensive grants are becoming available from the Carbon Trust for energy improvement projects.

◆ Exports, where support is available for example to attend overseas trade fairs.

◆ Employment of young people, where for example under the New Deal (www.newdeal.gov.uk) there are support grants available for the employment and training of young people.

◆ New business start-ups, particularly amongst young unemployed people where for example, the Prince's Trust (www.princes-trust.org.uk) provides support for those aged 18 to 30 with a business idea.

ASSISTANCE WITH OBTAINING GRANTS

There are a number of sites that seem to provide extensive guidance to what is available and how to apply for it, and which should therefore be your starting point for finding grants and obtaining assistance in accessing them.

◆ j4grants.co.uk (www.j4b.co.uk), a site run by a consultancy claiming to provide comprehensive information on 'government grants for both business and voluntary groups which is updated daily' as well as providing 'a database of publicly funded organisations that provide help and advice'.

The site provides a search facility to allow you to find what grants may be available for your type and size of business, in your location and for the purposes that you are seeking. They also offer a regular newsletter as well as an alert service to notify you of grants that become available that match your criteria.

It also includes a link through to grant-guide.com which provides details of grants available in Europe.

♦ Business Link (www.businesslink.gov.uk) – follow the links to 'Finance and Grants' and the Grants and Support Directory which is designed to allow you to search for grants and other support although even the Business Link website says that applying for a grant can be a highly complex process, and you may therefore want to contact your local Business Link for help and advice with your application.

♦ You can also try www.grantsonline.org.uk.

Once you have information as to what may be available you can then apply:

♦ on your own;

♦ using your local Business Link, which will have advisers who should be able to assist you in the process and who will have a good knowledge of the grants that are locally available; or

♦ through a private sector agency. These agencies will charge for their services, but can obviously offer no guarantee that they will be able to obtain a specific grant for you, so you should check their terms of business very carefully.

Your eligibility for a grant will normally be determined by the following factors.

♦ Your location: some schemes operate across the whole of the UK, but since many grants are available from local councils or regional development organisations, these will by definition only be available to businesses in those localities.

The European Union provides funds to help develop the poorer regions in the EU. This is done by targeting European and government funding and assistance on what are known as assisted areas which come in three levels:

Tier 1	Areas with the greatest economic need as their gross domestic product per head has been running below 75% of the EU's average. There are four such areas in the UK including Merseyside, South Yorkshire, West Wales and the valleys, Cornwall and the Isles of Scilly.
Tier 2	Areas of need which also combine with major areas the opportunity to create employment or to regenerate industry. These areas are much more localised than Tier 1 and can be found across the country from the Cumbrian coast in the northwest down to areas in London and Kent in the southeast.
Tier 3	Further areas extending beyond Tiers 1 and 2 where additional assistance can be available to businesses employing up to 250 people (sometimes known as enterprise grant areas). These typically include areas around ex-coalfields and rural development areas as well as urban spots of high unemployment.

Any business proposal which involves investing in an area covered by these tiers and offering the prospect of substantial job creation may be eligible for substantial support.

♦ The status of your business, where some grants may only be available to limited companies.

♦ The length of time your business has been operating, where some grants are restricted to businesses in their first few years.

♦ The size of your business, where some grants may be only available to SMEs. The European Union's definitions differ slightly from those in the Companies Act for small and medium-sized businesses while adding the concept of a micro business as follows:

EU definition	Micro	Small	Medium
Maximum number of employees	9	49	249
Maximum turnover (Euros m)	2.0	10.0	50.0
Maximum balance sheet value (Euros m)	2.0	10.0	43.0
Companies Act definition (see note)			
Maximum number of employees		50	250
Maximum turnover (£m)		2.8	11.2
Maximum balance sheet value (£m)		1.4	5.6

Note – for a company to qualify under the Companies Act as small or medium in a year it has to meet two out of the three criteria during that year.

♦ The sector you operate in, where funds may be targeted on the development of particular industries.

By contrast the EU has imposed specific restrictions for grants supporting a number of sectors. The ability to obtain grant support in the areas of retail, agricultural and food processing, transport, and some heavy industries such as motor vehicles, shipbuilding, coal, and steel are therefore very limited.

♦ The purpose of the grant, where these are usually awarded for a specific project or purpose such as relocation, developing exports, or investing in plant and machinery. You will not get a general grant providing you with general working capital or cash with which you can do what you like.

The provider will therefore generally be looking for specific targets and results to be met which will contribute towards the funder achieving their own targets and objectives.

From this it follows that in order to have the best chance of obtaining funding you need to find out what the funder's objectives are and ensure that your project is aligned with these. Generally it is a good idea to try to talk to the awarding body before putting your application in so that you can tailor your application to the criteria they are looking for, and ensure that your application is in an area that is relevant to that particular funder.

It also means that the funder will be looking:
– for your business to be committed to making the project a success, as otherwise the result will not be delivered; and
– for the project to be viable within a reasonable timescale.

Since you have to demonstrate the project's viability and that it is likely to achieve the result that you and the grant provider will be looking for, your application for a grant really has to take the form of a well constructed business case and plan which includes the items below.

◆ A detailed description of the project.

◆ A detailed and fully costed project plan.

◆ As much detail as possible of the potential benefits of the project, including as much quantitative information as possible about targets that will be hit (such as new jobs generated or employees acquiring qualifications) which meet the objectives of the funder.

◆ The other normal contents of a business plan such as cashflow forecasts and projections, as well as management CVs.

◆ Fully completed application forms.

To stand the best chance of getting a grant you should ensure that:

- the facts in your business plan are fully supported with detailed and up-to-date information;

- you have clearly demonstrated the impact of the project on both the business and, where appropriate, the local community;

- you can demonstrate that you have the appropriate matched funds and/or a private/public sector partner as appropriate;

- you have demonstrated that the grant funds are required for the project's success.

KEY POINTS

- As the www.j4b.co.uk website memorably puts it:
  Finding out what grant schemes you are eligible for is only half the battle. There is no such thing as free money and your application will require anywhere from a few hours to several days or even weeks for the bigger schemes.

- Obtaining grant funding is:
  - an uncertain and time-consuming process;
  - focused on providing part funding for a specific project, usually in arrears (although you will have to pay in advance);
  - from a myriad of local, regional, national and international, governmental and non-governmental sources;
  - where your eligibility will be determined by your location, business size and sector; and
  - determined in part by the strength of your arguments and business plan, but in part by how well this fits in with the funder's own objectives.

- It is therefore an area where to maximise your chances of success you may need to obtain assistance from a Business Link adviser, a supplier of services who may have existing links for obtaining grant funding, or from a private sector consultant.

(11)

Equity Finance

The money that your business can raise as debt will generally be limited by the assets available to give as security. Any money that your business needs in order to trade or invest for the long term into the business, which cannot be raised as debt or grants, will have to be invested into it by either introducing capital (which is to say money) from outside (in shares in a company) or later by leaving profits in the business. It is this owner's cash that is referred to as equity.

A provider of equity is putting money into the business normally in return for a share in both its ownership and its profits and future value. An equity provider is therefore in a fundamentally different position from a normal lender when it comes to risk and return:

	Provider of debt	Provider of equity
Risk	Will normally seek to take sufficient security to be able to recover their money if the business fails.	Has no security and is taking a risk. If the business fails they will be at the end of the line when it comes to returning any funds to creditors and shareholders.
Commitment	Usually defined by a set term and a schedule of payments whereby the cash lent is repaid.	Open ended as there are normally no arrangements in place for this capital to be repaid.
Return	Normally has a set rate of return (the interest rate). Has no share in the upside if the business is very successful.	Has no contractual return that they can rely on. They are putting money into a business in return for a share in its ownership, and therefore in its hoped for future success and are entitled to their share of its profits by way of any dividends paid which are dependent on the business's profitability, or increase in value.

As a result, if you seek other equity investors for your business (such as backing from a **VC** firm), you will be selling part of the ownership of your business to these investors, and as a result reducing (diluting) your own percentage holding in the business and, in the process, your control over it as well as your share of its present and future value.

Other than in respect of capital raised by you from your own resources to put into your own business as a sole trader or partner in a partnership, this type of funding is really only applicable to limited liability companies through the issue of shares. This chapter therefore covers:

◆ how shares work;
◆ the sources of external equity investment; and
◆ the process of raising these types of funds together with the issues that any business will face in doing so.

SHARES AND DIVIDENDS

Shares

For most small businesses in their earliest days of trading, shares simply reflect the ownership of the company and have nothing to do with raising finance as they tend not to be tied to any particular sum or investment.

The number and value of the shares that your company is allowed to have (known as its authorised capital) and how this is to be divided up into individual shares will be set out in the company's memorandum of association, which is a key part of the company's constitution. Most off-the-shelf companies will, for example, be incorporated with 100 £1 ordinary shares giving a total authorised capital of £100.

However, not all of the shares need to be issued at once. At the founding of the company the organisers will arrange for some of these shares to be issued to the initial shareholders (who are known as subscribers for the shares) and who therefore become shareholders or members of the company. Again typically in an off-the-shelf company this will be two £1 shares, giving the company an issued share capital of £2.

The company should in turn have received payment of £2 from the shareholders for their shares so that the shares are paid up. If cash has not been paid for shares that have been issued then, in the event that the company fails, those shareholders who have not paid up the value of their shares can be called on to do so.

Should you then wish to buy this off-the-shelf company, the subscribing members will complete stock transfer forms signing their shares, and therefore the ownership of the company, over to you. Since you will now own both of the only shares issued, you will own 100% of the company (as you own 100% of its issued share capital), despite the fact that 98% of its authorised share capital has yet to be issued.

So long as they are authorised to do so by either the company's constitution or by resolution passed by the shareholders, the directors of the company can then go on later to issue (allot) the remaining shares subject to the rules set out in the company's articles of association, which is the other key document of its constitution. The shares might be issued for the payment of their nominal face value of £1 each (at par) or the company might set a price which includes a premium so that, for example, a new investor might be required to pay the company say £500 for each share they received, which would mean that the company received £1 for the share and a £499 share premium into its reserves.

Requirements for PLCs

There are additional requirements in respect of Public Limited Companies (PLCs), which must have a minimum of £50,000 of issued share capital of which at least 25% (together with any share premium) must be fully paid up before the company is allowed to trade.

Alternatively the existing shareholders may sell part or all of their shareholding to a new investor, in which case the price of the shares is paid to the old shareholder and liabilities may arise for stamp duty or capital gains tax on which the seller should take the appropriate tax advice.

The company will need to report the details of new shares issued and transfers of shares to Companies House using the appropriate forms, most of which can now be downloaded from the Companies House website (www.companieshouse.gov.uk).

Dividends

Dividends are a payment made by the company to its shareholders out of its profits. The decision to pay a dividend is a matter for the board of directors and dividends can only be paid when the company has made sufficient profits to do so (and therefore has what are known as 'distributable reserves'). In some cases companies can be found to have paid unlawful dividends, where it is later apparent that they did not have sufficient reserves, in which case the company can request that these are repaid.

Since dividends are paid per share, the more shares that an investor has, the higher the dividend payment they will receive.

Other types of shares

So far we have only talked about ordinary shares. They might be regarded as a standard form of share, giving a full share in the business with regards to both ownership and value, but no particular rights over other shareholders.

However, the company's constitution can allow (or be amended to allow) for the creation of a variety of other types of share which will generally be given rights in advance of the ordinary shareholders. These types of share usually arise later in a business's life, where it is negotiating some form of formal investment in its equity from an outside party when that investor wants to try to safeguard their likely return on the investment.

These types of shares include:

♦ *Preferred ordinary shares*, which have voting rights like ordinary shares, but are agreed to have priority in the order and value of dividends paid, and the return of capital over the ordinary shareholders.

♦ *Preference shares*, which give the holder the right to a specified dividend to be met before any dividends are paid to ordinary shareholders. This means that should the company become short of cash the preferential shareholders have a better chance of being paid a dividend than the ordinary shareholders. Preference shares do not, however, normally carry a right to vote.

Preference shares can be the following.

- *Cumulative*, which also carry the right that even if a dividend is not paid in a particular year, this liability of the company to pay the shareholder carries over into following years so that it is not lost. This means that cumulative preference shareholders have an even stronger chance of being paid than preference shares as they are not reliant on the cash in any one particular year.
- *Convertible*, which have a right to be converted into ordinary voting shares.
- *Redeemable*, which carry an agreement that the company can buy them back at either a set date or the company's discretion, sometimes at an agreed level of premium, and which therefore provide a mechanism for returning the capital invested to shareholders.

Changes to share capital

Whatever arrangements are written into the company's constitution at the outset, the company's directors have the ability to amend these arrangements by putting suggested changes to a vote at a meeting of the shareholders.

These changes can involve:

◆ increasing the level of authorised share capital;

- decreasing the levels of authorised share capital by cancelling unissued shares;

- consolidating shares into larger nominal values where, for example, a million 1p shares might be consolidated into 10,000 £1 shares; or more commonly;

- subdividing shares into smaller amounts where, for example, an authorised share capital of 100 £1 shares might be subdivided into 1,000 10p shares.

As should be clear by now, the ownership of shares determines the ownership of the company which therefore determines two important aspects: control of it and entitlement to its profits and value. There may be circumstances, however, where you want to treat these in different ways and this can be done by creating different classes of shares.

For example, if a company wished to incentivise its staff by setting up an employee share scheme so that staff could share in rewards, whilst the original owners wanted to keep clear control of the direction of the business, they could achieve this by setting up two classes of shares:

- Class A shares, which would be voting shares the old owners would retain and which determined the control of the business.

- Class B shares, which would be non-voting shares which could be sold to the employees and which would entitle them to receive dividends.

Again, all such changes to the nature of the share capital will need to be reported to Companies House using the appropriate forms.

FINANCIAL PROMOTIONS

Before considering raising any sort of equity from any third party you do need to be aware of the onerous levels of regulation that surround this, as failing to comply can lead you into considerable problems.

The starting point is to look at raising equity funding you are going to need to approach investors. But as soon as you send out a business plan, or contact people to discuss the possibility of investing in your business, this is defined as a '**financial promotion**' under the Financial Services and Markets Act (FSMA). The rules under the FSMA are essentially designed to protect investors from being enticed into investing their cash in fraudulent or excessively risky schemes. So unless your approach falls under one of a number of exemptions set out in the Financial Promotions Order (FPO), it will need to be issued by an authorised person, which is generally someone regulated by the Financial Services Authority (FSA). If you fail to do so, not only might you be committing a criminal offence in issuing a financial promotion, but the other party may be able to walk away from any agreement entered into.

The FPO therefore specifies a number of exemptions to the overall prohibition in the FSMA on sending out proposals, the most important of which are as follows.

♦ Investment professionals (Section 19), such as employees of venture capital firms whose business is in considering and making investments and who are therefore considered sufficiently sophisticated to understand the risks involved in an investment put to them.

◆ High net worth investors (Section 48), who have obtained a certificate from either their employers or accountant certifying that they have income of over £100,000 a year, or net assets of over £250,000, were able to receive some classes of communication. However, in a Catch 22 clause they have to have provided you with a copy of this certificate before you can communicate with them. Under new rules introduced in 2005, individuals can now certify themselves and some types of proposal can be sent to people you reasonably believe are certified (although in practice this probably still means that you need to have a copy of their certificate).

◆ High net worth companies (Section 49), and those of their employees who are directly involved in investment, where high net worth means assets or issued share capital of over £5m (or £500,000 for a company with more than 20 shareholders).

◆ Sophisticated investors (Section 50), if they could find an authorised firm willing to take the risk of issuing them with a certificate stating they were sophisticated enough to understand the risks involved, can also be sent some types of proposal (although these have to carry heavy caveats). Given the obvious potential legal risk to a firm issuing such a certificate, it was rare for people to be able to obtain this type of certificate and again Catch 22 applied in that they needed to have provided you with their certificate before you could approach them in the first place. Under the new rules individuals can now self-certify themselves on a variety of grounds, which range from being a member of a business angel group to having been a director of a £1m turnover company within the past two years.

◆ Associations of high net worth or sophisticated investors (Section 51) such as business angel networks (so long as the investor will have no liability over and above the level of the investment) can receive proposals.

- Sale of a body corporate (Section 62), where essentially either the whole of the company or a controlling interest of over 50% of the shares is offered for sale.

Even if the potential investor that you wish to approach falls within one of these categories you will still need to be careful as the FPO specifies differing:

- notices that have to be given to each group, such as clear health warnings on any communication relying on the sophisticated investor exemption; and

- types of communication that you can send each group as the FPO distinguishes between communications that are:
  - real time or non-real time;
  - those which are parts of a marketing campaign or one-off approaches to a single investor or limited group that might be expected to act together; and
  - solicited or unsolicited.

The FSMA also prohibits the making of any misleading statements in any papers provided to potential investors that are involved in persuading or inducing investors to invest, which will obviously include your business plan. But your business plan, for example, will inevitably include a number of assumptions, some of which, in the absence of a 100% reliable crystal ball, may turn out to be completely wrong. So how can you tell what a court might subsequently hold to be a misleading, deceptive, or false statement made sufficiently recklessly for you to deserve sentencing for up to seven years? You may wish to remember at this stage that you are not a bank robber, but simply someone trying to raise finance for your business.

As a result of this regulatory minefield, you should therefore generally seek professional advice before speaking to any party about raising equity finance for your business.

WHAT ISSUES DO YOU NEED TO CONSIDER?

In all cases where you are bringing in outside investors you will need to consider the following.

- How much control you are handing over, what percentage of your business you will be selling and how actively involved the investor will then want to be in the business.

- The need for a business adviser to help you in the process of deciding what are the right sources of investment for your business, finding suitable investors, preparing the necessary documentation and then negotiating an investment through to completion on acceptable terms.

- How long it will take to raise the money, as all investors will have to go through some form of process to decide whether to invest, before which you will have had to go through some form of process in drawing up a business plan or proposal to interest them in investing.

- How certain you are of getting the cash, as you are ultimately reliant upon an investor deciding to risk their money.

- The costs involved in attempting to raise cash which can be substantial, as a proportion of the cash raised (and to what degree your advisers will require an upfront payment or will work on success only fees).

Some of the particular characteristics of the different potential sources of investment in relation to these points are discussed in the next chapter.

HOW MUCH IS YOUR BUSINESS WORTH?

If you are looking for an investor to buy part of your company to provide it with cash, an obvious issue that you are going to have to think about at an early stage is: how much is your company worth? After all, this will determine the size of stake you are going to have to sell your investor in return for their cash, since if I am investing £1m to buy 50% of the business this implies that the business as a whole is worth £2m. It is therefore important to know how the size of the investment sought relates to the business's value overall, so that you know whether the £1m you are seeking really represents 25%, 50% or 100% (or more) of the company's value.

There are six broad bases of business valuation, many of which are interlinked. These are:

Asset valuation	Total of the value of all the individual assets, tangible and intangible, in the business.
Market valuation	A comparison against the prices achieved for other businesses that have sold recently.
Discounted cashflow	Takes estimates of cash to be generated by the business in future years and uses accounting techniques to discount these back to a present value (or an implied internal rate of return that putting cash into the business will generate for the investor).
Return on investment	Essentially creates a variety of ratios of the return (the earnings that the investor will achieve) divided by the cost of the investment made.
Sector specific	Particular sectors will have their own rules of thumb about how to value a business based on the characteristics of the business (eg the number of beds in the hotel, pub barrelage, value of mineral reserves, multiples of fee income).
Basic multiple	As a rule of thumb businesses with certain characteristics will be valued at a certain multiple of earnings.

The first thing to appreciate is that the valuation techniques most commonly used are based on estimates of future net cashflows or earnings, as the investor is really buying a share of the future cashflows and profits of the company.

It may come as a surprise in looking at these items that both the investor and your professional advisers will almost always make significant adjustments to both past and projected earnings information to establish an estimated sustainable level of earnings. This will involve the stripping out of any excess charges you are putting through the company for tax reasons and the insertion of market rates for costs such as rent and directors' earnings. This is a normal part of the process and nothing to be particularly concerned about in principle, although it can lead to some major changes in the level of sustainable earnings shown for your business, which can in turn lead to a major change in the estimated value of the business.

The most commonly used basis of valuation in dealing with small owner managed businesses is the multiple of earnings approach.

This is calculated simply on the basis of:

- earnings/profits (before interest and tax, known as **EBIT** or **PBIT**)
- times the appropriate multiple.

The level of multiple to be applied is then obviously a matter of judgement, given the strength of the business and the current economic circumstances. If, for example, you had an established manufacturing business with a good market position and established management team you might expect this to achieve a multiple of say five to seven times current earnings.

Obviously, the worse the competitive position or reliance on strong management, the lower the multiple that should be expected. The clearer the competitive advantage and steadiness of the earnings stream, the higher the multiple that can be sought.

Most corporate investors, including venture capitalists, will also use discounted cashflow or **net present value** techniques to value a business. These are based on the assumption that £1 today is worth more than £1 in a year's time because:

◆ an expectation of receiving £1 in a year's time is by definition more uncertain than an actual receipt of £1 now and therefore there needs to be some reward for taking this risk; and

◆ £1 in a year's time is actually worth less than £1 now as over the year, a £1 receipt now could be invested to earn interest.

Discounted cashflows are therefore used as a way of estimating what an investor is prepared to pay now, for the future stream of cash that is going to be generated by having bought a particular asset, business or project.

The advantage for you in a business that is expected to grow swiftly is that these are explicitly based on the future expected cashflows of the business, whereas multiple figures tend to start from a multiple of existing trading figures and so tend to take much less direct account of growth potential.

The key issue for this type of exercise is therefore not only the nominal value of the cashflow forecast, but the discount rate used. This comes from either of the following.

- A financial theory, called the capital asset pricing model based on:
  - the risk free rate of interest that an investor requires for investing their money in shares rather than in a safe investment such as government stocks;
  - times a risk factor for investing in a particular sector, known as beta, which is generated by looking at returns generated by quoted companies.
- Or a weighted average of the investor's cost of the capital (WACC) where at its simplest, if it costs the investor 10% a year to raise cash and they can expect a return from your investment of say 20% a year, they are going to expect to make money by investing in your business.

If you would like more details on the basis of business valuations, two chapters are devoted to this issue in each of my books *Buying a Business and Making It Work* and *Selling Your Business for All It's Worth*, also published by How To Books.

KEY POINTS

- Equity is risk capital that you need to use when you don't have security on which to borrow.

- Ordinary shares give their owners the right to participate in the ownership of the business and to receive dividends in proportion to the number of shares they hold.

- A company can issue other classes of shares designed to give specific shareholders particular rights and advantages.

◆ Seeking investment is now a heavily regulated area which can carry criminal penalties for breaches and you are likely to need professional advice.

◆ It is also a process that can be time consuming, costly and uncertain, whilst if successful will lead to major changes in how you run your business.

◆ You need to be realistic about the value of your business as this will determine the share of the company that someone is going to need in return for the investment you are looking for.

12

Sources of Equity Finance

Potential sources of equity for your business fall into two broad camps.

- Informal sources, by which I mean people or businesses who may be interested in investing in your business for a variety of reasons, but who are not set up to act as professional investors, or are actively looking for investment opportunities. These can include:
  - you;
  - the three Fs – family, friends and fools;
  - employees;
  - trade partners.

- Formal sources: people or institutions who are professional investors actively looking for opportunities to invest and for whom making such investments is one of their principal business activities, such as:
  - business angels;
  - venture capitalists;
  - the public through institutional investors such as pension schemes.

Since the characteristics of the informal sources differ significantly from those of each of the formal sources, these are looked at separately below.

INFORMAL SOURCES

You
The first informal source of finance for your business is of course you, yourself.

You can invest your own cash, or cash that you have raised by borrowing against your other assets (for example by raising a mortgage against your house) into the business.

The advantage of this approach is that if you are providing all of the equity funding, you will retain full control and ownership of your business.

The disadvantages, however, can be that you may find:

◆ you may not have sufficient resources to fund the business properly to the level required; and that

◆ your personal assets (and personal financial health) are now mortgaged to the success of the business.

Nevertheless, for many new businesses, raising your own money to go into the business may be the only approach available and this will either involve:

◆ using your savings;
◆ selling off assets to raise cash;
◆ raising personal loans or borrowing on credit cards; or
◆ if you're a homeowner, borrowing against the equity in your property.

Personal loans
As many readers will be aware either from the frequent adverts in the press or indeed from the junk mail that pours through your letterbox, most people who own a home and who have a reasonable credit history will be able to obtain an unsecured loan

of up to £25,000 (which is a limit imposed under consumer credit legislation) over say ten to 15 years. As unsecured loans these tend to be expensive when compared with loans secured against your property such as a mortgage or second charge. However, they do tend to be quick to organise and can provide a valuable resource for business start-ups.

Credit cards

Similarly, most people who have a reasonable credit rating will also receive a large number of offers of credit cards. As is well known, interest rates on credit cards are extremely high in comparison with most other forms of borrowing. However, some small businesses are taking advantage of the competition in this marketplace whereby many of the offers of new cards have an introductory period of up to six months at 0% interest, including on balance transfers.

For those who are sufficiently organised and brave, these can be used to provide a source of finance at 0% where a personal credit card is used to meet business expenditure. The minimum payments are then made on a regular basis and the balance is transferred to a new card with another 0% balance transfer rate at the end of each introductory period.

The risk is obviously that at some point you will need to either repay this borrowing to clear the card, or you may end up with funds borrowed at a very high rate, so it's not a strategy that I would recommend.

Borrowing against personal property

Most individuals' major store of personal capital is the equity in their house. Therefore when looking to raise business capital, borrowing against this is usually the only realistic option.

It is also true that cash raised against the security of residential property can be amongst the cheapest sources of financing available as it is raised at domestic mortgage rates. If you simply want to arrange a top-up loan by borrowing against your house without disturbing your existing mortgage using what is called a second charge (because the lender will take a second charge on the property behind your mortgage lender) there are a number of websites which will allow you to apply for such money direct (try www.creativehomeloan.co.uk).

If you need to seek a full remortgage, this is now an area that is highly regulated and you will need to take professional advice from an independent financial adviser. Contact Creative Business Finance (see Useful Contacts p 429) for referral to one of the appropriately qualified advisers with which they work.

In any event, you must always remember that, as it says in the small print, your home is at risk if you do not keep up the payments on a mortgage or other loan secured on it.

There are obviously an enormous number of mortgage products on the market which change all the time. It is worth noting, however, three types of product in particular which may be of assistance in buying a business.

Fleximortgage – flexibility
This is a residential mortgage that provides a revolving loan

against your property that can be drawn down and repaid up to a specified number of times a year without penalty.

It can therefore provide a ready source of flexible funding at domestic mortgage rates, which gives you the ability to draw down your domestic equity over short periods at short notice without the high costs of bridging.

Loans of up to 85% of open market value (OMV) are generally available up to an upper capital limit of £250k (but higher loans may sometimes be available by discretion). A satisfactory prior lender reference is required, but a small amount of adverse credit history is generally acceptable. Loans are normally for up to a 25 year term and rates are similar to high street rates.

15 day mortgage – speed

Some lenders have stripped down the search and credit referencing procedure to provide a residential mortgage which can deliver a draw down of funds within ten to 15 days from application.

Again the advances available are normally up to 85% of the property's value on a self-certified basis with no requirement for an accountant's confirmation or lender reference in most cases. These loans are available to individuals with a significant adverse credit history and are for terms of up to 25 years. Rates tend to be slightly higher than normal high street levels and there will be redemption penalties.

Domestic bridging

If you only require the cash on a very short-term basis, as for example you believe that you will be able to take sufficient cash out of the business to repay this equity within three to six months, you might consider taking out a bridging loan rather than completely remortgaging the whole of your property.

Loans of up to £500k at up to 70% of OMV with rates from 1.1% per month are normally available from a range of lenders and can be swiftly put in place.

These are, however, very short-term funds and if you have any doubt about your ability to repay the bridging at the end of an arrangement you should not go into it.

Planning for personal investment

While you will obviously not need to prepare a pitch in order to sell yourself the idea of investing in the business in the way that you will have to if you're seeking money from other people, it is still always a good idea to prepare a formal business plan to help you think through how much money the business is going to need and where you're going to raise this from. The old insolvency saying about putting enough fuel in the plane to only fly halfway across the Atlantic has already been mentioned. If by preparing a business plan, including a cashflow, it becomes obvious that you cannot arrange sufficient funds from your own and the business's resources to make it through to a sustainable trading position, you need to either find another investor at the outset or rethink or abandon your existing plans.

One tip, however, is that while lenders will always be looking for you to put in as much as possible both to demonstrate your commitment to the business and to reduce the amount of money you need to borrow from them (and therefore their risk) you should always try to keep something in reserve. This is because if your business ever gets into difficulty, *in extremis* you may decide to pay in funds to see you through, where a third party funder such as a bank, which doesn't have such an emotional stake in the outcome or a financial incentive in terms of the value of the business, may not.

Of course, as covered in the section on turnarounds in Chapter 16, if your business ever does get into difficulty you need to think very carefully about pouring more money into it and the risk of simply sending good money after bad.

In practice, many small business owners start off by funding much of the business's initial expenditure from their own resources, bearing expenses like rent or stationery or advertising from their own funds, because until the business has achieved a successful level of trading, it simply doesn't have the funds to do so. Once the business is up and running the owner then has the choice as to whether these expenses should be repaid, or the cash left in the business by way of a director's loan, or treated as an equity investment. This is something that you might want to talk to your accountant about as it may have an impact on your tax position.

Your family, friends or others known to you

The second group of people that you might turn to are people with whom you have a personal connection, sometimes dismissively referred to by finance professionals as the three Fs of family, friends and fools. However, it is wrong to be dismissive as this type of funding has been vital for the start-up of thousands of businesses over the years, right up to well-known examples such as the garage owner who invested a few thousand pounds in a small new venture called Body Shop being started by Anita Roddick and ended up with a multi-million pound investment.

Through your personal network you may have direct access to people who may be able to provide cash. What's more you can do so without incurring the significant costs of trying to access this type of cash through more formal means. You will also have some idea as to whether they are actually likely to invest or not whereas, as discussed below, some formal sources may be much more uncertain.

However, you should think very carefully about the implications of using such money and how these relationships will be affected by the arrangement, because of the serious questions it raises such as the following.

♦ Do they understand the difference between a loan with a regular payment of interest, and a structured repayment back to them of their capital, and a shareholding with dividends only when the company both makes a profit and decides to distribute some to its shareholders?

♦ How long can they afford to wait to have their money back?

♦ Do they understand that they may have to wait and won't simply be able to ask for it to be repaid if they need it for something else?

♦ What are they going to get out of it? A full commercial level of return or a more limited one as they are providing funds for other personal reasons?

- To what extent do they understand the risks? Are they providing the money on your say so? Are they taking professional advice and undertaking some due diligence or are they simply taking your word for it?

- What happens if there is a business problem? How much can they afford to lose? What will this do to your relationship?

To get over these sorts of issues, in the same way as you should draw up a loan agreement if you are borrowing money from relatives or friends, you should draw up a clear shareholder agreement if they are investing in your business. This should spell out their interest in the business and the overall arrangement to avoid as far as possible any later disputes.

Employees

As people intimately connected with the business, your employees can be a source of funds, but more often employees' share schemes are set up as a way of incentivising and retaining key staff.

If you are considering approaching employees about investing in the business you should take tax advice. There are significant tax breaks for employee share schemes, including arrangements that allow employees to reinvest dividends received into shares which are held for three years attracting no income tax.

Trade partners

You should also think about whether there are any potential trade partners who might be interested in a stake in your business or in helping to fund a project in some kind of joint venture (JV).

The advantage here is that you'll be dealing with somebody who already knows your business and, to a degree, your market. They should therefore be in a good position to make a judgement about the attractiveness of investing.

You need to be careful about how such an arrangement may affect your business, however. If you have a joint venture with a supplier, are you then tied to them for supplies or are you free to shop around? If you have a joint venture with a customer, does this give you problems with other customers who might be their competitors?

BUSINESS ANGELS

Business angels are usually successful business people who have:

- made sufficient money to have retired or sold their own business;
- are now interested in investing in small businesses both as a way of:
  - making money; and
  - continuing to be involved in business.

They are therefore usually interested in investing in small businesses with potential for high growth, where by taking equity they can look to become involved, while potentially obtaining a high return on their investment.

Business angels therefore bring not only cash but usually significant business experience and often a good network of business contacts. The downside for the entrepreneur can be that they will often seek to be actively involved in the direction of the business which can lead to conflict, so it is important to see how hands-on they want to be and how you feel about this.

For most businesses looking to raise less than say £250,000 (such as for a start-up or seed development money), business angels usually offer the only realistic option (other than some smaller specialist regional venture capitalists). Some business angels are prepared to invest quite small amounts, say from £10,000 upwards, whilst at the top end of business angel investment, over £500,000 may be possible although this would usually be through a syndicate of such investors rather than a single individual. The typical business angel investment is generally reckoned to be somewhere between £75,000 and £100,000.

One advantage of dealing with a business angel is that since it is their money it is also their choice. There is therefore no anonymous credit committee involved; when you speak to the business angel you are speaking to the decision maker, so if you can convince them you can get the money.

Obviously as individuals business angels will each have their own criteria and approach to assessing any proposal, so for example the degree to which they will rely on professional due diligence will vary significantly. Nevertheless this will be a serious decision and therefore you need to prepare a professional business plan as discussed below to give yourself the best chance of success.

The things that a business angel will be looking for will be the same as for all professional investors and include the:

- quality of the people involved in the business and their commitment to it;

- strength of the business's competitive advantage or unique selling point;

- potential for growth in the market;

- realism and strength of the plan to take the business forwards;

- realism about the current value of the business and the stake in it that the proposed investment will require;

- preparedness to actually go through with selling some of the company shares (so that they are not wasting their time);

- degree to which the business's and investor's interest in the opportunity and view of the way forward are compatible such that they will be able to work together.

As most are interested in proactively helping the companies they invest in by using their own skills, experience and contacts, this means that they tend to invest:

- locally, so as to be able to be in regular contact with the business; and

- in businesses in sectors where they have some existing experience and contacts.

Some business angels invest on their own, while some work as part of clubs. There are a number of networks around the country which have been set up to enable prospective businesses to be put in touch with such investors, for example by circulating a regular digest of opportunities to a database of investors, or by running investment fairs where candidate companies seeking funding can take stalls and offer presentations on their proposals (see the British Business Angels Association as a starting point, www.bbaa.org). But since you are most likely to find an investor locally, you will also find that a good local business adviser such as an accountant specialising in corporate finance will have working relationships with local active business angels.

Whilst in some ways making the process of attracting business angel investment more difficult by way of the regulations discussed above, the government has also taken steps to try the following.

◆ Encourage business angels to invest under the Enterprise Investment Scheme, which provides tax incentives for business angels investing in companies that meet the criteria.

◆ Attempt to make more funds available by schemes such as:
   – the Early Growth Funding scheme which can invest up to £100,000 in small businesses to match commercial funding and which can usually be accessed via the DTI's Small Business Service or some business angel networks; and
   – a proposed scheme to be known as Enterprise Capital Funds, which is intended to provide extra cash for SMEs of potentially up to £2m by following or matching business angel investment, although at the time of writing it is not yet clear how these will actually work. In addition, there are suggestions that the government will require to have first claim on cash coming back out of the business which may make this unattractive for some investors.

The disadvantages of business angel funding include the following.

◆ It's true to say that most business angels will only make a limited number of investments and for much of the time may not be actively looking for opportunities. It can therefore be extremely difficult to find the right investor and the process is often very time consuming.

◆ It can also be expensive, as some of the networks are privately owned and charge high levels of fees to companies seeking to access their network of investors, which will be in addition to the cost of your own professional advisers.

◆ As they are investing their own hard earned money, however, business angels tend to be very choosy about which businesses they invest in and potential business angel investments have a reputation amongst some business advisers of falling away at the last moment.

◆ Finally, as people who have already made their money, some can be seen to be quite arrogant and overbearing by the owners of the businesses that are still on their way up, so it is absolutely vital to ensure that any such investor is someone that you will be happy to work with over the lifetime of their investment in your business.

VENTURE CAPITALISTS

For sums larger than are available through business angel finance you will need to turn to one of the over 150 venture capital firms operating in the UK today.

Venture capitalists (VCs) are businesses that exist to raise funds from institutional investors such as pension funds (or for bank related VCs, their parent bank) which they are then looking to invest to provide them a higher return than they can achieve from other sources.

A venture capital firm (VC house) therefore regularly goes through a cycle of:

◆ raising a fund and investing the cash raised;

◆ managing a portfolio of investments for the life of the fund which might typically be seven to ten years;

◆ before then selling off its investments in order to realise a capital gain, and pay back their investors' capital together with a sufficient return to attract investors for their next round of fundraising.

This structure obviously puts pressure on the VC house to get a good return so as to make its next round of fund raising easier, which will be passed on to you. But it also puts pressure on the VC house to exit from its investments by the target date and investments that are still held by a closed fund can find themselves under pressure to achieve a sale.

A Venture Capital Trust (VCT) raises funds slightly differently in that it is a publicly quoted company that raises funds from private investors who get a tax incentive for putting money in for three years. The operation and investment of a VCT is usually managed by a VC house on a contract basis so VCs of all types will therefore be looking to:

◆ invest in unquoted companies with high growth potential and ambitious, experienced management;

◆ be more willing to commit a material amount of their own money into the venture;

- be prepared to sell a realistic stake in the business for the funding required and the risk the VC is taking;

- expect to be able to sell their investment on within say three to seven years which will mean the:
  - sale of the shares back to the company;
  - sale of the company; or
  - a **flotation**; and
  - return on their investment by way of a capital gain on their exit of say over 20% to 30% a year.

This means that before considering venture capital (or business angel) investment your business needs to be an entrepreneurial one that is looking for a high rate of growth, rather than a lifestyle business which gives you a decent standard of living, but which is unlikely to provide the financial returns to make it worth an outside investor risking their money in the business.

Dealing with a VC as a potential investor, however, has some advantages over dealing with a business angel, in that a VC house will have a process of investment appraisal which is likely to be extremely tough, but you can at least assume that if you clear the high hurdles set, they are likely to invest and will not suddenly get cold feet and put their cheque book away as business angels can do.

Another advantage for many business owners of VCs over business angels is that a VC will not generally become involved in the day-to-day operations of your business as the management of the business will remain your responsibility, whereas business angels will often actively seek a role. The VC firms' approaches differ, but they will normally want a seat on the board and may also wish to appoint a chairman of the board to both provide guidance to the business and act as the VC's eyes and ears. There are some exceptions to this general rule, most notably a VC house specialising in turnaround such as Alchemy Partners, which because of the nature of the situations they are investing in become very actively involved in the hands-on management of the business.

Of course, not all investments will work out as planned and so VCs will generally work on a portfolio basis. That is to say that out of any ten investments they might expect say two to fail, seven to survive and succeed at a moderate to good level but not deliver the super returns of a star, and one to really shine and deliver a phenomenal return.

The equity gap

Other than some smaller regional funds that specialise in smaller amounts (as discussed below), most venture capitalists are also looking for large investments to justify their time and costs in undertaking a transaction. The minimum level of deal that a VC will be interested in will obviously differ from house to house, but for most mainstream VCs this is likely to be in excess of say £2m. Since business angel finance can generally only deliver funds of a few hundreds of thousands of pounds, this presents a difficulty for businesses seeking from say £500,000 to £2m in investment, known as the equity gap.

In order to try to bridge this equity gap the government with European support has introduced the Regional Venture Capital Funds (RVCs) listed below, which are managed by professional fund managers, can advance up to £250,000 and will often work in concert with business angels.

Region	Fund	Fund size	Website
North East	Capital North East	£15m	www.insight-capital.co.uk
North West	North West Equity Fund	£35m	www.nwef.co.uk
Yorkshire	Yorkshire & Humber Equity Fund	£25m	www.yfnventurefinance.co.uk
East Midlands	East Midlands RVCF	£30m	www.catapult-vm.co.uk
West Midlands	Advantage Growth Fund	£20m	www.midven.com
East of England	CREATE East of England Fund	£20m	www.createpartners.com
Southeast	South East Growth Fund	£30m	www.segrowthfund.co.uk
London	The Capital Fund	£50m	www.thecapitalfund.co.uk
South West	Southwest Ventures Fund	£25m	www.southwestventuresfund.co.uk

There is some justified criticism that given the level of funding available from the RVCs they are not actually addressing the real equity gap which lies in the region of £500,000 to £2m. From this point of view the introduction of the Enterprise Capital Funds discussed above, which are expected to be able to invest up to £2m, may present more of a solution to this problem if they can be made to work in practice.

There are also a number of other schemes which include the following.

- Regional funds managed by local development agencies such as invest in Northern Ireland, Scottish Enterprise and Welsh Finance which can offer ranges of funding up to £1.5m.

- Bridges Community Ventures, which is a government scheme designed to regenerate deprived areas of England that can invest up to £2m.

In addition, listing your shares on **Ofex** or **AIM**, the junior UK stock markets discussed below, may also provide a solution for some companies.

Types of investments

Venture capital firms distinguish between a number of different types of investment based on the use the money is going to be put to and the stage of the company's life cycle. These can be summarised as below.

Seed capital

Seed is the first stage of developing a business idea and perhaps manufacturing a prototype to demonstrate its potential, through sometimes to small scale manufacturing or piloting. Given the small scale of seed capital requirements, and the huge risks involved in an untried business and relatively small management team which can then require a lot of handholding and support, few venture capital firms are interested in this type of funding which traditionally relies more on business angel finance.

Start-up and early stage funding

These are normally designed to support the development of existing products, and the launch and commercialisation (or taking to market) of a product at commercial levels of operation.

As a small business grows and demonstrates its potential it may require further rounds of funding in order to exploit the opportunities that it is creating and continue its expansion, as it requires investment in machinery to increase production levels or additional working capital to deal with the level of trade being generated. These types of development or growth capital investments are one of the main uses of venture capital in the UK. Where there is an existing business angel or venture capital investor in the business, this process is sometimes referred to as **second round funding**.

Buy outs

Here venture capital funding is used to buy an existing established business from the owners. Buy outs can take a number of forms including:

◆ Management buy out (MBO) where the existing managers in a business seek to buy it from the shareholders.

◆ Management buy in (MBI) where a manager or managers from outside the business seek to buy it.

◆ Buy in, management buy out (**BIMBO**) where existing managers team up with some external managers to acquire the business.

◆ Institutional buy out, where a venture capital firm buys a business directly and may then sell on a stake in it to existing or new managers.

◆ Public private, where funds are used to buy control of a listed company in order to take it off the stock market and back into private ownership.

◆ **Secondary buy out**, where a VC house purchases another VC's stake in a business.

◆ Rescues and turnarounds, where a business in difficulty is bought, normally at a very low value to reflect its circumstances, with a view to turning it around and resale at a profit.

Refinancing

Refinancing can involve the following.

- Replacement equity, where a VC house is brought in to replace an exiting investor or to provide the funding to redeem an investor shareholding.

- Replacement of debt, where a company may need to restructure its balance sheet and replace some level of debt with equity in order to reduce its gearing.

- Bridging finance, where a company requires a very short-term level of funding. For example, a highly seasonal VC funded business with a turnover of £90m had a short-term requirement for a six-week overdraft facility of £1.5m, without which it would undoubtedly have failed, but for which it could offer no security without the VC house providing a guarantee to the bank.

Different firms have different levels of appetite for each of the above types of investment, with some specialising in seed and early stage investments whilst others are only interested in buy outs or even rescue and turnaround situations.

These differing types of investment can also lead to a degree of confusion concerning the terms venture capital and private equity, as they have slightly different meanings in the UK (where the terms are essentially interchangeable) and in the US (where they are used to refer to the two different ends of the scale).

	UK	US
Early stage investments (seed and start-ups)	Venture capital	Venture capital
Business buy outs such as MBO/MBI	or	
transactions or the purchasing of public listed	private equity	Private equity
companies to take them into private hands		

For the purposes of this book I am using the UK convention.

Finding a VC

Obtaining VC investment is undoubtedly difficult, with some sources quoting a rate of 1% of business plans submitted to VCs actually attracting investment.

So what can you do to stand the best chance of being in the 1% that attract funding?

As different VCs will have different appetites, the first step in obtaining VC investments is to find the right one to put your proposal to. The key criteria for finding the right VC are outlined below.

◆ The stage or type of investment, as discussed above.

◆ The value of investment sought, where for reasons of scale and the relative costs of undertaking transaction, for thousands or millions of pounds, the bulk of VCs are seeking larger levels of investment, but where there are some specialists who will look at smaller transactions.

◆ Your industry or sector as some VCs may have:
  – particular sector skills;
  – raised a fund designed to be specifically invested into a particular sector (such as a biotechnology fund that will be targeted on investments in that sector); or
  – particular sectors that they either do not wish to invest in or may be barred from investing in (for example funds raised from some ethical investment sources are unlikely to be available to invest into say a defence or tobacco related business).

- ◆ Your location, as some VCs will have specific geographical preferences, which in one case, for example, meant that a London based VC declined to receive a business plan from a company based in Hull as 'we would never travel that far north'. VCs vary in that:
  - some VCs are regionally based and are looking to invest in their local region;
  - some only have an office in London but will operate UK wide;
  - some only have an office in London and don't deal elsewhere (as illustrated by the example above); while
  - the best known of the VCs, 3i plc, has a network of offices nationwide.

The British Venture Capital Association (BVCA) has a directory of members available at www.bvca.co.uk that you can search online using all the above criteria.

Corporate venturers and incubators

Depending on which industry you are in, you can also find that larger companies on the lookout for emerging products and talent have set up internal funds to act as a quasi VC in order to invest into smaller innovative businesses. Since these activities are always industry related, they are generally reasonably well known and a study of your trade press may be sufficient to identify companies operating in this way.

Some of the leading universities have recognised the potential of businesses being spun out from the research work they do and are therefore seeking to provide support to the businesses to get off the ground. During the dot com boom this approach was taken one step further when a number of private businesses were set up described as incubators, where potential entrepreneurs with a viable idea could be provided with funding to help set up in business together with other managerial and facilities support as appropriate. Since the demise of the dot com boom much less is heard about this type of approach.

Achieving investment

If you are looking to raise venture capital you will undoubtedly need a business adviser both to sell the proposal to the venture capitalist and to help you in structuring the deal. This leads to the second major step you can take, which is to appoint good professional advisers who will give you credibility with the VC houses that you approach.

With a 1% investment rate, VCs look to advisers to screen deals before presenting them to the VC. They will build relationships with advisers who build a reputation for only bringing the VC sensible, doable deals that have been well thought out and tested before presentation. As a result, any deal introduced to a VC by such an adviser is likely to attract more attention and to be taken more seriously than a business plan received directly.

Which brings us onto the next key point which is to have a good business plan.

There are entire books available on how to write a good business plan which I do not intend to try to reproduce here. The key points that I would make in respect of any business plan used to raise finance are the following.

- It has to be your business plan. Professional advisers can be vital in helping you to shape it and test it so it stands up when subjected to critical examination by an investor, but fundamentally it has to be your creation which you can convince the VC that you live and breathe.

- The numbers are important in terms of robust financial projections, but they are not the be all and end all. As important are the reasons that the numbers will happen, which are:
  - the details of the market;
  - the opportunities for major growth;
  - the reasons why your product or service is going to fly; and critically
  - the strength of your management team. VCs will often say they don't back businesses, they back people, so they need to be convinced about the skills, experience and commitment of you and your team to making the business funded with their money a success.

- It has to consider what the investor will be looking for in terms of an understanding of the purpose to which their cash is to be put, the likely risks and the expected return, which in the case of a VC will need to include a discussion of the likely exit routes and timetable.

- It has to be readable, short enough to be easily digestible and to interest an investor; but long enough to cover the subject in sufficient depth to show that you have considered all the key issues. If you need to include detail, put this in as appendices.

- It has to be professionally (but not ostentatiously) produced, with the contents clearly structured to show a logical progression of thoughts, data clearly presented using tables and graphs so as to assist the reader in understanding the proposal, and carefully spelt and grammar checked, as failure to do so can give an impression of lack of attention to detail. Given the sums involved, using a professional copy editor and proof reader to check the final product before it goes to press can be a worthwhile investment (try pabulum@hotmail.co.uk).

♦ It needs to be carefully drafted to ensure it doesn't trip up on any of the regulatory issues discussed above.

Investment structure

Where a venture capital firm invests in a business it can structure its holding in a number of ways. This can be a complex area and is one where you are likely to require guidance from your professional advisers, particularly where this involves issuing shares.

As equity investors the VC will obviously require a shareholding in return for their investment. In order to match the required return to the business's circumstances this may well mean the creation of special classes of shares in addition to the normal ordinary shares that will already be authorised. The VC will typically want to structure part or all of their holding in some form of preferred ordinary shares which will carry voting rights, but also rank ahead of the ordinary share capital for both dividends and payments out of capital; as well as holding preference shares designed to give a specific rate of return on the investment which, as discussed above can be cumulative, convertible and/or redeemable.

In addition, the structure of the investment and the specific levels of shareholding may actually be determined by the business's performance as the transaction could include the following:

- An 'earn out', where the total value of the payments and therefore the funding required from the VC house is in part determined by the business's performance after the buy out.

- Or a '**ratchet**' (also known as an '**escalator**'), whereby the shares allocated to the management team can be increased if the business achieves specified targets.

In order to maintain control of the business's structure the transaction will usually also specify pre-emption rights. These are essentially an agreement between the shareholders that in the event that a shareholder wishes to sell their shares, they are normally required to give first refusal to the other shareholders.

In addition to equity, a VC may put in part of the funds required by way of a loan which can be unsecured, although where there is security available, including PGs from the directors, the VC will usually take it. These loan elements tend to be expensive, particularly if they are unsecured, and they tend to be required to be paid down relatively quickly. This then often puts significant cash pressure on the business in the early years and is a factor that probably contributes to the failure of a number of buy outs.

As has already been discussed, there is usually a tax advantage in having debt finance rather than equity, as the interest charge is deductible from profits before calculating any corporation tax due. As a result, many VC investments have traditionally included a significant amount of debt in their structure. However, HM Revenue & Customs appears to be taking the view that this is an abuse of the process in that it is simply structuring what would otherwise be an equity investment in order to gain tax advantages.

At the time of writing there is therefore a change in the rules being proposed under which interest on loans that are provided by the major source of finance of a company may not be treated as an expense for tax purposes. You will therefore need to take professional tax advice about the current state of legislation in this respect if debt of this kind forms any part of a VC investment in your business.

Process

You should remember that raising money by way of finding equity essentially involves selling part of your business. The process therefore follows that of a business sale very closely, in that once the marketing of your business plan to potential investors has led to a VC firm being interested in buying a stake, the process then involves the following.

- An offer letter, which although not legally binding sets out the terms of the VC's offer of finance which will always be subject to both due diligence and final contract negotiations.

- Due diligence, which is essentially a form of legal, financial and commercial audit of the business, its plan and the proposed investment in order to give comfort to the VC firm about investing.

- Completion of a contract, which will involve you providing warranties to the investor about the state of the company and the information provided to them on which they have based their investment decisions.

More detail on how to manage each of these stages can be found in *Selling Your Business for All It's Worth*, also published by How To Books.

One difference from a normal sale of a business, but one that is only of relevance if the investment is very large, as in for example a major buy out or taking a listed company private, is that a VC investment may require **syndication** if it is too large or too risky for a single VC firm to do alone. Syndication involves a number of VC firms coming together to participate in the deal, each providing part of the funding package and holding a stake in proportion to their contribution, the syndicate being put together by a lead investor.

PUBLIC LISTING

By floating or listing your company on a stock market through an **initial public offering** (IPO) you are selling some of the company's shares to the public, either directly as individual shareholders, or indirectly where your shares are bought by pension schemes and other institutional investors.

There are many reasons why you might want to float your business which can include:

- finding capital to fund growth at a greater level than family and friends can afford to invest, or you can attract through a business angel or VC funding;

- enabling a founder or investor in the business such as a VC house to exit by selling their shares to the public;

- enabling you to use your shares as currency with which to buy other businesses;

- providing incentives for your staff by using shares or options; or

♦ improving your standing with customers and in the market, where being perceived as a listed business can give you an advantage over your competitors.

In the UK, the idea of listing is usually associated with the main market of the London Stock Exchange where the country's main publicly known businesses are traded and is thus very much associated with big business. However, listing can also be of relevance to small and medium-sized businesses as a real alternative to raising venture capital.

There are actually three stock markets in operation in the UK today, which in ascending order of size are listed below.

Ofex

Ofex is an independent exchange operated by PLUS Markets that has been running since 1995 and which is fully regulated by the FSA.

This is a service where shares can be sold mainly to private investors and it offers a route for small companies that need to raise in the order of £1m to £10m. At the time of writing Ofex has just under 150 companies listed. For some advisers Ofex can be seen as one of the answers to the equity gap, particularly as the cost of listing on Ofex, which has a low regulatory burden, are significantly lower than those of AIM as discussed below.

Ofex, however, has a number of disadvantages which mean that many advisers are still sceptical. It has a relatively limited number of investors and those investors have only a relatively limited ability to trade their shares, which means that institutional investors are rare. These factors have therefore limited both the cash available through this market and the price obtained on flotations.

As a result, businesses which grow on Ofex will often trade up to list on AIM in order to access a wider variety of investors. Some advisers then see this as a double whammy as the businesses will incur the cost of listing on AIM as well as Ofex, when they could in theory have listed on AIM in the first instance.

There are suggestions at the moment that Ofex will be introducing services which will allow for greater trading in shares and which may therefore help to address this problem in future.

Alternative Investment Market (AIM)

AIM is part of the London Stock Exchange (LSE) and has also been running since 1995 since when about 1,200 companies have been listed.

As with Ofex, the AIM market is designed for small companies, including start-ups where no trading record is required, and as a result almost 30% of the listed businesses have a market value of less than £5m.

With stricter requirements, including the production of a full **prospectus**, the professional costs of listing on AIM are higher than those for Ofex, being estimated by *Corporate Financier* magazine in the order of £300,000 to achieve a £5m listing on AIM (as against £100,000 to £150,000 on Ofex). To be listed you will also need to have a nominated adviser (**Nomad**) at all times, who essentially will be responsible to the exchange for your conduct of the flotation.

The advantages of AIM over Ofex are, however, that it is a higher profile exchange, being part of the LSE (although as a market designed for small businesses its regulation is much lighter than the main market), and there is a wider range of shareholders who have a greater ability to trade their investments. As a result there is a much greater participation by investment institutions and therefore more cash in the market.

It is also a market that attracts private investors because of the tax breaks available. Investments in companies with less than £15m gross assets that are not property investment or financial services companies can give investors under the Enterprise Investment Scheme 20% income tax relief and 40% capital gains tax rollover relief, while qualifying AIM shares that are held for over two years are free of inheritance tax.

In addition to floating a company on AIM in the normal way, many businesses have become listed on AIM by reversing into cash shells. These cash shells are companies which have raised cash and obtained a listing, but have no actual trading business. By allowing your business to be purchased by one of these shells you can have immediate access to not only the cash but their listing. Since a large number of these shells had become registered on AIM but were not conducting any transactions, the stock exchange has recently completed an exercise requiring all those shells which held less than £3m to have either completed an acquisition or started the process of delisting.

If you do list on AIM you will find that there are some restrictions. For example if your business has been trading for less than two years, you will have to keep your shares for at least a year after the flotation.

The London Stock Exchange main market (LSE)

Being listed on the LSE is known as having a full listing. This is usually only available to larger companies with a strong trading track record. If you are considering this step you will undoubtedly need to discuss all aspects of it with a firm of professional advisers.

Flotation issues

Whichever market you choose, flotation will be a complex and expensive process which will have huge implications for the way in which you manage your business before, during, and after the event, which is beyond the scope of this book. However, the LSE produces a very useful guide called *The Practical Guide to Listing*, which covers:

- all the issues surrounding the decision to float;
- its implications for how you manage your business in terms of corporate governance;
- the process of listing; and
- your ongoing obligations thereafter to your investors.

While it is clearly directed at companies looking to float on the main market is also quite applicable to companies listed on the other two exchanges, so if you are seriously considering whether a flotation is for you, you should download a copy from the LSE's website at www.londonstockexchange.com.

KEY POINTS

♦ You are likely to be your business's key early stage investor by way of cash freed up from personal assets such as your house.

♦ Informal sources of equity investment such as joint ventures with trade partners can be significant sources of funds for small businesses.

♦ Business angels as individuals are a traditional source of funding for sums up to say £100,000.

♦ Venture capitalists tend to be interested in larger opportunities (from say £2m to £5m upwards).

♦ Between these levels exists what is referred to as the equity gap, and the government is introducing some schemes to try to bridge this gap.

♦ Achieving an AIM or Ofex listing can be expensive, but can represent a real opportunity for smaller businesses to raise equity investment, including sums that otherwise fall into the equity gap.

C

SPECIFIC FINANCING SITUATIONS

The chapters in this section are designed to be read as stand alone briefings on each of the particular topics covered. They will therefore to a degree repeat some of the information already provided, if in less depth. You may therefore want to refer back to the earlier sections of the book for more details where this is appropriate.

13

Funding a Start-up

A start-up business faces some particular problems in raising finance when compared with an already established business, in that as the business does not yet exist or is in its very early stages it does not have the following.

- A track record of trading with which to demonstrate its viability and its ability to meet its forecasts, which obviously adds a degree of uncertainty to any investor's or lender's consideration of putting money into the business.

- Significant business assets to act as security for loans.

- Reserves retained in the business from prior years' profits that can provide a cushion when things get tight.

They also tend to have a requirement to invest cash in the early stages of setting up; arranging premises, hiring staff and taking products or services to market, before they can hope to start to see some cash coming back through achieving sales. There is an American phrase '**burn rate**', which describes the speed at which a business uses up its available cash.

These characteristics mean that while start-ups tend to use the same types of sources of finance as more established businesses, as covered in Section B, these tend to be in a different order of priority which runs thus.

◆ You as the business owner, in a mix of both cash and unpaid time (sometimes known as sweat equity).

◆ From within the business itself, by way of bootstrapping or running it in such a way as to maximise the cash generated and retained within the business in order for the business to support its own growth.

◆ Before relying on external funders for grants, equity or loans.

It should be stressed that each of these areas is covered in more detail in Section B and this chapter therefore simply gives an overview of the issues involved.

When you are preparing your business plan and its cashflow forecast, you should at first leave out any injection of finance as the important thing to start with is to establish how much is required. Only once you have a view on this, should you then start to think about how you're going to fund it.

One tip, however, is that while lenders will always be looking for you to put in as much of your own cash as possible, both to demonstrate your commitment to the business and to reduce the amount of money you need to borrow from them (and therefore their risk), you should always try to keep something in reserve. This is because if your business ever gets into difficulty, in extremis you may decide to pay in these reserve funds to see you through, where a third-party funder such as a bank, which doesn't have such an emotional stake in the outcome or a financial incentive in terms of the value of the business, may not want to advance additional funds.

YOU AS THE BUSINESS OWNER

Many businesses are funded in the first instance by the owner's own cash.

The advantage of this approach is that if you are providing all of the equity funding, you will retain full control and ownership of your business. The disadvantages can be that:

◆ you may not have sufficient resources to fund the business properly to the level required; and that

◆ your personal assets (and personal financial health) are now mortgaged to the success of the business.

Nevertheless for many new businesses, raising your own money to go into the business may be the only approach available and this will involve:

◆ using your savings;
◆ selling off assets to raise cash;
◆ raising personal loans or borrowing on credit cards; or
◆ if you're a homeowner, borrowing against the equity in your property.

While you will obviously not have to prepare a pitch in order to sell yourself the idea of investing in your business in the way that you will have to if you are seeking money from other people, it is still always a good idea to prepare a formal business plan. This should always include a cashflow forecast (see Chapter 4) to help you think through how much money the business is going to need and where you're going to raise this from. There is an old saying in the insolvency profession to the effect that there is no point putting enough fuel in the plane to fly halfway across the Atlantic. If by preparing a business plan including a cashflow, it becomes obvious that you cannot arrange sufficient funds from your own and the business's resources to make it through to a sustainable trading position, then you need either to find another investor at the outset, or rethink or abandon your existing plans.

In practice, many small business owners start off by funding much of the business's initial expenditure from their own resources, bearing expenses like rent, stationery or advertising from their own funds because until the business has achieved a successful level of trading, it simply doesn't have the funds to do so. Once the business is up and running the owner then has the choice as to whether these expenses should be repaid, or the cash left in the business by way of a director's loan, or treated as an equity investment. This is something that you might want to talk to your accountant about as it may have an impact on your tax position.

Personal loans

As you can see from the frequent adverts in the press or the junk mail that pours through your letterbox, most people who own a home and who have a reasonable credit history will be able to obtain an unsecured loan of up to £25,000 (which is a limit imposed under consumer credit legislation) over ten to 15 years. As unsecured loans these tend to be expensive when compared with loans secured against your property such as a mortgage or second charge. However, they do tend to be quick to organise and can provide a valuable resource for business start-ups.

Credit cards

Similarly, most people who have a reasonable credit rating will also receive a large number of offers of credit cards. As is well known, interest rates on credit cards are extremely high in comparison with most other forms of borrowing; however, some small businesses are taking advantage of the competition in this marketplace whereby many of the offers of new cards have an introductory period of up to six months at 0% interest, including on balance transfers.

For those who are sufficiently organised and brave, these can used to provide a source of finance at 0% whereby a personal credit card is used to meet business expenditure. The minimum payments are then made on a regular basis and the balance is transferred to a new card with another 0% balance transfer rate at the end of each introductory period.

The risk is obviously that at some point you will need to either repay this borrowing to clear the card, or you may end up with funds borrowed at a very high rate, so it is not a strategy that I would recommend.

Borrowing against personal property

Most individuals' major store of personal capital is the equity in their house and therefore when looking to raise business capital, borrowing against this is usually the only realistic option.

It's also true that cash raised against the security of residential property can be amongst the cheapest sources of financing available, as it is raised at domestic mortgage rates. If you simply want to arrange a top-up loan by borrowing against your house without disturbing your existing mortgage, using what is called a second charge (because the lender will take a second charge on the property behind your mortgage lender), there are a number of web sites which will allow you to apply for such money direct (try www.creativehomeloan.co.uk).

If you need to seek a full remortgage this is an area that is now highly regulated and you will need to take professional advice from an independent financial adviser. Contact Creative Business Finance (see Useful Contacts p 249) for referrals to one of the appropriately qualified advisers with which they work. Fleximortgages, which allow you to draw cash down against your property (and repay it again without penalty) can be a particularly useful source of flexible funding for business owners.

In any event, you must always remember that, as it says in the small print, your home is at risk if you do not keep up the payments on a mortgage or other loan secured on it.

BOOTSTRAPPING

Once your business has started, the way that you trade it has an enormous impact on the amount of cash it may or may not require. The practice of running a business in such a way that it generates the maximum amounts of cash internally, and both retains this and uses it as efficiently as possible, is known as bootstrapping, from the expression to pull yourself up by your own bootstraps. The techniques for doing so are covered in Section A, but essentially this is a matter of the following.

♦ Squeezing money out of the working capital (or to look at it another way, making whatever cash you do have go as far as

possible in funding trading) by actively managing to:
- minimise the investment in current assets (stock and debtors); and
- maximise the finance available from its normal sources of trade credit

where use of techniques such as consignment stocking can in effect help both sides of the equation.

♦ Retaining as much as possible of the profits from trading in the business, which is a matter of restricting the dividends paid out to shareholders (**dividend policy**) or cash drawn by the partners or owner.

EXTERNAL FUNDING

There is a wide range of external sources of finance that you can look at to start your business (each of which is covered in detail in Section B).

Grants

Grants are defined by the DTI as a 'sum of money given to an individual or business for a specific project or purpose', where as long as you keep to any conditions attached to the grant you will not have to repay it as you would with a loan, nor will you have to give up any shares in your business, as you would with an equity investor.

There are a large number of grant schemes across the country, particularly in depressed or deprived areas, designed to help support business start-ups. However, many of these only operate in a specific local area, or like the Prince's Trust are open to people of certain ages, so the first hurdle is finding out what grants are available for you and your business.

Your local Business Link should be able to advise on what is available in your region, while www.j4b.co.uk has a searchable database.

Equity

Equity is money put into your business by investors in return for a share of its ownership and profits.

Before going any further, however, a warning is required. To look at raising equity funding you are going to need to approach investors. But as soon as you send out a business plan or contact people to discuss the possibility of investing in your business, this is defined as a Financial Promotion under the Financial Services and Markets Act (FSMA). The rules under the FSMA are essentially designed to protect investors from being enticed into investing their cash into fraudulent or excessively risky schemes. So unless your approach falls under one of a number of exemptions set out in the Financial Promotions Order (FPO), it will need to be issued by an authorised person, which is generally someone regulated by the Financial Services Authority (FSA). If you fail to do so, not only might you be committing a criminal offence in issuing a financial promotion, but the other party may be able to walk away from any agreement entered into. You should therefore always take legal advice before attempting to raise equity from other people for your business.

Equity can come from a range of informal sources, sometimes sneeringly referred to by financial professionals as the three Fs of family, friends and fools. However, they should really know better, as this type of funding has been vital for the start-up of thousands of successful businesses over hundreds of years.

Through your personal network you may have direct access to people who will be interested in providing cash, without incurring the significant costs of other routes. However, your relationship with these people can then be a problem for the business, so you should always draw up a clear shareholder agreement spelling out their interest in the business and the overall arrangement, to avoid as far as possible any later disputes.

Business angels
Business angels are usually successful business people who have made money in business and are interested in investing in small businesses, typically sums of up to £100,000, both as a way of making money and of continuing to be involved in business.

They are therefore usually interested in investing in small businesses, normally in their local area and in an industry in which they have some knowledge, with potential for high growth businesses where by taking equity they can hope to obtain a high return on their investment. To access business angels' finance you will normally need to either find a local financial adviser with links to local angels, or approach one of the networks to which many belong (see the British Business Angels Association as a starting point www.bbaa.org).

Business angels therefore bring not only cash but usually significant business experience and often a good network of business contacts. The downside for the entrepreneur can be that they will often seek to be actively involved in the direction of the business, which can lead to conflict, so it is important to see how hands-on they want to be and how you feel about this.

Venture capitalists

Venture capitalists (VCs) are businesses that exist to raise funds from institutional investors such as pension funds (or for bank related VCs, their parent bank), which they are then looking to invest to provide them a higher return than they can achieve from other sources.

VCs of all types will therefore be looking to:

- invest in unquoted companies with high growth potential and ambitious, experienced management;

- management who are willing to commit a material amount of their own money into the venture;

- companies that are prepared to sell a realistic stake in the business for the funding required and the risk the VC is taking;

- where the VC can expect to be able to sell their investment on within say three to seven years, which will mean the:
  - sale of the shares back to the company
  - sale of the company; or
  - a flotation; and

- obtain a return on their investment by way of a capital gain on their exit of say over 20% to 30% a year.

This means that before considering venture capital (or indeed business angel) investment your business needs to be an entrepreneurial one that is looking for a high rate of growth, rather than a lifestyle business which gives you a decent standard of living, but which is unlikely to provide the financial returns to make it worth an outside investor risking their money in the business.

A VC will not generally become involved in the day-to-day operations of your business as the management of the business will remain your responsibility, whereas business angels will often actively seek a role.

Other than some smaller regional funds that specialise in smaller amounts of seed or start-up capital, most venture capitalists are also looking for large investments to justify their time and costs in undertaking a transaction. The minimum level of deal that a VC will be interested in will obviously differ from house to house, but for most mainstream VCs this is likely to be in excess of say £2m. Since business angel finance can generally only deliver funds of up to a few hundreds of thousands of pounds, this presents a difficulty for businesses seeking from say £500,000 to £2m in investment, known as the equity gap.

In order to try to bridge this equity gap the government, with European support, has introduced Regional Venture Capital Funds (RVCs) which are managed by professional fund managers, can advance up to £250,000 and will often work in concert with business angels. There are a number of other initiatives as discussed in Chapter 12.

Depending on which industry you are in, you can also find that larger companies on the lookout for emerging products and talent have set up internal funds to act as quasi VCs in order to invest in smaller innovative businesses. Since these activities are always industry related, the players involved are generally reasonably well known and a study of your trade press may be sufficient to identify companies that are operating in this way.

Spin-offs from research
Some of the leading universities have recognised the potential of
businesses being spun out from the research work they do and are
therefore seeking to provide support to these businesses to get off
the ground. During the dot com boom this approach was taken
one step further when a number of private businesses were set up,
described as incubators, where potential entrepreneurs with a
viable idea could be provided with funding to help set up in
business together with other managerial and facilities support as
appropriate. Since the demise of the dot com boom much less is
heard about this type of approach.

Listing
Finally, in the UK, the idea of listing is usually associated with
the main market of the London Stock Exchange where the
country's main publicly known businesses are traded and is thus
very much associated with big business. However, listing can also
be of relevance to small and medium-sized businesses as a real
alternative to raising venture capital.

In addition to the main market there are also two stock markets
in operation in the UK today, both regulated by the FSA, on
which new businesses can be listed to raise capital from investors.

◆ Ofex, which is an independent exchange where shares in about
  150 listed companies are sold mainly to private investors. It
  offers a route for small companies that need to raise in the
  order of £1m to £10m and so can provide a way around the
  equity gap, although the costs of doing so tend to be in the
  order of £150,000.

- Alternative Investment Market (AIM), which is part of the London Stock Exchange (LSE) and is also designed for small companies including start-ups where no trading record is required. As a result almost 30% of AIM's listed businesses have a market value of less than £5m, but with stricter requirements including the production of a full prospectus, the professional costs of listing on AIM are higher than those for Ofex.

Debt

Debt is money that has been lent to a business.

The most familiar type of debt is formal lending by a financial institution set up to advance funds to a business such as banks, building societies and a range of businesses known as Asset Based lenders (ABLs). These institutions offer a range of financing services such as overdrafts, mortgages, leasing, hire purchase, sale and leaseback, trade finance, factoring, and invoice discounting.

However, it can come from other sources such as:

- directors, or family loans into the business; or

- credit provided normally by a third party as part of the business's transactions which is the equivalent to a loan. Examples of these would include trade credit, sums due to the Crown by way of VAT or PAYE/NI and **vendor finance** where the seller of a business allows the buyer time to pay for some or all of the purchase price over a period of time.

When it comes to formal lending such as from a bank, start-ups have a particular problem as most bank lending is based on two legs.

♦ Confidence in the business's ability to meet its forecast
repayments, whereas a start-up has little or no track record on
which a lender can make a judgement as to its ability to
achieve its projections, and therefore its ability to manage
repayments, and banks tend to be reluctant to provide
overdraft facilities.

One way around this is for the business to borrow instead from
asset based lenders such as factors or invoice discounters where
the funding available is related directly to the business's assets.
With factoring, for example, as the business and therefore its
debtor book grows, so the funding available from the lender
will also grow.

♦ The assets available as security to enable repayment of any
borrowings in the event of default where start-ups tend to have
few assets to offer as security.

To address the problem of start-ups with a viable business plan
requiring a loan, but which do not have the security required,
the DTI operates a scheme with a number of participating
lenders called the Small Firms Loan Guarantee (SFLG)
whereby the government will provide the lender with a
guarantee against default by the borrower.

To qualify for this scheme your business must be less than five
years old and have a turnover of less than £5.6m. Under the
SFLG, the government provides the lender with a guarantee for
75% of the loan amount in respect of loans of up to £250,000
and terms of up to ten years, which can be used for most
purposes although there are some business sectors which are
not eligible.

The cost to the borrower of this guarantee is a payment to the DTI of a premium of 2% of the outstanding loan, in addition obviously to the lender's own charges and interest.

In summary then, the question whether your business's cash requirements can be met by borrowing, and if so from which source, or will it require an equity investment will generally come down to the question of the available security. Whilst it is a bit crude, the flowchart in Figure 17 provides a rough and ready guide to the likely answer to this question.

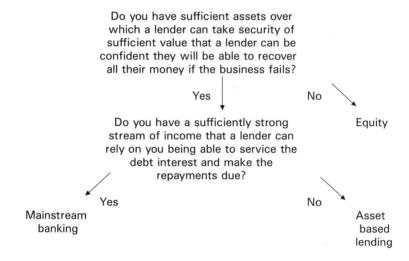

Fig. 17. Supplying your business's cash requirements.

Franchises

The purchase of a franchise can solve some of the above problems in that the track record of other franchises can give a lender some comfort as to the viability of your business's projections.

Additionally, since the franchising organisation has an interest in enabling prospective franchisees to buy and run franchises, many will have set up financing arrangements to enable them to do so.

14

Financing an Acquisition

Purchasing a business can mean that you have to raise a large amount of cash. When doing so it is important to remember that you are going to need to raise finance to cover significantly more than just the purchase price. To make a success of the deal, the funding you have available will additionally need to cover the following.

♦ Clearance of any debt to be satisfied as part of the deal.

♦ The working capital required post-sale to trade the business. It is no good buying the business only to find that you do not have the cash with which to run it. You will therefore need to work closely with your advisers to ensure that your financial projections are robust and that you raise sufficient funding to see the business through.

♦ Any restructuring costs that you will incur to make changes you want to put through such as redundancy costs.

♦ Any investments required in the business following the sale. These might range from some simple expenditure on relaunching the business under new management through to significant expenditure on updating the products, introducing new lines or replacing machinery. Don't forget that the old owner may have been considering the sale of the business for a number of years, and it is not unknown for such owners to run the business on a harvesting strategy, whereby rather than reinvesting in the business to keep it up to date in the years leading up to the sale, instead they draw out as much of the free cash as possible for their own use. The result can be that a business requires significant refurbishment in order to ensure its competitiveness.

It's also true to say that you will always need more cash than you thought you did, for example as below.

◆ Management bought out a specialist pipework manufacturer that was turning over approximately £13m. Within a year turnover had increased significantly with prospects of hitting £20m following the failure of one of its main competitors. As a result the business began to need substantially more cash than had been planned in order to support the increased levels of trading, and within a year the business came very close to collapse, only being saved by a sale and leaseback of the property which raised approximately £1m in cash.

◆ At the same time (and only 20 miles down the road) the managers of an electronics business had bought their plant out of a receivership. Unfortunately in this case, rather than turnover recovering from the receivership level of £30m to the expected £40m, things got worse, falling to closer to £20m. Given the business's cost structure this translated into severe losses which there was insufficient cash to cover and as result the business failed again within 18 months.

Since neither you nor your advisers will have a 100% reliable crystal ball, you will always want to ensure that you have a significant contingency reserve built into your cash to cover the inevitable ups and downs.

This point is especially true if you're buying a business that is in difficulty as it is likely to have stretched its creditors. Once you have bought the business you will not be able to rely on obtaining the same lengths of credit period as the business currently has. Creditors will have been giving these periods unwillingly and, on seeing that a new owner has purchased the business, will often make the assumption that there is now more cash available. You may therefore find that doing the deal precipitates a rush for payment by existing creditors, so planning your working capital must take into account provision for payments to bring overdue creditors up to date, or a plan for how these are otherwise to be dealt with.

Finally, do not forget to build into your valuation of the business, and the financing requirement shown by your cashflows, the level of interest and capital repayment in respect of the borrowing you undertake.

WHERE DO YOU GET THE MONEY?

Funding a business purchase is a large subject, but in essence there are four main sources of money to consider at the outset.

Equity

Equity will come from a mixture of:

- your own equity (which in many cases essentially means borrowing against equity in your house);
- friends and family;
- your business;
- a venture capitalist (VC) who is backing the purchasing team;
- a business angel;
- joint or co-venture partners;

♦ the seller, if you can persuade them to take paper (shares in your company) as payment in whole or in part, rather than cash.

Grants and soft loans

These are of particular relevance in development areas.

Debt

This is by way of borrowing against the assets being purchased.

Most forms of borrowing money to finance a business (including mortgages, leasing and hire purchase, factoring and invoice discounting, and most overdraft arrangements) require the business to provide some form of security by way of charges over business or personal assets. The level of borrowing obtainable is therefore determined by the level of security you or the business have to offer.

The only usual sources of significant unsecured lending to your business will come from credit given to you by suppliers, and any unsecured loans you or friends or family decide to put into the business.

The seller

This is by way of vendor finance (a form of debt) such as deferred consideration or an earn-out, or by paying the seller with shares in your company rather than cash.

In addition, once in control of the business you may look to run its finances in such a way as to maximise the cash retained in the business, a process known as bootstrapping. This usually involves:

- reducing or eliminating non-essential expenditure (what you don't spend you get to keep);

- agreeing terms with suppliers that allow you longer to pay;

- keeping the level of stock held (and hence cash tied up) to a minimum;

- ensuring that customers pay you as quickly as possible so that you do not have excess money tied up in debtors.

This then allows you to build up the business's financial reserves by retaining profit within the company and growing the shareholder's funds.

The degree to which you believe you'll be able to reduce the business's requirement for working capital by use of bootstrapping techniques obviously reduces the overall amount of cash that you need to seek to raise.

Over-reliance on bootstrapping can, however, be dangerous, as for example, an MBI team bought out a £20m turnover manufacturing business. Critical to their assumptions was an expectation that they would be able to reduce both their costs and working capital requirements significantly by better purchasing. In practice they found that the old owner had already beaten suppliers' prices down to rock bottom and there was little further saving therefore available to be made. The MBI ran out of cash and failed within a year.

Each of these sources is discussed below, but for more detail you should refer to the relevant chapters in Section B.

WHAT FORM OF EXTERNAL FINANCE IS RIGHT?

The way you finance the purchase will affect the following.

- To what degree you own and control:
  - if you are able to fund the purchase from your own resources and by raising borrowings, then the business will belong to you alone; but
  - if you fund the business by way of equity raised from a third party such as a venture capitalist, they will require a significant share of the business in return.

- And how financially stable it is, as:
  - a business with high levels of borrowings (high gearing) will have a high level of interest and capital payments that it has to make irrespective of its trading results; while
  - a similar business which you have funded from equity can in theory decide not to pay a dividend if times get tough. I say in theory, as if this is equity you have raised by borrowing against your house you will need to take sufficient out of the business to service the interest, while a VC will generally structure part of their investment as preference shares which have rights to be paid a set level of dividend.

The decision as to the appropriate mix of debt and equity is therefore a fundamental one with huge implications for the business.

If you are funding the business with borrowings then generally it is good practice to do the following.

- Match the type of finance used to what you are going to use the cash for. So to buy an asset with a long, useful life such as a property, it is better to borrow over a long period by using a mortgage so that the cost of the finance is spread over the useful life of the asset. Short-term working capital needs are better met with short-term flexible facilities such as an overdraft or debtor finance.

◆ Borrow long and pay short. If you think that the business can pay off a mortgage in ten years, borrow over 15 instead (making sure that there are no hidden penalties for early repayment). Then, if times get tougher than you had expected, the repayments you are committed to are less than they would have been, while if everything goes well, you can still pay off in the ten years you planned.

As with any exercise in raising external finance, doing so for a business purchase will require at the minimum the preparation of a business plan and full set of forecasts, including cashflows which act as the main tool for communicating to the finance provider:

◆ who you are;
◆ what your business does and why it will be successful;
◆ what you are going to do with the money;
◆ how much you need;
◆ how long you need it for;
◆ how you are going to repay the debts; or what return the investor will get on their equity (which for a VC will always need to involve a discussion as to the exit by which they will be able to sell their interest in the business);
◆ what risks the lender/investor is taking and how these are to be managed.

As a vital sales document you may well find it helpful to obtain professional advice and assistance in preparing this in a suitable form. At the same time, you should also take advice on the most appropriate financing structure for what you are proposing.

EQUITY

The money that can be raised as debt will generally be limited by the assets available to give as security. Any money that the business needs to trade, which cannot be raised as debt or grants, has to be supplied by the shareholders, either by introducing external money by investing (in shares in a company) or later by leaving profits in the business.

An equity provider is taking a risk. They are putting money into a business in return for a share in its hoped-for future success. As a result, if you seek other equity investors (such as backing from a VC firm), you will be selling part ownership of your business to others, diluting your own holding and ultimately, perhaps, your control over the business.

Raising equity is now a highly regulated business with potentially severe criminal penalties for breaches of the rules, so you should always seek legal advice before approaching potential third party investors.

Potential sources of equity for your business are as follows.

You

By investing your own cash, or cash that you have raised by borrowing against your other assets (such as by mortgaging your house).

The advantage of this approach is that you retain control of your business. The disadvantages can be that you do not have sufficient resources to fund the deal and business properly and your personal assets are now mortgaged to the success of the business.

Most individuals' major store of personal capital is within the equity held in their personal property. When you are looking to buy a business and need to put cash in as equity, borrowing against this capital is therefore many people's only option.

It is also true that cash raised against the security of residential property can be amongst the cheapest sources of financing available as it is raised at domestic mortgage rates.

Personal borrowing through mortgages is, however, an area that is regulated. If you are seeking to raise finance against your property you must take professional advice from an independent financial adviser or deal with an appropriately regulated mortgage broker (contact me at mark@theoss.freeserve.co.uk if you would like to be referred to an appropriate broker). In any event, you must always remember that, as it says in the small print, your home is at risk if you do not keep up the payments on a mortgage or other loan secured on it.

There is obviously an enormous number of mortgage products on the market which change all the time. It is worth noting, however, three types of product in particular, which may be of assistance in buying a business.

Fleximortgages
These are residential mortgages that provide a revolving loan

against your property that can be drawn down and repaid up to a specified number of times a year without penalty. They can therefore provide a ready source of flexible funding at domestic mortgage rates, which gives you the ability to draw down your domestic equity over short periods at short notice without the high costs of bridging.

Loans of up to 85% of open market value (OMV) are generally available up to an upper capital limit of £250k (but higher loans may sometimes be available by discretion). A satisfactory prior lender reference is required, but a small amount of adverse credit history is generally acceptable. Loans are normally for up to a 25 year term and rates are similar to those of the high street.

Fifteen day mortgages

Some lenders have stripped down the search and credit referencing procedure to provide a **residential** mortgage which can deliver a draw down of funds within ten to 15 days from application.

Again the advances available are normally up to 85% of the property's value on a self-certified basis, with no requirement for an accountant's confirmation or lender reference in most cases. These loans are available to individuals with a significant adverse credit history and are for terms of up to 25 years. Rates tend to be slightly higher than normal high street levels and there will be redemption penalties.

Domestic bridging

This can be used if you only require the cash on a very short-term basis. If, for example, you believe that you will be able to take sufficient cash out of the business to repay this equity within three to six months, you might consider taking out a bridging loan rather than remortgaging the whole of your property.

Loans of up to £500k at up to 70% of OMV, with rates from 1.1% per month, are normally available from a range of lenders and can be swiftly put in place. These are, however, very short-term funds and if you have any doubt about your ability to repay the bridging at the end of the arrangement you should not go into it.

Your family, friends or others known to you

Here you have direct access to people who may be able to provide cash without incurring costs and you have some idea as to whether they are actually likely to invest. However, think very carefully about the implications of using such money and how your relationships will be affected by this arrangement (for example, what happens to your relationships if there is a business problem?).

Business angels

These are usually successful business people who have made sufficient money to have retired or sold their own business and are now interested in investing in small businesses both as a way of making money, but also as a way of continuing to be involved in business. They therefore bring not only cash but usually significant business experience and often a good network of business contacts. The downside for the entrepreneur can be that they may seek to be actively involved in the direction of the business, which can lead to conflict, so it is important to check how hands-on they want to be and how you feel about this.

Business angels are a main source of equity investment for most businesses looking to raise less than say £250,000, but they tend to be interested in investing in start-up or other early stage businesses rather than backing business purchases.

They tend to invest locally and a good business adviser will have working relationships with locally active business angels and/or can put you in contact with some regional and national networks of business angels.

Venture capitalists

Other than some smaller regional funds that specialise in smaller amounts, most venture capitalists are looking for large investments to justify their time in undertaking the transaction and funding business buy outs.

They will be looking for businesses with high growth potential and ambitious experienced management; where they can expect to be able to sell their investment on within say three to seven years by way of a sale of the shares back to the company, sale of the company or a flotation; and obtain a return on their investment of over 30% a year.

If you are looking to raise venture capital you will undoubtedly need a business adviser both to sell the proposal to the venture capitalist and to help you in structuring the deal.

Trade partners

You should think about whether there are any potential trade partners who might be interested in joining with you to purchase the business by way of a joint venture.

While this can assist in raising funds and sharing risk, you need to be careful about how this arrangement may affect your business. If you have a JV with a supplier, are you then tied to them for supplies or are you free to shop around? If you have a JV with a customer, does this give you problems with other customers who might be their competitors?

In all cases where you are bringing in outside investors you need to consider:

◆ how much control you are handing over;
◆ the need for a business adviser to help you in the process;
◆ how long it will take to raise the money;
◆ how certain you are of getting it; and
◆ the costs involved in attempting to raise cash (and to what degree your advisers will require an upfront payment or will work on success only fees).

GRANTS

Obtaining grants can be a long and frustrating process that involves the following.

◆ Finding out what grants are available for your business. This can be difficult as there is a wide variety of grants available across the country funded by local authorities, central government, European and non-government organisations such as the Prince's Trust. To find out what is available in your area contact a business adviser or your local Business Link, or log on to www.j4b.co.uk which has a facility to search for grants by postcode.

- Finding out if you have to apply before you incur the expenditure. Many grants are not retrospective.

- Finding out if you can obtain cash prior to the expenditure. Many grants provide repayment to you of part of an expense or investment that you have to make and cannot be retrospective.

- Completing the application process, which you will generally find includes attempting to estimate how many jobs will be created, or staff helped to obtain NVQs etc, as a significant part of the form of selection criteria.

- Awaiting approval of your application and payment of the funds required, which may take some time.

All of the above tend to suggest that grants will have little relevance to most business purchases, although they may well be important for funding investment required downstream.

Nevertheless there are some occasions, particularly in relation to buying out businesses from insolvency, where grants can play an important role, particularly Selective Finance For Investment in England. These grants are made towards capital expenditure, where all other sources of funds have been exhausted, and are available in what is known as Tier 2 and 3 development areas.

Be careful if you take up such a grant, however. The terms will normally make specific reference to the number of people employed. This can cause a problem downstream, as for example an electronics business MBO had obtained sizeable grant aid which specified that it was to secure 600 jobs. When the industry suffered a downturn and its competitors laid off staff, the company was unable to do so as this would trigger repayment of the grant. The company staggered on without reducing its cost base until eventually it failed.

There are, however, two sources of government funding or support that you should be aware of.

♦ The DTI operates a department called the Redundancy Fund which will step in to pay employees for statutory redundancy in the event of insolvencies. What is less well known is that if persuaded that by making some staff redundant, other jobs can be preserved, the Redundancy Fund will sometimes lend companies the money to make statutory redundancy payments, with repayments typically over a three-year period. If you anticipate needing to make redundancies as part of a restructuring, this may therefore be assessed in meeting part of the cost.

♦ The DTI also operates the Small Firms Loan Guarantee Scheme (SFLG) under which a business which has a viable business plan, but which is unable to get bank lending due to lack of available security, can have the borrowing underwritten by the DTI. Again this is not really of relevance to raising the finance for the immediate purchase of the business, but may be of great assistance in helping to fund the ongoing working capital or future investment in the business.

DEBT

The finance you can raise by way of loans against the company's assets will comprise a structured finance package of borrowings against its:

- property by way of commercial mortgage, or sale and leaseback;

- plant and machinery by way of sale and leaseback; and

- debtors (and sometimes stock) by way of a factoring or invoice discounting facility.

Providers of this type of funding include the following.

- Banks, which will have a range of financing subsidiaries (and don't forget that you will also need a trading bank account anyway). Banks are, however, unlikely to want to fund such deals by way of overdraft facilities.

- Package lenders, who are normally invoice discounters who are also able to offer financing against property and/or plant and machinery, as well as in some cases stock. While such funders are key to many successful MBO/MBIs, some limit their overall exposure to a certain percentage of debtors (for example by being no more than 150% of the debtor book value).

- Stand alone independent specialist funders who will finance against any one particular class of asset (such as a factor to cover debtors, a building society to lend on the property, and an asset financier to cover the plant and machinery). Some commercial finance brokers specialise in putting together packages of such funders in order to provide greater financing (headroom) than use of a package funder alone.

The types of borrowing available are discussed in more detail below, but the levels of advance available are generally the following.

- Property – 70%– 85% of the OMV by way of a commercial mortgage, or 100% by way of a sale and leaseback, which therefore removes the requirement to fund the deposit out of equity. In fact in some cases the actual sales price achieved can be well in excess of the surveyor's OMV for borrowing purposes, resulting in an injection of working capital into the business at the outset.

◆ Plant and machinery, from 70% to 100% of the machinery's valuation dependent on the lender, on a three to five year sale and leaseback basis.

◆ Debtors, up to 85% of available debt, which is to say of the right type, under 90 days old and subject to credit limits etc.

◆ Stock will be by way of an increased ability to draw down against debtors (say up to 100% or more of the debtor book) but such borrowings will only be against finished goods stock.

The basic information that an asset finance broker will need to establish how much debt funding can be raised for purchase is set out below.

TYPES OF DEBT FINANCE

Borrowings divide into short or long-term funding. For accounting purposes, anything due for repayment on demand (such as an overdraft) or due within the next 12 months (such as trade creditors or the next year's worth of lease instalments) will count as current liabilities on the company's balance sheet, whilst money not due until in over a year's time will count as long-term liabilities.

Short-term sources

Short-term sources include the following:

Management buy-out
financing information checklist

Tick box when information collated

1   The deal

Type of sale (share purchase or business and assets)

Purchase price

Expected working capital requirements following sale

Equity, grants, vendor financing (by way of deferred consideration or earn out) or other funding being put in (including details of MBO teams' investments in the deal)

2   The business

Industry and nature of trade

Trading history covering three years (with last audited and current management accounts)

The business forecasts (with underlying assumptions)

If in difficulty, details of the turnaround plan

3   The management team

CVs for all key team members

Personal wealth statements (house values less mortgages, other assets)

4   The assets and liabilities

Property: freehold or leasehold, valuation and description, details of any environmental/contamination issues, existing mortgages

Plant and machinery: valuation (or if not, asset listing with sufficient information re machinery make, model, age and condition to allow 'desktop' valuation), outstanding HP/lease liabilities

Debtors: aged debtors, aged creditors, sample invoice, contract and delivery note

Stock: list of finished goods stock and confirmed order list

Fig. 18. Management buy-out financing information checklist.

Trade creditors

When a supplier provides goods and allows the company time to pay, this is in effect an interest free loan (although the supplier should have costed in the credit they will allow the company in pricing the job). The more the company is able to borrow from suppliers with their agreement in this way, the less you have to borrow elsewhere.

Overdraft

Much UK business funding has traditionally been by way of overdrafts as they tend to be the most flexible banking facility offered.

An overdraft is a short-term facility intended by banks as a revolving credit to cover temporary timing differences between payments you have to make to suppliers and receipts from customers. Banks will therefore expect to see the account swing back into credit on a regular basis and do not expect to see it used for purchasing long-term assets. As a short-term facility, an overdraft is usually repayable on demand.

The bank will also generally look to take some form of security for an overdraft by way of charges over a parcel of assets, particularly debtors and, where not already used to support other borrowings, property.

Because of this approach to taking security over a range of assets (some of which, such as stock and debtors will vary in value significantly from day-to-day), banks will take a relatively cautious view in assessing the real value of their security, while specialists at lending against specific types of asset may be able to lend more.

Overdrafts are also time consuming for banks to manage, so you can expect to see banks moving more and more customers across to factoring facilities as an alternative to overdrafts.

Factoring/invoice discounting

These allow a business to raise money against its debtors by assigning the outstanding invoices to the lender who will advance you say 80% of the approved invoices immediately.

As the lender takes over the debtors as security, these are then not available for a bank to secure its overdraft. So completion of a factoring deal usually involves paying off the overdraft out of the proceeds of factoring the ledger being taken over.

In factoring, the lender takes over management of the sales ledger and actively chases in payment, which can in itself be an advantage if the business's credit control has been poor. In some cases factors will allow a CHOCs arrangement for key accounts (client handles own customers) whereby the company retains control of the contact with the customer.

Invoice discounting is usually only available to businesses with turnovers of greater than £1m. It differs from factoring in that the company continues to run its own sales ledger and collect in the debtors. As the company is continuing to do the work, it is therefore possible to have confidential invoice discounting (CID), which means that the customers will not be aware of the arrangement.

Some invoice discounters will take stock into account and are then able to offer higher levels of advance against invoices (sometimes exceeding 100% of the debtor book).

The issues you need to consider are the following.

- With factoring you will lose control of how your customers are chased for payment.

- Your facility will be based on a percentage advance against approved invoices. The actual advance you receive as a percentage of your total debtors can be significantly less than this headline percentage as the factor may disallow debts over three months old, overseas debts, or may set concentration limits where individual customers' debts cannot be more than a set percentage of your sales ledger. You need to look at the nature of your debts and ensure that you will not run into such problems with your factor.

- Some debts are difficult to factor. They have to be business to business debts, and not sales to consumers and there are only a limited number of factors who will deal with contractual debt involving stage payments (such as construction contracts).

- As the advance is tied directly to invoicing, factoring is well suited to fast growing companies as the financing automatically expands as the business grows, reducing the danger of overtrading.

- However, as the facility is tied to sales volume, if sales fall, so does the funding available (which may be just the moment that you need finance the most).

- Once you have this type of facility in place, it can be extremely difficult to get to a position where you can exit the arrangement.

- There is still a stigma attached to factoring in some circles as it has been seen as financing of last resort. However, as banks have moved more customers to this form of financing, and this type of finance becomes a standard part of the funding package for buy outs, this stigma is disappearing (and of course is avoided with confidential invoice discounting).

◆ Factoring and invoice discounting are often perceived as expensive; however, when comparing costs against bank facilities it is important to compare against the total cost of equivalent bank facilities including interest, management charges, etc to get a fair comparison.

Block discounting

Where you have a long-term stream of income such as a rental income from property or machinery that is rented out, you may be able to borrow what is in effect an advance against this future income through block discounting. This is a specialist market where each deal is very much a one-off, so you are likely to need to use an independent broker to explore this if it is appropriate.

Bridging loans

Bridging loans are normally short-term loans that typically allow you to spend income that is anticipated (usually from the sale of an asset such as a property), before the cash has been received.

There are some specialist funders who will offer bridging loans against property essentially as emergency funding. However, while this can raise say 70% of the security value of a property within two weeks, this type of funding is extremely expensive and interest rates can often run at 2% a month together with substantial arrangement fees.

Long-term sources
Long-term sources include the following.

Bank loans (term loans)
If you are looking to invest in long-term assets, such as plant and machinery or property, you should borrow over a period that matches the expected useful life of the asset being bought, so that it repays the borrowing over its useful life.

Fixed rate loans
These offer you certainty over the payments you will make (but can therefore be inflexible and have repayment penalties built in).

Variable rate loans
These tend to be more flexible, but leave you exposed to uncertainty as interest rates change over time. If you are borrowing significant sums (say over £250,000) you may be able to buy what is in effect an insurance policy against interest rates going up in the form of a rate cap.

Mortgages
Mortgages, which are simply an example of a long-term loan secured against a property, and all the points above apply.

Where a business has a property that is not fully lent against, remortgaging this is usually the cheapest and easiest way to obtain finance.

Hire purchase
Hire purchase involves you in agreeing to purchase an asset by making payments in instalments over a set period.

Hire purchase agreements vary widely in their terms, offering fixed or variable interest rates. You need to check the rates carefully (particularly where there is an interest free period as rates for the balance of the term are likely to be high).

Some hire purchase agreements are structured with low ongoing payments and a large (balloon) final payment in settlement at the end.

In general, while you will be responsible for maintaining and insuring the asset from day one, legal ownership will remain with the finance company until the last instalment is paid.

Leasing

Leasing, by contrast, involves a finance company retaining ownership of the asset which is then rented to you. There are three basic types of lease:

♦ Finance lease, usually used for major items of plant and equipment where the finance company buys the asset and the business pays a long-term rental that covers the capital cost, interest and charges and is responsible for insurance and maintenance. Once the capital is repaid there may be an option to purchase the equipment outright, or to continue to rent it indefinitely for a small fee (peppercorn rent).

♦ Operating leases are typically used for smaller items such as photocopiers, where the equipment is rented for a specified period and the finance company is responsible for servicing and maintaining the equipment.

◆ Contract hire is a type of operating lease where the renter is
responsible for day-to-day maintenance and servicing (for
example, often used for motor cars).

You may need to pay an initial deposit in setting up a lease and,
from a tax point of view, while the rental can usually be treated
as a cost, as you do not own the asset you cannot usually claim
capital allowances on it (nor can you generally use the asset as
security for other borrowings as it does not belong to you).

Sale and leaseback
Sale and leaseback is an alternative to borrowing against an asset,
where it is sometimes possible to arrange to sell the asset (plant and
machinery or property) to a finance company to release cash and
then to rent it back so that you can continue to use it. The amount
of cash you can obtain will depend on the value of the asset being
sold. This is a specialist area (particularly in relation to property,
where this is only normally applicable to properties worth over
£500,000) and you will need to engage a good finance broker.

Directors' loans
There is nothing to stop you as a director putting money into the
business by way of a loan rather than equity if you have the funds
available. This should be considered when discussing the
appropriate financial structure of the business with your advisers.

PG tips
Don't do personal guarantees if you can avoid them. The taking
of personal guarantees from company directors by lenders is
becoming increasingly common. By giving a personal guarantee,
you are promising that if your company cannot repay whatever
has been guaranteed, then you will do so personally.

If you have to give a personal guarantee then try to follow these steps.

♦ Have the guarantee limited to a specific amount (such as up to £25,000 of the company's overdraft) rather than unlimited, which would mean that you are liable for the whole of the company's borrowings.

♦ Avoid giving a supported guarantee (where the guarantee is backed up by charges over specific assets such as a charge on your home) and instead give an unsupported guarantee, not tied to any particular asset that can be seized.

♦ Ensure that you understand the circumstances under which the guarantee can be called and in practice you (and your spouse if there is to be a charge on your matrimonial home) will be advised by the lender to obtain legal advice.

How much you can borrow

To allow you to estimate how much you may be able to borrow against the target business's assets from these different sources, a ready reckoner is given in Figure 19. By completing this with estimates as to the value of the business's assets, you can calculate how much you are likely to be able to borrow either from a mainstream bank or from a mix of asset based lenders.

In particular this form only takes into account the security value available from the business's assets. It does not make any allowance for other security you may be able to provide, eg personal guarantees, or that may be available through schemes such as the Small Firms Loan Guarantee Scheme.

HOW DO YOU RAISE CASH?

To raise cash externally you will need to prepare some form of

Business Borrowing Ability Ready Reckoner

To calculate a business's indicative borrowing ability, complete the form below using:

* the basis of valuation noted to calculate the security value of the assets; and
* the percentages shown to calculate the likely borrowings available.

Your actual borrowing ability will be determined by a number of factors and the table below can act as a general guide only.

	Estimated open market value	Bank	Mix of specialist lenders	Package lender
Property	£	£ 60%	£ 75%–85%	£ 75%
Plant and machinery	£	£ Usually nil although may advance if significant	£ 75%–100%, less existing HP/leasing liabilities to be settled	£ 75%–100%, less existing HP/leasing liabilities to be settled
Debtors	£ Debts under three months old	£ 50%	£ 75%	£ 75%
Finished goods stock	£	£ Nil	£ Can be used to top up advance against debtors to say 100%	£ Can be used to top up advance against debtors to say 100%
Total		£	£	£
Restriction			£ Limited to say 1.5 times debtor book	
Net available		£	£	£

Reproduced with the permission of Creative Business Finance Ltd

Fig. 19. Business borrowing ability ready reckoner.

business plan and cashflow forecasts (but it is worth checking when you need to consider the possibility of raising cash internally). While doing so, bear in mind the banker's CAMPARI checklist as you will need to satisfy this for almost any external lender or investor.

Character

Will the investor or lender see you as honest, do they trust your integrity and reliability, or have you made exaggerated claims in the past?

Ability

Do you and your management team clearly have the necessary skills and ability to run the business?

Means

How much are you worth (both as a guide to your past money making performance and your ability to provide cash to cover any short-term problems)?

Purpose

What are you intending to do with the money? Is it a feasible idea, that matches funding against the need appropriately? Are you also looking to do something that the investor or lender finds acceptable given its own policies (for example, the banks may not be interested in lending to businesses in your sector due to its internal policies)?

Amount

How much are you putting in compared with the risk you are asking the lender or other investors to take; and are you asking for enough to properly see the project through to completion?

Repayment/return

How long do you need the money for and how is it to be repaid (or what return is an investor going to make on their money)?

Insurance

What sort of security is available to cover the loan from:

◆ the business assets;

◆ you by way of a personal guarantee (PG) which may also be backed up by a charge over your personal assets (supported PG);

◆ or the Small Firms Loan Guarantee Scheme?

Additionally, many lenders will need you to take out insurance cover (such as key man life cover) as part of their assurance that their money is safe.

Alternatively, it is increasingly common for business sellers to arrange an indicative package of **asset based finance** with lenders (known as **stapled finance**) that a potential purchaser can take advantage of if they wish. The advantage from the seller's point of view is that this helps the sale process along by removing one element of uncertainty. How much the buyer can raise by way of debt against the business assets has already been decided. From the buyer's point of view this also means that they then only have to concentrate on raising the equity element.

VENDOR FINANCE

A business for sale will typically have been valued at a multiple of its annual earnings. This can easily mean that even a relatively small business may come with a target purchase price of many hundreds of thousands of pounds.

This is, however, a problem for both you as a buyer and the seller, as you or any other buyer will only be able to afford to pay the amount of cash that you are able to raise. Not many people actually have hundreds of thousands in cash available with which to buy a business, even having taken into account the amount you may be able to raise from remortgaging your domestic property; while the funds that can be raised against the business's assets may be limited as shown by the percentages given above.

This means that the only realistic source of payment to the seller for much of the business's goodwill is likely to be from the future profits generated by the business under your new ownership. But because this does not provide any realisable form of security, you are unlikely to be able to borrow against this from banks or other lenders apart from the seller.

So sellers who are not prepared to allow you some degree of credit (vendor finance) are in effect reducing the amount of money they can be paid for the business.

In allowing credit they are, however, taking a risk that they will not be paid this deferred consideration, and so will want to look to cover themselves by charging interest and taking security.

Bonding solution

There is a solution to this problem for business sales with a value in excess of £2m as there is now a service available backed by a major institution which will guarantee payment of up to 100% of the deferred consideration to the seller by way of an insurance policy. This bonding approach therefore eliminates the seller's risk in offering such credit, covering up to 100% of vendor consideration of £2m–£50m in transactions of £2m–£250m, with deferred consideration periods of up to five years.

The policy is non-cancellable and 100% underwritten by an investment grade backer with very limited exclusions covering vendor fraud or deliberate misrepresentation. It can also be combined with raising asset based finance against the business's assets to fund payment of the premium.

This approach has benefits that can be shared by both you and the seller:

◆ the seller can have confidence that they will receive their payment whether or not the business is a success;

◆ the seller does not have to take further security and the phasing of payments can give tax planning advantages; while

◆ agreement by you on the seller's headline price is easier to achieve; and

◆ you can reduce the level of gearing needed to buy the business, reducing the financial burden on the business and the risk of failure.

Price structuring

How you structure the purchase price can also have a large impact on the amount of cash you will need to raise.

- In an earn out, the final value to be paid for the business is determined in part by the way the business performs in a period after the sale. This type of arrangement will therefore affect both the total amount you have to pay, but also its timing, as the impact will be to delay part of the consideration at least until some time after the transaction has completed.

- Consultancy agreements can be used to retain the old owner's involvement in the business as a way of obtaining a controlled handover. Again, making part of the purchase price payable by way of such an agreement can be a way of deferring part of the total cost over the period of the consultancy arrangement.

Alternatively, a seller may be willing to take shares in your business as part or all of the payment, which again obviously reduces that amount of cash you will have to raise. However, this is only usually practical where your shares are listed on a market such as Ofex or AIM on which they can rely to be able to sell again in order to obtain cash.

FINANCIAL ASSISTANCE

In many business sales you will be acquiring significant business assets such as land and buildings or plant and machinery against which, as discussed above, you would expect to be able to borrow. And indeed, if the value of these assets forms a significant part of the value of the business this would appear to be one of the most logical routes to raising the money with which to buy them.

The Companies Act

However, this is to reckon without the vagaries of British company law, where to borrow against the assets being purchased is actually normally against the **Financial Assistance** rules of the Companies Act.

These rules prohibit you from pledging the assets of the company to be bought as security to a lender for money to be raised to buy the company's shares. These provisions were designed to prevent asset stripping, where a company with significant assets could in the past be bought by someone with money raised from financial institutions on the basis that the business would be broken up and the assets sold off as soon as the deal had been completed, with the proceeds used to repay the borrowed money.

In practice, the Act provides a mechanism whereby so long as certain procedures are met, you can borrow against the value of the assets being acquired in order to fund the deal. You will, however, need to instruct professional advisers, who will be required to prepare what is known as a **whitewash** report to allow the borrowing to take place.

For a whitewash report the target company's directors have to swear a statutory declaration that the business will be able to meet its debts in the year following the sale and this declaration has to be confirmed by the business's auditors.

The Companies Act also imposes restrictions on the sale of substantial business assets from the business to the directors (designed to prevent directors looting the company's assets without the knowledge of the shareholders). The effect of this is that if you are a director and you wish to buy either substantial assets (in effect anything with a value of over £100,000 or 10% of the balance sheet) then under Section 320 of the Companies Act, the transaction requires the approval in advance of the shareholders. This has obvious implications if, for example, you are looking to undertake a management buy out of part of your existing business.

Funding Property Development

In some ways, property development is a business like any other. However unlike most businesses, property developments are usually one-off projects that may even be carried out using a company specifically incorporated for the project (a single or special purpose vehicle, or SPV) which may be wound up once the project is completed.

Similarly, the funding requirements are somewhat peculiar in these respects.

- Projects need to raise cash to both:
  - purchase the site; and
  - undertake the development (or build out).

- The cash inflows tend to come largely towards the end of the project as the units are completed and sold off.

So the funding often needs to be held for a long period before being repaid. Unless you are arranging to pre-sell some of the units off plan (which generally involves giving some kind of discount) to generate cash as you go, there may well be little or no funds available to pay interest during the bulk of the project.

These specific requirements mean that property development tends to require the use of either:

- specialist funding products specifically designed to meet the particular needs of such projects; or

♦ very clever use of standard funding products.

Whichever you use, you will need to be very careful in order not to come unstuck, as given the sums involved in most property transactions, running into problems can quickly lead to very serious financial issues.

The funding options available generally fall into one of five categories which are:

♦ specialist property development funding products for developers;

♦ commercial bridging loans and mortgages;

♦ **top-up funding** for projects by way of either
  – joint ventures with equity partners; or
  – mezzanine loans;

♦ joint ventures with developers for owner occupiers;

♦ self-build development loans for owner occupiers.

Each of these sources and their uses are discussed in turn below.

SPECIALIST PROPERTY DEVELOPMENT FUNDING PRODUCTS

These are loans specifically designed to fund property development and which are available from both the high street clearing banks and specialist lenders.

A normal package of this type will typically be to advance:

- 60% or so of the site value; and
- 100% of the development costs on applications.

This lending is usually subject to an overall limit of 65% to 70% of the expected value of the completed development.

Lenders will be interested in understanding the planned sales process from the completed development, whether agents have been instructed and whether units are expected to sell off plan or on completion (as obviously the more units pre-sold, the lower the lender's risk).

There are, however, issues in the standard approach to funding development.

- While funding of 100% of development costs on applications provides a seemingly sensible basis of funding for the build out, the lender's desire to see the developer put in equity early means that any advance against the site cost is usually limited to 60% of the purchase price, leaving the developer to find 40% of this cost out of their own capital.

- The ability to draw down the funds on the basis of applications is fine in theory, but what if you have costs that you need to meet as you go? You will need to ensure that you have sufficient funds available in hand to meet such expenses.

- A loan of in theory 65% to 70% of the completed site value seems competitive, but of course this is always less the professional costs. These will often bring the total possible advance down to closer to 60% by the time the developer has paid for a quantity surveyor's site visit for every drawdown and the lender's top quality legal team.

- Then there's the simple sounding 1% in, 1% out facility fee, which often tends to turn into £500 to £1,000 exit fee per unit, which can be rather more than the 1%.

- All this is in addition to the ongoing 3% to 4% over base rate charges.

In some cases therefore this type of standard approach is better replaced by careful use of ordinary commercial loans as covered below. In others it will need to be topped up with funding from other sources.

Developers using this type of funding also need to be on the look out for other issues, as below.

Potential cashflow problems

Some developers will not look to raise finance to cover the full costs of the build out, relying instead on the assumption that they can achieve some sales of units while the build is progressing, either off plan or as completed units come on stream.

The danger with this approach is if sales do not complete as forecast, the project's cashflow can run into difficulties, sometimes leading to the failure of the whole scheme part way through.

Using the buy to let insurance route outlined below can mitigate this risk, but the best solution in our view is generally to ensure that you have finance in place for the full build out costs.

Many development projects will have cost overruns and again, if sufficient funds have not been negotiated to cover these, the project can run into difficulties.

Cost overruns

One solution to this which we have arranged on larger cases is to negotiate a B tranche of funding which can be drawn down if necessary. This type of tranche may, however, be on the basis of a profit share or penalty interest rates, so calling on it is generally to be avoided wherever possible.

Pressure from the bank

It is worth pointing out that most high street lenders take the view that interest must always be paid as the project goes. The impact of this is that problems with the cashflow, such as the delay of a planned sale, can be fatal to a project where the lender's interest is then not met.

In one example the owner of a small retail business decided to undertake some property development and arranged funding with their normal bank, based on an assumption that he would make sales as he went. When the sales failed to happen on time, the business came under pressure from the bank to meet the interest charges that were expected to be covered by the site sales. The owner attempted to service this borrowing from the retail business, but eventually the project failed.

Some of the specialist lenders may, however, take a more flexible view.

Impact on the overall project

Finally, when setting up the financing of a project it is also always worth considering how this can impact on both the feasibility and profitability of the overall project.

For example, the residential spec builder's worst nightmare is that your build comes to an end and the properties do not, for whatever reason, sell. It could be that another development in the area that has completed before yours has soaked up demand; or it could be that willing buyers are simply unable to sell their existing properties. Whatever the reason, all the time the properties remain unsold, the compound interest clock will be ticking on the relatively expensive development debt, which can very quickly mean the developer is in serious trouble.

There is a way to take some of the risk out of this equation by use of financial products. The answer surprisingly can be to take out insurance in the form of another mortgage, which can actually also make it easier and cheaper to borrow at the outset.

This technique involves arranging a mortgage at the outset against each of the properties to be built on a buy to let basis, based on 100% retention until completion. As this implies therefore, these mortgages can only be drawn down following practicable completion of the build.

Now if all goes well and the properties sell, you need never call on the mortgages. But this also means that if for any reason they do not sell, you have the option to draw these down. This enables you to mitigate your potential losses by:

- redeeming the expensive development funding and replacing it with cheaper buy to let rates; and

- then letting out the property so that you have an income producing rather than vacant asset. It might not be what you had planned at the outset, but it's a better outcome than no buyer and spiralling debts at compounding development rates.

This approach can be used flexibly as, depending on the size of your project, you may need to use a mix of buy to let funders on any development as no one lender will want to be too exposed to any one particular site. This then also allows you to only draw down as required, so you can mix and match sales and letting as required.

The final piece of good news with this approach is that this sort of arrangement should make it both easier and cheaper to find development funding in the first place. After all, by having this type of underwriting facility in place, all the properties are in effect pre-sold with full financing in place, which should help in making your build an attractive one for lenders.

In considering any project lenders will be looking for the following.

- The nature of the scheme and its planning status, how real or speculative it is.

- The anticipated market for the development and the professional opinion of the intended sales agents as to the values that might be achieved.

- The degree of pre-sales achieved to date (if any).

- Your experience as a developer, your track record in this area, and the team of professionals that you have assembled to make the project a success.

- The costs of the project, in part to ensure that you have not overlooked any key cost, which is also a guide to your experience and professionalism.

- The project's cashflows.

- Your capital commitment to the project.

The form in Figure 20 provides a useful checklist of the main items required to put together a **property development finance** application, including a checklist of the main categories of cost to consider.

COMMERCIAL BRIDGING LOANS AND MORTGAGES

As an alternative to property development loans you may be able to raise funds more flexibly by the use of normal commercial loans, particularly bridging loans, against the specific site being purchased or by commercial mortgages, for example against an existing portfolio of properties.

Bridging

Bridging loans are short-term loans, typically of six to 12 months length with a three month minimum period, secured against property.

- They are generally quick to put in place, taking a week or two if all goes well, and do not tie you in long-term to a particular funder.

- They can usually provide funds of up to 70% of the property value (or even higher using some top-up funders).

- They can be open or closed where arrangements to repay the borrowing are in place from the outset.

Creative Business Finance
www.creativefinance.co.uk

Property Development Financing Enquiry Form

Introducer name _____

Introducer contact details _____

Client name _____

Scheme

	No of units/% split	Value per unit	Sales
Residential			
Social housing			
Commercial/retail			
		Total end value	

Site

Planning status		Location	
Cost		Commission	
Stamp duty		Legal fees	
		Total site costs	

Development cost

	SQ FT	£/SQ FT	
Build costs			
Contributions			
Utility connections			
NHBC registration			
Site development			
Car parking			
Landscaping			
Professional fees			
		Total development costs	

Selling/marketing costs

Agents	
Promotion	
Solicitors	
Total selling costs	
Return before financing costs	

Finance required

Site purchase		Development	

Additional documents required (tick box when documents collated)

Client CV and net worth		Professional advisers	
Project cashflow		Site details	
Planning consent		Pre-sales details	

When complete, please fax back to 0870 220 8587

Fig. 20. Property development financing enquiry form.

- They are generally non-status where the borrower is simply operating on a pawn broking basis, in that if the borrower defaults, the lender can recover their money simply by a sale of the property.

- They tend to be based on the property's value and not simply its purchase price.

Mainstream banks will offer closed bridges on a status basis. For open bridges and non-status loans there are a limited number of serious players in the commercial property bridging market, mainly lending up to £2m. Larger bridging loans can be arranged, but this is an area where specialist advice is required in syndicating and placing the proposal.

Bridging loans are, however, expensive. As well as valuation, broker and legal costs, you can expect to pay a lender's arrangement fee of 2% to 3% and discounted interest rates currently of between 1.25% and 2.5% per month. Interest is either collected upfront by way of a deduction of the total interest charge for the facility period from the initial drawdown, or monthly or weekly in advance, or more rarely rolled up into a bullet payment at the end of the arrangement. So you should always be looking from the outset at how you are intending to repay the bridge, either by selling the asset on or refinancing it (known as takeout finance). In the event that you default you will lose the right to pay the discounted rates of interest which can lead to charges accruing at up to 5% per month and lenders will take swift recovery action. You should never go into a bridge without having both your exit and your interest servicing planned and, if anyone you are dealing with appears to be advising you to take out a bridge without having both this and the funding of the ongoing interest charges covered, you should seek another adviser immediately.

Against this being interest only, bridging loans can in some circumstances have short-term cashflow advantages over a normal commercial mortgage where regular payments would include an element of loan capital.

However, bridging is also an area fraught with risks. It is therefore vital to deal with reputable funders to avoid the following.

- **Predatory lenders**, by which I mean lenders who may have another agenda such as an interest in acquiring properties for their own portfolio, or unfair terms such as excessive repayment penalties, or the ability to impose changes in their terms at short notice, or hidden charges.

- **Advance fee fraudsters** who will take an upfront fee to arrange financing, together with collecting cash to arrange valuations and, sometimes, even a monthly retainer until such time as they manage to raise finance but never deliver the funding promised.

  While the cash paid out to this type of fraudster is bad enough, things can get even more serious when the victim then goes ahead with a transaction based on the understanding that they have finance in place when this is not the case, leading to situations for example where:

  - an individual put down a multi-million pound deposit on the purchase of a commercial development property based on an offer of funding, but was then unable to complete and not only lost his deposit but was also facing an action for costs and interest from the vendor; and

- an individual who had completed on the purchase of a development property using a bridging loan at high rates of interest; and who then thought that they had arranged replacement finance, only to find that when they went to sign the completion papers for the loan they were dealing with an empty accommodation address and rates of default interest of up to 5% per month.

A finance broker such as Creative Business Finance Ltd will charge you for arranging a facility, typically based on:

- 1% of the sum borrowed;

- a success fee only basis on your acceptance of a sanctioned offer (and not simply an offer in principle which does not actually commit the lender to lending to you); which is

- deducted from the advance drawn down.

Using an asset finance broker can assist you in raising all types of property development finance, but you do need to be careful to find and use a reputable broker in whom you can have confidence that they will look after your interests and you do not find yourself in the types of situations below.

- A broker arranged a multi-million pound bridging loan for a client to buy a development property (and took their fee for doing so), but failed to arrange for either the interest to be rolled up until the bridging loan was repaid or development funding put in place to service the interest, leaving the client in immediate default and facing a bankruptcy petition.

♦ A client found a development site and spoke to a broker to arrange financing, but it appears that the broker brought in his own property investor and bought the site to undertake the development themselves instead.

The National Association of Commercial Finance Brokers (NACFB) is the trade body for asset finance brokers and was set up in the first instance to tackle the issue of advance fee fraud. Any reputable brokerage should therefore be a member and a list of members can be found on their website www.nacfb.org.

Uses of bridging

So if bridging loans are such a risky area, why might you consider using them?

They can enable you to move quickly to secure the purchase of a site where it would take longer to get financing in place for the full project.

Smart use of bridging lending's property value based approach, combined with clever structuring of deals, can also allow developers to achieve almost 100% funding levels for projects, including the site purchase price. Two examples show how this can be done.

♦ A developer with an option to buy an old approved school site wanted to fund its purchase and development. Having obtained planning permission for the project that increased the site's value over the purchase price, the developer was able to take out a bridging loan against the site's current value which provided sufficient funds to both complete the purchase and to complete the refurbishment of the first few units. They could then go on to sell these units to repay the bridging loan and use a series of **rolling bridges** to fund the subsequent phases of the build out, without having to put up any equity other than the small initial option payment.

◆ Another developer purchased a site using a conditional sale dependent on obtaining a change of use from the existing office use. Once planning was granted, again they were able to borrow against the uplifted site value to raise sufficient funds to complete the purchase and start development. As a result, the client needed to put up no equity other than the initial option payment, which meant that by using syndicated loans they obtained over 99% debt funding of a £15m project.

The key information that a bridging lender will require is relatively simple, as set out on the bridging enquiry form shown in Chapter 8.

Borrowing against a property portfolio

You may of course already have a portfolio of properties either from previous developments or bought as investments that you let out. When these have been acquired over the years you may well have a mix of different lenders in place. While this is a good way to manage all risk exposure to any one lender it has the disadvantage that you are unlikely to be maximising your capacity to borrow against these properties as a whole in order to fund further deals.

By consolidating all your borrowings with a single lender you can therefore take advantage of your equity across all your holdings in order to achieve borrowings of up to 85% of the entire portfolio's value. In fact some lenders will on this basis provide you with a free, underwritten agreed facility to allow you to make further purchases. This type of approach can cover unlimited numbers of properties, including portfolios of over £5m with up to 25-year terms and three-year fixed rates available.

Lending is usually based on both:

♦ property value; and
♦ rental cover where a ratio of loan repayments to rent: 125% seems to be the current industry average.

Assessing the scope for raising this type of portfolio finance therefore requires reviewing the makeup of the portfolio, residential or commercial, its value, and its rental income as set out in the portfolio funding equity form included in Chapter 8.

TOP-UP FUNDING

The mainstream specialist property development solutions discussed above involve borrowing a percentage of the site's value. This means that unless you are able to avoid this by way of a bridging solution as discussed above, there will be some gap between the sums that can be raised and the finance required to undertake the scheme, which will need to be met from some other source as illustrated below.

	Project £000	Normal development funding %	£000
Site cost	500	60%	300
Total build out cost (including normal interest)	500	100%	500
	1,000		800
Funding requirement			200
			1,000

This can obviously come from your own funds, but if you do not have sufficient you will need to turn to an external provider for this top-up funding.

This requirement has traditionally meant entering into a joint venture with an equity partner on a profit share arrangement, but there are now also some specialist lenders coming to the market who are able to offer top slice loans as an alternative.

Equity funding joint ventures

These external partners will all generally operate on the basis of agreeing a profit share in the completed development, which as a rule usually starts at 50%. One issue to be aware of here is in defining the profit on the project, or more precisely, defining the costs that will be taken into account when calculating the profit. The equity providers will usually, for example, seek to insist that only the direct costs attributable to the project are included. This will exclude any recovery of your general business overheads which will have to come out of your profit share.

The funder will need a separate valuation addressed to them from a firm of their choosing and will expect you to bear this cost.

They will also generally want the scheme to be reasonably fully leveraged, so that the amount of equity required is kept to a minimum. In some cases they may wish to provide the debt funding themselves and charge a margin on this.

They may also provide a funding line against cost overruns, but this will usually be on bridging finance style interest rates.

And finally, to protect themselves, the equity providers may also seek the right to step in and take over the build to complete it if it is not going to plan. These rights could obviously be open to abuse so the developer needs to ensure they are carefully drawn.

Institutional funding

The institutions involved in such cases can include local building societies which will set up off balance sheet joint venture projects to develop sites, but these will usually be limited to their local area, while the merchant banks are sometimes involved in larger transactions. There are also some specialist property funds who will fund equity requirements of £250,000 to £500,000.

Where a project is larger than a particular funder wishes to undertake on their own, the project may be syndicated into a club deal across a number of investors. As with many areas of finance it is a case of knowing who to talk to or finding a broker who does.

Individual funding

The alternative to institutional funding is finance provided by high net worth individuals. Here the market is quite fragmented and it is difficult to contact such individuals. Instead, developers are generally dealing with an arranger who has (or claims to have) put together a network of wealthy individuals (their investors).

This leads to problems in establishing the *bona fides* of an arranger and their purported investors which, even with good references, can remain uncertain right up until the point when a transaction has been concluded.

This is another area where advance fee fraud can occur so any request for upfront fees should be considered very carefully. While a request from an individual arranger for an initial fees of £15,000 plus a retainer might put you on guard, particularly where there is a refusal to provide much evidence of a track record or references, some quite reputable networks charge a significant commitment fee to ensure that enquirers are serious before putting proposals to their investors. In these cases it is a matter of taking advice and attempting to take whatever references are available.

An exception to this can be a request for say £1,500 as a deposit, as an upfront fee of this level can often be being used by the funder to cover their initial legal fees in the event that the transaction does not proceed.

However, even if *bona fide*, the arranger themselves may well have difficulty in tying their investors down to a decision, or even to committing to a timescale within which to make a decision. The investors will often be busy, sometimes travelling extensively, and this practical issue can lead to significant delays and uncertainty.

Since the investors are funding each transaction with their own cash, they can also tend to be very choosy about which investments they will fund, again leading to uncertainty right up to the point of completion.

Top-up and mezzanine debt funding

The obvious disadvantage of equity funding is that you will end up giving away normally at least half of your profits to an equity partner.

As an alternative there are, however, some specialist lenders who can introduce funds on a debt basis which you may be able to use to eliminate the requirement for an equity partner.

One source, for example, offers a second charge top-up facility of loans from £250,000 to £750,000. These can be used to top up the level of funding that can be raised for the purchase of a site purchase through normal development funding of say 60%, so that you can actually borrow 90% of the site value and only need to find 10% yourself. You can then use the normal development funding of 100% of costs to complete the build out.

Another source is currently offering a similar facility which can provide a top-up to give up to 98% funding of the entire development project, including interest in professional fees.

This type of top-up facility is expensive as the lenders are stepping in to what would otherwise be an equity risk and therefore interest rates can run at 3% to 4% per month, although some lenders will be prepared to take this as a bullet payment at completion of the project. And of course you will need to be careful as to whether this is compounding or not, as a monthly interest rate of 4% will compound over a year to a rate of 60% (4% in month one and then interest on the principal plus the 4% interest in month two and so on), not simply 48% (4% times 12 months).

However, despite this cost, this type of borrowing can still be attractive compared with an equity investor, as illustrated below taking the example already used and assuming a one-year project:

	£000
Total project cost	−1,000
Sale value	1,500
Profit	500
Funding required	200
Return to an equity investor at 50% of £500,000 profit	250
Top-up interest on £200,000 at compounding 4% per month for a year	120
Saving	130

JOINT VENTURES WITH DEVELOPERS FOR OWNER OCCUPIERS

In some cases an owner occupier will hold a property which has development potential, but does not have the capacity or skills in-house to develop the site themselves.

These situations can be resolved by entering into a joint venture with a developer. So for example, a company operating from a large industrial site at the edge of town, with excess capacity, badly laid out buildings that had evolved over time and surrounding spare land had decided that:

◆ it wished to relocate to smaller purpose built premises;
◆ it did not have the expertise in-house to manage a property development project; but it recognised that
◆ the site might be of interest for a major retail development provided that the planning issues could be dealt with.

The solution to this problem was a joint venture with a developer under which the developer sought the necessary planning permissions. Once these were obtained the developer would then:

◆ build an alternative site for the company on a new site to be let to it on a normal institutional lease; while

- the developer then developed the original site, with the company having a share in the profit.

Each such arrangement will need to be tailored to the precise circumstances of the site and business involved.

SELF-BUILD DEVELOPMENT LOANS FOR OWNER OCCUPIERS

Finally if you are considering a self-build project for your own use as an owner occupier (or in some cases to retain for letting) there is a range of mortgages designed to meet your requirements.

These will typically involve a commercial mortgage of up to £5m taken over from five to 25 years at interest rates close to normal commercial lending terms, plus a lender's arrangement fee.

In other respects these loans are much like normal development finance in that they will lend:

- up to 70%–75% of the final value and occasionally more in respect of commercial units; with

- money released at stages as agreed, based on valuation certificates, which in some cases during the build phase can mean that funds are available at up to 90% of the current valuation.

RAISING PROPERTY DEVELOPMENT FINANCE

For a successful property development you obviously need to have the right:

- site;
- plan as to what you are going to create; and

◆ process for controlling and completing the build.

To this list I would add a fourth factor: funding.

Given the scale of finance involved in most property development transactions, successful funding arrangements are usually a critical element that can play a major role in helping determine the success or failure of the project. So in seeking whatever sort of funding for your project, there a number of general guidelines that you should bear the following points in mind.

◆ Undertake contingency planning for any problems with your planned funding. By doing so you can ensure you have a strategy for dealing with the worst case scenario that you can put into place if needed (such as when the developer exchanged contracts to buy the site only to find that their equity investor then failed to complete on their £750,000 investment in the project).

◆ Know who you are dealing with. By which I mean that if you are going to rely on someone to organise finance for you, you should check to ensure that they have the expertise to put in place what you need them to arrange. In one case a developer needed to raise a bridging loan within a tight timescale to complete a purchase, or risked losing a multi-million pound deposit. Unfortunately the broker they had instructed had little experience of raising such specialist loans and failed to take the steps required in speaking to the appropriate lenders in order to do so.

◆ Ensure you understand the risks involved in any arrangement, such as those outlined above in any bridging loan, that you are entering into.

- Look to add value to your project by the work that your brokers do and the financing options that you choose, which should be the most appropriate ones for your venture and not simply the cheapest.

A developer had built a block of flats as an investment property to be retained and let and simply wanted to replace the development finance with cheaper buy to let mortgages. In arranging the borrowing the broker advised him to restructure the property holding from a single building into individual long leasehold flats. The results were these.

- The value of the property went up by 20% – as a single property this building could only realistically be marketed to other property investors. By creating individual leasehold properties these could be sold on the normal open market, increasing the total value.

- The level of funding available increased and the cost of borrowing went down – an individual institution looking to lend against the block as a whole would be concerned about concentration of their exposure to the number of flats in one location. This would lead to caution in the loan to value offered and an element of risk premium in the rate. By being able to spread the lending amongst a number of the retail buy to let providers against individual flats, the client could obtain normal high street rates and terms.

- The flexibility of the arrangement was improved – as now there were individual leaseholds the owner could realise these piecemeal as required, rather than having to dispose of the entire block in one transaction, thereby reducing some of the risk.

16

Funding a Turnaround

A business turnaround is usually precipitated by a cash crisis so funding a turnaround usually involves two steps:

◆ managing the business's finances so as to survive through an initial crisis and to stabilise the business; and then

◆ refinancing to fund the regrowth and future trading of the business.

At both points in a turnaround, lenders' confidence in both the business's management and its ability to meet repayments of borrowings out of future forecasts of cashflows are likely to be low, given the business's current situation or recent history. Funding for turnarounds therefore tends to rely on:

◆ whatever funds you can generate from within the business; together with

◆ asset based lending from sources whose principal concern is the value of the security available, at its most extreme on a pawn broking basis.

The focus of this chapter is therefore on surviving an immediate cash crisis. The type of funding you will need to raise to finance the business's future development will depend very much on the nature of the business and your plans for it, and you should therefore refer to the whole of the prior section for guidance as to the best sources of funding.

WEALTH WARNING

You must not simply use the techniques outlined in this section to obtain more cash, particularly by increasing borrowings or taking further credit simply in order to stave off an inevitable collapse.

You should seek to raise money to support a business in difficulties if you have a real plan for turning it around, which will involve making major changes in how it is operating.

If you simply put more money into a business without making such changes, or insufficient money to see the changes through, all you will be doing is simply sending good money after bad as the business will burn through the new cash introduced. But in doing so you may have actually worsened your position in that you may have:

◆ converted your own assets, such as money held in a pension scheme, into cash to invest into the business which is then lost;

◆ had to give personal guarantees for new borrowings; and/or

◆ become personally liable for the business's debts as a result of wrongful trading, which is essentially where you took credit from suppliers and carried on trading after the point when you knew, or ought to have known, that there was no reasonable prospect of avoiding failure.

The purpose of this chapter is to help you to weather a cash crisis in order to put a turnaround plan, with some reasonable chance of success, into place. If you are in a cash crisis and you have (or it would be reasonable to have) any concerns about whether there is a reasonable prospect of the business surviving, you must take professional advice to protect your personal position. If you are faced by a turnaround situation you can find more guidance on all aspects of achieving a successful turnaround in *Turning a Business Around* published by How To Books.

The key questions in a cash crisis are:

♦ **Is the company insolvent?** Because if it is, whilst you do not necessarily have to cease trading, there are potential implications and risks of personal liability for the directors (which includes *defacto* and shadow directors) that can arise out of your legal duties on which you need to obtain advice.

♦ **Does the company have sufficient cash for the immediate/ foreseeable future?** If not, you have just answered the first question.

♦ **Will the lenders continue to support you?** This may well determine the answer to the second question.

IS THE COMPANY INSOLVENT?

In principle, insolvency simply means that the company is unable to pay its debts as they fall due. Where a winding up is sought on these grounds, the Insolvency Act (1986) sets out four tests, failure of any of which is taken to prove insolvency:

♦ **failure to deal with a statutory demand**;

♦ **failure to pay a judgement debt**;

♦ the court is satisfied that the company is failing to pay its debts where due (**the cashflow test**);

- the court is satisfied that the company's liabilities (including contingent and prospective ones) are greater than its assets (**the balance sheet test**).

Insolvency is important because if the company fails, a liquidator can potentially:

- act to set aside some transactions made when the company was insolvent; and

- hold you personally liable for the company's losses.

Additionally, your responsibility for the insolvency will be taken into account when considering company director disqualification proceedings.

If you are not trading through a company, but are acting as a sole trader, however, you have unlimited liability for all your own debts (business and personal). If you are trading in a partnership, all the partners are liable together and individually for the partnership's business liabilities (jointly and severally).

The moral is, when in doubt, if you are concerned about solvency, you should seek professional advice concerning your balance sheet position and your short- and medium-term cashflows. This advice may then enable you to legitimately continue to trade your way through while meeting your legal responsibilities.

DO YOU HAVE SUFFICIENT CASH FOR THE IMMEDIATE/FORESEEABLE FUTURE?

To answer this you need a cashflow forecast. At this stage you usually need to concentrate on the short-term and prepare a forecast on a weekly basis for the next 13 weeks, but in extreme cases you may need to prepare one on a daily basis, covering only the next few weeks.

The cashflow forecast will be a vital document, for:

◆ actively managing the cash to ensure survival;

◆ obtaining proper advice as to whether to continue to trade (to protect your personal position);

◆ obtaining and maintaining bank support.

Cashflow forecasting is essentially straightforward as you are dealing with real cash movements into and out of your business, not more abstract accounting transactions, such as accruals, prepayments or depreciation.

For a weekly forecast, all you are looking to calculate is:

◆ the cash you are going to get *in* that week;
◆ less the cash you are going to pay *out* that week;
◆ to give a **net** movement (**flow**) of cash into or out of the company.

Adding the net inflow (or deducting the net outflow) of cash to the balance held at the start of the week gives the balance at the end of the week as shown below.

	Period 1	Period 2
	£000	£000
Cash in	100	100
Less cash out	−50	−125
Net cash in (out) flow	50	−25
Balance brought forward	25	75
Balance carried forward	75	50

The secret of cashflow forecasting is to keep it simple, and to work methodically and logically down the page through all the cash coming in and going out of the business. You can now total all these to obtain your estimated total weekly inflows and outflows.

Apply the following when preparing a cashflow:

◆ Be realistic in your estimates of timings and amounts of cash and when in doubt, be prudent. Be pessimistic about when and how much people are going to pay you and when you are going to have to pay others.

◆ Make your assumptions explicit. If your forecast assumes sales are going to increase by 20% next month because a new contract comes on stream then you should say so, otherwise lenders who may be looking at the figures may just think that you are relying on the new sales fairy to wave a wand and make this happen.

◆ Experiment with sensitivities by flexing some of your key assumptions (what if sales go up by 5% instead of 10%, what if customers take 60 days to pay instead of 45?) to see how sensitive the forecast is to these fluctuations.

- Think widely. Check that you have allowed for all possible payments that may need to be made by comparing the type of items you have allowed for with last year's detailed profit and loss account and/or your old cheque books. Have you allowed for any unusual or one-off payments such as corporation tax, redundancy payments, pension top-ups, capital expenditure or repairs if any of these are likely to fall due in the period? Turnarounds tend to require professional assistance. Have you allowed sufficient to cover the accountants', lawyers' and bankers' fees?

- Finally, remember that you do not have a 100% reliable crystal ball. Build in a margin as a round sum contingency to allow for the things that will inevitably come crawling out of the woodwork. The more uncertain your starting point, the larger this needs to be, up to say, 10% or 20% of payments in some cases.

Part of the reason for cashflow forecasting is to build your lender's confidence that you are in control of your finances. Having a contingency in place is not only prudent, but if it helps to ensure that you beat your forecast cash performance, it will also help to ensure that your lender's confidence in your management skills will increase.

Once you have prepared your forecast on a prudent and realistic basis, you should then use what you have produced to plan and actively manage your cash on a day-to-day or week-to-week basis.

- Compare the balance at the end of each week with the facility you have with your bank to see whether you have headroom or are going to be in excess.

◆ If you are going to be in excess, plan what you are going to do about it. Look to see what scope there is for moving payments further back or bringing forward receipts. Speak to your lender in advance to agree a temporary extra facility. Use the cashflow forecast to explain why the excess will occur, how much it will be, how long it will be for, and how you are going to then reduce your borrowing to return to your normal facility.

◆ Monitor your actual performance against forecast and where they differ ask yourself why: is this telling you anything that you need to take into account to improve your forecasting?

WILL YOUR LENDERS CONTINUE TO SUPPORT YOU?

The good news is that lenders will tend to support customers in difficulties where:

◆ the lender trusts your integrity;

◆ you talk to them in time (and seem likely to continue to talk to them);

◆ you seem to be in control of your business (and its numbers);

◆ you have a plan;

◆ the plan sets out clearly what support you need (how much, how long, how it is to be paid back);

◆ you are prepared to get in help where you need it;

◆ the lender is confident your plan can work;

◆ the lender is confident you can make it happen; and

◆ your plan does not materially increase the lender's risk.

This last point is concerned with the current level of the lender's security and the simple questions:

◆ can the lender currently get out or not? and
◆ how does your plan affect this ability going forwards?

A full estimate of a bank's security position will be a complex matter, requiring specialist assistance in the valuation of assets and assessing reservation of title clauses.

For the purposes of most businesses, simply looking at the position in respect of the two main assets of property and debtors provide a reasonable broad brush view of the lender's position. It should provide you with a sufficient basis to understand and discuss with your bank how confident or exposed they feel about your business. If your business has a significant value of plant and machinery you will need to add lines in for this as well.

By rolling this calculation forward, based on your forecast balance sheet, you can also see how the lender's security position is likely to be affected by further trading. By discovering whether you are asking them to become more exposed or if your action will help them to improve their position, you can help to ensure their support.

So for example, a company may want to borrow more in order to fund making cost cuts and reorganising their product lines which will result in a short-term dip in trading. But then as a result of the reduced costs and newly organised sales working through, the company expects to be able to reduce its borrowings to give a profile as shown below for, say, a year.

	Now £000	Qtr 1 £000	Qtr 2 £000	Qtr 3 £000	Qtr 4 £000
Property					
Market value	100.0	100.0	100.0	100.0	100.0
Borrowings secured on property	−70.0	−70.0	−70.0	−70.0	−70.0
Surplus/(deficit)	30.0	30.0	30.0	30.0	30.0
Debtors					
Book value	150.0	125.0	150.0	150.0	175.0
At realisable value of say 70%	105.0	87.5	105.0	105.0	122.5
Borrowings secured on debtors (eg overdraft)	−125.0	−150.0	−175.0	−150.0	−125.0
Surplus/(deficit)	−20.0	−62.5	−70.0	−45.0	−2.5
Total surplus (deficit)	10.0	−32.5	−40.0	−15.0	27.5

The above example assumes all finance is through a single lender, such as a bank. Despite the projection that its position will have improved at the end of the year as a result of the plan, the lender will, however, clearly be concerned about backing this plan without some other security being made available, such as meaningful personal guarantees. This is because overall you are asking the lender to take a further £50,000 risk in allowing their current potential surplus of £10,000, which is the margin of safety they have that they can recover their borrowings if your business fails now, to fall to a projected peak deficit of £40,000, before any insolvency costs.

Of course these days you may not have a simple single bank funding position and for many companies the debtors may be funded separately, by a factor or invoice discounter, from the lender providing a mortgage on the property, so each funder will have to look at their own particular position.

MANAGING A CASH CRISIS

In a cash crisis, your business's short-term survival depends on taking emergency measures to conserve and generate cash to buy time for longer-term issues to be addressed. Unfortunately you may need to take action before making a full assessment of your business's problems or deciding on your recovery strategy. There is therefore always a risk that the short-term actions you take will be detrimental to your business's long-term interests.

While surviving the short term must take priority at this stage in order to have a long-term future to worry about, where possible you should try to consider the long-term consequences and adopt an approach that balances:

◆ short-term survival; and
◆ long-term regeneration.

But when in doubt, short-term survival must come first.

A cash crisis can arise for a number of reasons, ranging from operating losses or excessive levels of debt draining the cash away; to excessive capital expenditure or inefficient trading operations absorbing too much cash into illiquid assets; through even to a rate of growth that is too fast for your supply of cash to keep up.

The key areas to focus on to survive a cash crisis are to:

◆ control the cash you have;
◆ get more cash in from normal trading;
◆ get in more cash or credit from elsewhere;
◆ reduce and/or control the cash going out;

- ◆ reduce the amount of cash you need to trade;
- ◆ improve profits.

One way to prioritise actions is to use a matrix like the one in Figure 21 to plot your estimates of which actions will have the largest/fastest relative effects, so that you can focus on the ones that will make a real difference.

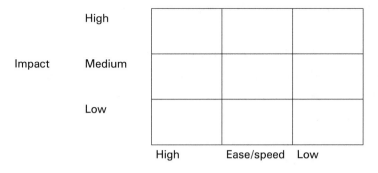

Fig. 21. Plotting which actions have the greatest effect.

The good news is that if you can demonstrate that you can identify, face up to, and deal with a severe cash crisis by taking the actions necessary to survive, you will be increasing your credibility with your lenders and therefore their willingness to support you through the process.

Control the cash you have

It is surprising how many businesses in a cash crisis fail to take the basic steps to control this scarcest of resources and to ensure it is used as efficiently as possible. As discussed, you will need to prepare a cashflow forecast. From this exercise it will logically follow that to efficiently manage the business's cash you need to take the following steps.

- Centralise control of cash receipts, payments and forecasting (and forecast daily on a cleared funds at bank basis). You can then prioritise and schedule payments so the available cash is best used for the benefit of the whole business, rather than being used, say, by individual managers, sites or branches as they see fit.

- Roll forward the cashflow forecast on a regular basis, reviewing performance against forecast each time you do so to pick up any variances that need to be investigated or which can be used to improve the next forecast's accuracy.

- Increase the level of authority required for ordering goods or making payments. Company credit or charge cards should usually be cancelled or restricted so that cash is not wasted or committed outside the central forecasting regime.

In using your cashflow forecast you may be able to identify where the cash is leaking out. Is it particular branches, sites or parts of the business? If so, you can target these areas for specific reviews and remedial action.

Get more cash in from normal trading

You are likely to have a lot of money tied up in debtors. As trading and sales becomes more difficult, many businesses feel less confident in demanding payment from customers for fear of losing future business, or are distracted from the day-to-day necessity of chasing in debts and by default allow debtors to enjoy longer or more extensive credit terms than normal. This ties up vital working capital and is often the first place to look for funds.

You should review your debtors ledger and take action to:

- reduce credit terms to customers;
- target and get in overdue debts.

If as a result you find that your credit control procedure or practices are poor, mark this as an area for specific action as part of your turnaround plan. In the meantime, introduce tougher credit terms for customers.

Get in more cash or credit from elsewhere

Other than trading, possible other sources of cash are from selling assets, raising new borrowings or obtaining investment.

Review the assets on your balance sheet to identify these.

- Surplus fixed assets (land and buildings, plant and machinery, motor vehicles) that can be sold.

- Assets that could potentially be made surplus (and then sold), for example by subcontracting out your manufacturing processes.

- Essential fixed assets that you need to continue to use, but which can be sold and leased back to provide cash.

- Underutilised plant and machinery capacity that can be hired out, or spare factory or office space that could be sub-let.

- Separable and saleable investments, subsidiaries or any parts of the business (such as a specific branch) that could be disposed of for cash.

- Is there any equipment lying around that is not even on the balance sheet that can be sold?

Using your cashflow forecast, seek to negotiate an extension of your existing bank facilities or other borrowings to cover the forecast requirement. If appropriate, seek to agree deferment of loan repayments or to roll up interest for later payment. Do you have any unpledged assets that can provide security for new loans, such as brands, trademarks, and other intellectual property rights?

Asset based lenders who specialise in lending against a specific type of security (such as factors who lend against your debtor book) will often advance a higher loan to value against these assets or security than may be available from normal banking arrangements. Can you use such sources to obtain more borrowings against your assets than you currently have available from your bank?

If seeking to borrow further funds, always consider carefully your business's ability to meet the payments in both the short and long-term before taking further money. You do not want to simply dig yourself deeper into debt that you cannot afford to service, particularly if you may be asked to give personal guarantees.

♦ Agree new stocking arrangements with supportive creditors such as sale or return; pay when paid; or agreed longer payment terms.

♦ Ask customers to supply free issue stock for you to work on so that you do not have to buy in materials.

♦ Seek injections of capital from shareholders or directors (your bank may well put pressure on for this to happen in any event as a sign of commitment to the turnaround, as well as a way of managing or reducing its exposure).

If you are being asked to make a further investment into a business in difficulty, or to personally guarantee further borrowings for a company, you must look very carefully at the commitment you are making, the likelihood of recovery and the impact it will have on you should the business fail. You should always consider getting professional advice in these circumstances.

Reduce and/or control the cash going out

Just as with everything else in life, what you don't spend, you get to keep, so you should look at the following.

◆ Cancelling discretionary expenditure such as payments of dividends.

◆ Cutting back or cancelling:
  − advertising and marketing (but only after assessing how immediate the link is between this and sales and do not cut advertising that is vital for short-term turnover);
  − training, but keep any required to meet statutory requirements;
  − research and development, but assess the risk that you may run of losing any key projects or staff that are vital to the long-term recovery plan;
  − capital expenditure, but assess how vital any such planned expenditure is to improving profitability in the short-term or the long-term turnaround plan.

◆ Increasing creditor payment periods by agreement with suppliers.

◆ Negotiating scheduled payments with key creditors, HM Revenue & Customs (an informal arrangement). If agreeing scheduled payments with suppliers, be clear as to what proportion of the payments made is going to be used by the supplier to reduce the total amount you owe and what proportion will be used to allow further supplies on credit.

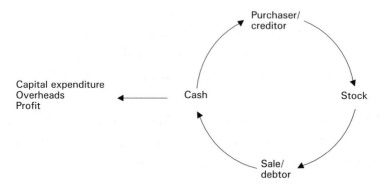

Fig. 22. The working capital cycle.

◆ Consider using an insolvency act procedure such as a Company Voluntary Arrangement (CVA) or administration to obtain protection or agree a formal binding deal with creditors.

◆ Consider whether any key creditors might be willing to convert their debt to shares in the business (a debt for equity swap) if this is acceptable to the existing shareholders.

Pensions warning

In the aftermath of the Maxwell affair, the regulations to protect employees' pensions have become more stringent, with strict duties and timescales in respect of the payment across of pension contributions.

The different type of possible pension schemes makes this a complex area, but the general rules must be:

◆ always pay over employee contributions deducted from salaries;

◆ always obtain professional advice on any proposal to reduce employer contributions before making any change.

Reduce the amount of cash you need to trade

Your working capital cycle should be a virtuous circle with stock turning into sales and debtors, and then into cash to provide funds with which to pay your suppliers, and contribute to covering your overheads and generating a profit (see Figure 21).

Whether this cycle requires funding is determined by your actual terms of trade with suppliers and the degree to which you are holding cash tied up in first stock and then debtors as if:

◆ you have 30 days from receipt of goods within which to pay your supplier; but

◆ goods sit in your stock for two months on average before being sold; and

◆ it takes you an average of a month to collect the cash from your customer; then

◆ you have a funding gap of two months between the period of credit you are receiving and the point when you are realising cash, which then tends to mean relying on an overdraft or other lending.

Obviously the higher the volume of trading you are undertaking, the larger the value of this gap, which is why high growth businesses can fail through running out of cash, a problem known as overtrading. Reducing the length of the funding gap means that what cash you do have can fund more trading.

In this case the company could reduce its investment in stock and debtors.

♦ If it only bought in goods when it had a firm order and could ship it straight out (a back-to-back deal), then the debtor would pay at exactly the same time as the creditor was due.

♦ If it only stocked what it could sell in a month for cash.

♦ Or if it took all its goods on a consignment stock basis, while it physically held the items on site, but only buying them from the supplier when a customer took one.

It could also seek to replace bank lending with supplier credit by taking three months' credit, which would match the date of receipt and payment.

Or it could seek a mixture by, for example, taking two months' credit from suppliers and only stocking items which sold within a month.

You should look at all aspects of your working capital to see where there is scope for reduction.

♦ Reduce finished goods stock (such as by a sale of slow moving or old items), but be careful with such strategies and consider the risks and consequences (for example, is dumping stock in your normal markets going to spoil your efforts to increase normal sales?).

♦ Complete your work in progress and turn it into sellable finished goods as soon as possible.

♦ Review your production management. (Particularly if you are building say batches of subassemblies, does this mean that you are deliberately tying up cash in parts that will not become finished goods for a long time? Can you move to just in time production?)

♦ Cancel or reduce any outstanding raw material orders so long as this does not give you a contractual problem or unacceptable risks of stock outs.

♦ Return any unnecessary stockholdings to suppliers, either by agreement or by stepping up your quality control standards and checks.

Improve profits

Fundamentally, to improve profits requires achieving some combination of the following, depending on which area is most responsible for the problem:

♦ *increasing turnover*, by increasing some or all of customer numbers, value of spend per customer or frequency of spend;

♦ *increasing margins*, by reducing costs of sales; and/or

♦ *reducing overheads*, which includes dealing with any non-performing parts of the business that are dragging the rest down.

In the situation of a cash crisis, the steps that have the highest short-term return tend to be focused on cost reduction.

Look to increase turnover.

◆ Can you raise prices? But check how sensitive your sales volume will be to price first. If you produce a commodity (such as pencils), customers will tend to buy largely on price and so raising prices above market rates will lead to a major loss of sales. If your product or service is differentiated so that customers cannot buy exactly the same thing elsewhere, the position is a more complex question of perceived value, and you must judge how much can you increase your price before customers decide that a cheaper product will do well enough for what they want.

◆ What opportunities can you identify to achieve quick, cost effective, and relatively certain increased volumes by attracting more customers, getting them to come back more often, or to increase their spending with you on each occasion?

Look to increase margins.

◆ Identify the key constraints on the business such as a production bottleneck and ensure that profit is maximised by focusing on the most profitable use for the capacity available at that constraint.

◆ Improve your productivity and output by looking at your processes, but solutions requiring capital expenditure (such as increased automation) tend to be long-term issues.

◆ Improve your efficiency in control of purchasing, distribution, contract control, quality assurance, or waste management. Look for any opportunities to reduce the cost of goods sold such as reducing raw material prices, reducing scrap, changing materials or lowering labour components.

- Reduce wage costs by introducing short-time working or a redundancy programme (compare your head count with competitors' or to that of two or three years ago), but be careful to ensure that this is understood to be a short-term step, and do not preclude the need to make further long-term changes.

  When making redundancies you will need to take care to meet current standards and legislation in respect of:
  - consultation with employees;
  - grounds for redundancy;
  - selection of employees.

  It is best therefore to obtain up-to-date advice from your solicitor. You will also need to fund any redundancy payments required. In some circumstances the DTI's redundancy fund will be able to make a loan available over up to three years with which to help fund the payments. Contact the DTI (Redundancy Fund helpline number 0845 145 0004) to find out what assistance is currently available.

Look to reduce overheads.

- Can you reduce manufacturing overheads?

- Are your selling, general and administrative expenses in line with industry standards or can you look for savings in some of the following areas:
  - Management salaries – should you share the pain?
  - Premises costs – can you consolidate and lease out extra space?
  - Vehicles – can you eliminate the car fleet, or have your employees bear the costs of cars?

- – Professional costs – can you reduce the costs of accountants, lawyers, etc?
- – Postage – do you really need overnight couriers, etc?
- – Telephone costs.
- – Advertising and promotion costs – is your advertising cost effective? Is it an investment in the future or a necessary expense for obtaining sales in the short term?
- – Selling expenses – can you cut the size of the sales force, or the number of sales offices without significant short-term costs?

♦ Consider closing or selling any of your business, subsidiaries or branches which have net cash outflows or are unprofitable.

KEY POINTS

♦ Can you pay your debts as they fall due? If not, you are insolvent. Don't panic, but do get professional advice.

♦ Create a cashflow to work out how much cash you are going to need in the short term. It is the first step towards making sure you have it.

♦ Work out how comfortable/exposed the bank is, and will become, before you sit down to talk to them about how much cash you need.

♦ Use these tools to keep track as you go.

♦ Explore the use of asset based finance to generate greater borrowing headroom than is available through bank finance.

♦ Actively manage your cash and the funds tied up in your working capital.

♦ Do not put good money in after bad.

Loan Repayment Table

This table allows you to calculate your monthly repayments on normal capital and interest loans such as a traditional mortgage where you pay off the capital borrowed as you go.

It shows the monthly cost per £1,000 borrowed. In order to find out how much the repayments would be on a loan of, say, £100,000 at 7% over 25 years simply:

◆ find the figure for 7% at 25 years (£7.07); and

◆ multiply by 100 to obtain a monthly cost of £707.

Capital and interest loan repayment table									
Interest rate	Period of loan in years								
	5	6	7	8	9	10	12	15	20	25
6.0%	19.33	16.57	14.61	13.14	12.01	11.10	9.76	8.44	7.16	6.44
6.5%	19.57	16.81	14.85	13.39	12.25	11.35	10.02	8.71	7.46	6.75
7.0%	19.80	17.05	15.09	13.63	12.51	11.61	10.28	8.99	7.75	7.07
7.5%	20.04	17.29	15.34	13.88	12.76	11.87	10.55	9.27	8.06	7.39
8.0%	20.28	17.53	15.59	14.14	13.02	12.13	10.82	9.56	8.36	7.72
8.5%	20.52	17.78	15.84	14.39	13.28	12.40	11.10	9.85	8.68	8.05
9.0%	20.76	18.03	16.09	14.65	13.54	12.67	11.38	10.14	9.00	8.39
9.5%	21.00	18.27	16.34	14.91	13.81	12.94	11.66	10.44	9.32	8.74
10.0%	21.25	18.53	16.60	15.17	14.08	13.22	11.95	10.75	9.65	9.09
10.5%	21.49	18.78	16.86	15.44	14.35	13.49	12.24	11.05	9.98	9.44
11.0%	21.74	19.03	17.12	15.71	14.63	13.78	12.54	11.37	10.32	9.80
11.5%	21.99	19.29	17.39	15.98	14.90	14.06	12.83	11.68	10.66	10.16
12.0%	22.24	19.55	17.65	16.25	15.18	14.35	13.13	12.00	11.01	10.53
12.5%	22.50	19.81	17.92	16.53	15.47	14.64	13.44	12.33	11.36	10.90
13.0%	22.75	20.07	18.19	16.81	15.75	14.93	13.75	12.65	11.72	11.28
13.5%	23.01	20.34	18.46	17.09	16.04	15.23	14.06	12.98	12.07	11.66
14.0%	23.27	20.61	18.74	17.37	16.33	15.53	14.37	13.32	12.44	12.04
14.5%	23.53	20.87	19.02	17.66	16.63	15.83	14.69	13.66	12.80	12.42
15.0%	23.79	21.15	19.30	17.95	16.92	16.13	15.01	14.00	13.17	12.81
15.5%	24.05	21.42	19.58	18.24	17.22	16.44	15.33	14.34	13.54	13.20
16.0%	24.32	21.69	19.86	18.53	17.53	16.75	15.66	14.69	13.91	13.59
16.5%	24.58	21.97	20.15	18.82	17.83	17.06	15.99	15.04	14.29	13.98
17.0%	24.85	22.25	20.44	19.12	18.14	17.38	16.32	15.39	14.67	14.38
17.5%	25.12	22.53	20.73	19.42	18.45	17.70	16.65	15.75	15.05	14.78
18.0%	25.39	22.81	21.02	19.72	18.76	18.02	16.99	16.10	15.43	15.17
18.5%	25.67	23.09	21.31	20.03	19.07	18.34	17.33	16.47	15.82	15.57
19.0%	25.94	23.38	21.61	20.33	19.39	18.67	17.67	16.83	16.21	15.98
19.5%	26.22	23.66	21.91	20.64	19.71	19.00	18.02	17.19	16.60	16.38
20.0%	26.49	23.95	22.21	20.95	20.03	19.33	18.37	17.56	16.99	16.78

Glossary

Like any other area of activity, business finance has its own jargon. This section sets out brief explanations for some of the common terms used.

The downloadable guide *The Practical Guide to Listing* available from the London Stock Exchange's website (www.londonstockexchange.com) contains a useful glossary of terms associated with floating a company on a stock exchange.

Acid test (or ratio) Ratio used to indicate the company's ability to pay its current liabilities out of its liquid assets (cash and debtors).

Accounting concepts The fundamental assumptions that underlie any set of accounts, see *prudence, accruals concept, historical cost convention* and *going concern.*

Accruals concept The accounting concepts that revenues and costs should be dealt with in the period to which they relate.

Adverse Items which adversely affect your credit rating such as mortgage arrears, County Court Judgements or insolvency proceedings.

AIM The Alternative Investment Market; a public UK stock market which has lower criteria for obtaining a listing than a full stock market listing.

Asset based finance Lending that is based on specific classes of asset, eg commercial mortgages based on property, factoring or invoice discounting based on debtor book (and sometimes stock), leasing, hire purchase, or chattel mortgages based on plant and machinery. Often an important element in the financing of buy-outs.

Asset based lenders (ABL) Lenders who will advance against the security of a particular class of assets, more generally lenders who will do so across a number of types of asset such as an invoice discounter who will also lend against property.

Assets Items owned by business which can be used by it and to which a value can be attached.

Availability The funds you have available to be paid to you (drawn down) by your factor or invoice discounter.

Benchmarking Comparison of your business against other similar competing businesses.

BIMBO See *buy out*.

Block discounting Lending against a stream of future rental income.

Book value The value of assets as shown in the accounts of the company. As book values are generally based on the historic cost of the asset less depreciation since it was purchased, they often bear little or no relation to the asset's current market value.

Bootstrapping The process of running a business so as to generate enough funds internally to support its own growth, from the expression 'to pull yourself up by your own bootstraps'.

Break-even The level of sales at which the gross profit or contribution is sufficient to cover the overheads so that the business makes neither profit or loss.

Bridging loan A short-term loan usually designed to bridge the period before another transaction can be completed.

Burn rate An American term used to describe the rate at which a company is using up (burning through) its cash resources.

Business angel A wealthy individual, often a retired businessman, who has already sold one business and is interested in investing funds personally in smaller or start-up companies. Will often be looking for an active role in management of the company.

Buy in See *buy out*.

Buy out The purchase of an existing established business from its owners, can be by its existing managers, an MBO, new managers coming in from outside (a management *buy in*, MBI), a combination (buy in management buy out, BIMBO) or where one venture capitalist buys out another's stake (secondary).

Capital A term which is widely used in a number of different but related ways. Capital essentially refers to a stock of cash which can be invested in assets, but this stock can be made up of differing elements and calculated in different ways depending on what you are looking to discuss.

Capital can therefore include:

♦ 'Loan capital' which is the sum borrowed by way of a loan (also known as the loan principal).

♦ 'Share capital' is the cash invested by the shareholders in the shares of the business.

♦ A 'capital account' is a partner's share of the retained profits of the business.

♦ A 'capital asset' is generally a fixed asset such as a property, or plant and machinery, which has absorbed cash.

♦ A 'business's capital' can make up the total funding base of a business, which usually means its shareholders' funds and its long-term borrowings.

So ensure you understand which sense is being used whenever the term is mentioned.

Capital expenditure (capex) Purchase of fixed assets.

Cashflow forecast A projection of a business's receipts and payments over a period.

Charge Security taken by a lender, can either be fixed where the lender has to give permission for the sale of the assets, or floating where you are free to buy and sell the relevant assets (such as stock) on a day-to-day basis.

Commercial asset finance broker Business that arranges borrowings on your behalf with appropriate asset finance companies.

Concentration Limit imposed by factor or invoice discounter on the percentage any single debtor can be of the debtor book.

Contingency Allowance in a cashflow forecast for unforecast payments.

Contract hire See *leases*.

Contribution See *gross profit*.

Creditor Person to whom the business owes money.

Creditor days A measure of the amount of credit being taken from suppliers by a business.

Crown debt Money due to HM Revenue and Customs for PAYE/NI or VAT.

Current assets Liquid assets used by the company such as debtors and cash, together with stock, which is intended to be sold as part of the company's normal trading operations.

Current liabilities All sums of money which are due to be paid by a business within the next 12 months.

Current ratio The value of the current assets divided by current liabilities. See also *acid test (or ratio)*.

Debenture Technically, a written acknowledgement of a debt, but more usually the document by which a lender such as a bank takes a charge or security. In the US, also used to describe a publicly traded debt or bond.

Debt Money lent to a business which has no right to a share of ownership or profits, will need to be repaid and usually carries an interest charge.

Debtor Person who owes the business money.

Debtor days A measure of the amount of credit being given to customers by a business.

Deferred consideration Where a seller of a business allows the buyer time to pay the purchase price.

Depreciation The writing off to the profit and loss account of the cost of a fixed asset over time.

Disallowed Debt that is not available for factoring or invoice discounting (eg because it is too old).

Discounted cashflow The value of money to be received in future periods, discounted back to its equivalent today (as money to be received at some future date is by definition less certain and therefore less valuable than cash in hand now).

Dividend Payment to shareholder out of profit.

Dividend policy A company's approach as to whether to pay dividends to shareholders or to retain profits within the business.

Drawdown See *availability*.

Due diligence The purchaser's process of detailed investigation and review prior to completing a purchase.

Earn out Where the price to be paid for a business is determined by its subsequent performance.

EBIT Earnings before interest and tax. The underlying profit from trading before it is affected by the business's tax status or financing. (Earnings is an American term and the UK equivalent is PBIT – profit before interest and tax.)

EBITDA Earnings before interest, tax, depreciation, and amortisation, used as a measure of the cash generated by trading activities.

Equity (1) Money put into your business by investors in return for a share of its ownership and profits.

Equity (2) The value of the difference between the market value of an asset (eg a machine on a finance lease or hire purchase arrangement, or property subject to a mortgage) and the outstanding borrowings.

Equity gap The difficulty faced when looking to raise equity funding at a level higher than business angels are likely to provide, but lower than the level at which venture capitalists want to invest.

Escalator See *ratchet*.

Excess Overdraft levels greater than the agreed facility.

Facilities Banking term for the package of loans agreed with the client (eg overdraft facility and mortgage on the premises), which will be set out in a facility letter.

Factoring Lending money based on the security of a company's debtors where the lender takes over the collection process (contrast with invoice discounting).

Financial assistance Rules under the Companies Act to prevent a company's own assets being used to buy it except by using a *whitewash report.*

Financial promotion The act of seeking investment, governed by tight regulation with potentially severe criminal penalties.

Fixed assets Assets owned by a business such as property or plant and machinery to be used over a number of years, the cost of which is written off each year by a depreciation charge.

Fixed charge See *charge.*

Floating charge See *charge.*

Flotation The process of listing a company's shares for sale on a stock exchange, also known as listing or an Initial Public Offering (IPO).

Funding gap The difference between the amount of credit you are receiving from your suppliers and credit you are providing to customers (your terms of trade) together with the time it is taking to turn purchases into sales; which determines the degree to which your working capital required funding.

GAAP – generally accepted accounting practice This means that your accounts have been prepared in accordance with normal accounting conventions. Note that American and UK GAAP have some significant differences and you will need professional advice if this is an issue.

Gearing Borrowing. A company is said to be highly geared (in US: leveraged) if it is largely funded by way of loans rather than share capital.

Going concern The accounting assumption that the business will continue to trade into the future.

Grants Cash provided to you without you having to pay interest or give a share in your business, which you do not have to repay if you meet the terms on which it is provided.

Gross profit Your turnover or sales, less the costs of the goods sold.

Hardcore Apparently permanent level of overdraft.

Headroom Available level of unused overdraft facility.

Hire purchase Arrangement where an asset can be bought using instalment payments.

Historical cost convention The assumption that the value of assets on the balance sheet is recognised at the original cost of purchase, less any depreciation or subsequent write-down to reflect a loss of value.

Initial public offering (IPO) See *flotation.*

Insolvency Being unable to pay debts as they fall due. The Insolvency Act sets out a number of tests including failure to deal with a statutory demand or to pay a judgement debt, and liabilities exceeding assets, each of which would be taken by a court as proof of insolvency.

Internal rate of return (IRR) The discount rate at which a net present value calculation gives a zero result, which in turn means that the discount rate equates to the return generated by the project or investment.

Invoice discounting Lending money based on the security of a company's debtors where the borrower remains responsible for the collection process (contrast with *factoring*).

Joint and several liability The position in a partnership where all the partners are jointly liable for the partnership's debts, while each partner is also individually (severally) liable for all the debts of the partnership.

Lease Arrangement where a finance company purchases an asset and rents it to you. Can be long-term finance leases, short-term operating leases or contract hire, where you have responsibility for maintaining and servicing the asset.

Letter of credit (LC) Document issued by bank to a supplier confirming that the bank will settle their invoice on presentation of the appropriate documents.

Leverage American term for *gearing*.

Liabilities The amounts of money a business owes to others.

Limited liability company (Ltd) Company where the shareholders' (members') liability to contribute to the company's assets is limited to the unpaid amount of the shares that they own, which means that they are not liable to contribute any further cash even if the company cannot pay its debts.

Limited liability partnership (LLP) New form of partnership structure which gives the partners some protection from the business's debts.

Liquidity Availability of cash to meet liabilities.

Listing See *flotation*.

Loan to value Ratio of the sum a lender is prepared to advance against the value of the asset to be taken as security.

Management accounts Periodic accounts prepared for use within the business rather than for public filing.

Mark to market Accounting approach which states assets and liabilities at current market values. Contrast with *historical cost convention*.

Matching (1) The principle that the type of finance should match the type of use the funds are to be put to, eg long-term stable finance for long-term investment, short-term flexible finance for working capital requirements.

Matching (2) Accounting concept, see accruals.

MBI See *buy out.*

MBO See *buy out.*

Mezzanine finance Loans made in excess of normal available security.

Mortgage A term loan secured on property (or when on plant and machinery, a chattel mortgage).

Net present value A discounted cashflow, less the amount of money you have to pay to acquire it.

Nomad Nominated adviser to a company seeking a stock exchange listing.

Non-status lending Lending based on the value of the security (such as pawn broking) rather than on an assessment of the borrower's ability to keep up repayments.

Ofex A privately traded listing where shares are dealt in on the basis of individual trades. Often used by small companies to obtain speculative money as an alternative to venture capital, but is significantly less liquid than other stock market listings as there are no active market makers trading the shares.

Off balance sheet debt Types of arrangements such as sale and leasebacks where a business has the equivalent of a loan but without having to show a liability on the balance sheet.

Open market value How much an asset will fetch if sold on the open market. Also known as fair market value.

Overdraft The extent to which cash has been drawn out of a current account to leave a negative balance.

Overheads Expenditure on a business's indirect costs which are not specifically attributable to the costs of particular goods sold.

Overtrading Trading at a higher level than your available cash is able to support.

Package lender See *structured loans.*

Partnership Two or more people engaged in business together for profit. See *joint and several liability.*

Payable See *creditor.*

PBIT See *EBIT.*

Personal guarantee (PG) Agreement that an individual will pay a company's debt if the company is unable to do so.

Preference shares A share in the company with rights to dividend payment, superior to ordinary shares, but do not normally have voting rights.

Preferential creditors Nowadays limited to some sums due to employees, preferential creditors are paid out of the floating charge assets before the floating charge holder, see *charge.*

Priority agreement Agreement between lenders to vary the normal order in which their security would rank for payment.

Private company Any company that is not a public company and is therefore not entitled to offer its shares for sale to the public.

Property development finance Finance to cover site purchase and building costs designed to fund property development.

Prospectus A package of information prepared for provision to potentially interested investors in a *flotation*.

Prudence The accounting concept of recognising losses as soon as they can be identified, but profits only once they have been earned.

Public limited company (PLC) A company that meets statutory requirements about the level of its issued share capital and which may therefore be entitled to sell shares to the public (although not all PLCs are listed on a stock exchange).

Ratchet Arrangement for increasing management's shareholding if business hits targets.

Receivable See *debtor*.

Recourse Arrangement where a factor or invoice discounter can recover any advance made to you in respect of any debt that is subsequently not recovered. In a non-recourse arrangement you have protection from this happening.

Regulated loan A loan where a first charge is given on a domestic property or on a commercial property where over 40% of the area is used as your residence.

Reserves (1) A business's retained earnings.

Reserves (2) Reduction of your availability applied by a factor or invoice discounter to cover any potential exposure (eg to supplier contras).

Rolling bridges The use of a series of bridging loans typically to fund a phased property development project.

Sale and leaseback A way of raising cash by selling an asset and then renting it back.

Second round funding Further equity investment into a business with an existing external investor (eg by a venture capitalist to develop a business that has had start-up or seed money from a business angel).

Secondary buy out See *buy out*.

Section 320 Provision in the Companies Act that prevents a director purchasing substantial assets (broadly anything worth more than £100,000 or 10% of the net assets of the company) without first obtaining the consent of the shareholders.

Security (1) A source from which a debt can be repaid if the borrower does not make repayments in the normal way, such as a charge over property or other assets.

Security (2) A document acknowledging that the holder has certain rights (eg repayment of a debt from the issuer).

In the US can be extended to cover a share certificate.

Self-certification The process whereby a borrower confirms that they are able to make repayments on a loan rather than proving it by providing accounts.

Share capital The capital contributed to a company by its shareholders.

Shareholders' funds The total book value of a company (the net assets on its balance sheet) which is owned by shareholders.

Small Firms Loan Guarantee A DTI scheme where the government provides a guarantee to lenders for loans made to young businesses.

Sole trader An individual in business in their own name.

Stapled finance A package of potential borrowings prearranged for the buyer by the seller of a business.

Statement of source and application of funds Statement showing how profits generated by the business combine with investment in or realisation of assets, together with credit received or repaid, result in a movement in the business's cash.

Stock (1) A company's trading stock comprising raw materials, work in progress, and finished goods stock.

Stock (2) A company's shares.

Stock days A measure of the time taken to convert goods purchased into sales.

Stock exchange A market in which shares and other securities can be traded.

Structured loans Loans from an asset based lender across more than one type of asset (eg factoring and a property loan).

Sub prime Borrowers with significant levels of adverse making them unattractive to mainstream lenders.

Swing Movement in a bank current account.

Syndication Situation where a number of funders join together to each fund a share of a project.

Term loan A loan repayable by an agreed level of instalments over a period of years.

Terms of trade See *funding gap*.

Top-up funding Additional mezzanine or equity finance to cover the difference between total costs of a property development project and the sums available under normal property development finance.

Trade finance Specialist funding of trading transactions such as importing goods for resale.

VC Venture capital or *venture capitalist.*

Veil of incorporation The protection offered to shareholders by a company's limited liability.

Vendor finance See *deferred consideration.*

Venture capitalists (VC) A firm set up to hold investors' money and to invest it in high growth opportunities. Generally look to achieve a return of 30% per annum and hold investments for three to five years before selling. Generally tend not to be interested in deals below say, £0.5m investment. (See *equity gap, business angel.*)

Whitewash report or agreement Accountant's report used to enable a business's assets to be used as security on which to raise money to buy it.

Work in progress A contract which is not yet complete or goods which are in the process of manufacture but which are not yet finished.

Working capital A business's current assets less its current liabilities.

Working capital cycle The concept that a business's working capital turns over as it goes through its cycle of trade; suppliers providing goods which become stock and then debtors once sold, with the cash received from debtors then being used to pay suppliers.

Yield The amount of return received (E for earnings) for the price (P) paid. Usually shown as a percentage.

Useful contacts

Please feel free to contact me: mark@theoss.freeserve.co.uk:

◆ for an introduction to any of the specialist advisers mentioned in the book; or

◆ for advice on any aspect of finance covered in this book where I may be able to provide an answer; or

◆ with any comments or queries about the content or suggestions for incorporation into future editions.

DEBT
www.creativefinance.co.uk
Full service commercial asset based finance brokerage.

www.nacfb.org
National Association of Commercial Finance Brokers, the trade body for brokers.

www.thefda.org.uk
Factors and Discounters Association, the trade body for these types of lenders.

www.creativehomeloan.co.uk
Online application for second charge home loans.

EQUITY
www.bbaa.org
The British Business Angels Association provides a starting point for seeking business angel finance.

www.bvca.co.uk
The British Venture Capital Association (BVCA) has a directory of members which can be searched by stage of funding, size of investment sought, and location.

www.londonstockexchange.com
The London Stock Exchange's website, good source of information on all aspects of having a public listing.

GRANTS
www.4jb.co.uk
Private sector grant-finding consultancy with searchable online grants database.

www.grantsonline.org.uk
Another private sector grants consultancy.

www.businesslink.gov.uk
Small business support from the Department of Trade and Industry (DTI).

www.lsc.gov.uk
Training grants from the Learning and Skills Council.

www.dti.gov.uk/regionalinvestment
Information on regional selective assistance grants from the DTI.

www.newdeal.gov.uk
Information on government training grants under the New Deal project.

www.princes-trust.org.uk
Support from the Prince's Trust for those aged 18 to 30 with a business idea.

GENERAL
www.companieshouse.gov.uk
Companies House website.

www.howtobooks.co.uk
Source of a wide variety of specialist business books including those covering business planning.

Index